VISUAL QUICKSTART GUIDE

Quark XPress 3.3

FOR MACINTOSH

Elaine Weinmann

Peachpit Press

Visual QuickStart Guide
QuarkXPress 3.3 for Macintosh
Elaine Weinmann

Peachpit Press
2414 Sixth Street
Berkeley, CA 94710
510/548-4393
510/548-5991 (fax)

Peachpit Press is a division of Addison-Wesley Publishing Company.

Permissions
Definitions on page x from *The Oxford Encyclopedic English
Dictionary*, 1991, edited by Joyce M. Hawkins and Robert Allen
reprinted by permission of Oxford University Press.

ISBN 1-56609-128-4
Eleventh Printing

Printed on recycled paper

Printed and bound in the United States of America

Dedication

To Peter Lourekas, artist, teacher, partner, and computer wizard, without whose love and support I would not have dreamed of writing this book.

P 92 – Expanded/Condensed Type
✳P 101 – Resize Picture
P 110 – Transparency/Layers.

P 55. Master Pages.

P 163– Layering

Thank You.

Bert and ***Richard Weinmann,*** for their nourishment.

Pamela Wye, artist, writer, and editor par excellence.

Quark, Inc., for continuing to redefine the standard for page layout software, and ***Michael Johnson,*** technical support.

Ted Nace and ***Peachpit Press,*** for giving me the freedom to write the book I wanted to write.

LinoGraphics Corporation of New York City, for their output services.

Adam Stock of ***Electronics for Imaging, Inc.*** (EFI) for his comments on the EfiColor XTension section.

Stan Pinkwas, managing editor of Video Magazine, for editing Appendix C.

Peter Lourekas, for his technical advice.

Theodora, Christ, Harriet, Steve, Nia and ***David,*** for being there.

My students who are brave enough to ask questions when they are confused.

And ***Chester*** the kitten, without whom writing this book would have been a million times easier.

Table of Contents

Chapter 6: **Text Flow**

Chapter 7: **Paragraph Formatting**

quark[1] /kwa:k/ n. *Physics* any of a group of (originally three) postulated components of elementary particles. Quarks are held to carry a charge one-third or two-thirds that of the proton. Many predictions of this theory have been corroborated by experiments but free quarks have yet to be observed. In a sense, quark theory recapitulates at a deeper level efforts earlier this century to explain all atomic properties in terms of electrons, protons, and neutrons. [coined by M. Gell-Mann, 1964, from phrase 'Three quarks for Muster Mark!' in James Joyce's *Finnegans Wake* (1939)]

quark[2] /kwa:k/ n. a type of low-fat curd cheese.

THE BASICS 1

Introduction.

QuarkXPress is complex. That's why you bought a book. People rave about QuarkXPress because it's a great typesetting and layout tool and offers so many features for making documents, but having so many options can be daunting to a newcomer. The purpose of this Visual QuickStart Guide is to direct you down the main thoroughfares with step-by-step instructions and lots of illustrations. There are also many special tips to help you avoid getting "stuck."

This is a guidebook, and it is designed for page-flipping, complete with thumb tabs, though I recommend that you read Chapters 1 and 2 first. Like a visitor in a foreign country, give yourself time to get acquainted with the turf, where the various menus, features, screen icons, and commands are located, as well as with the QuarkXPress language.

Don't worry if you feel confused or clumsy at first. Remember how you felt the first time you tried to ride a bicycle or drive a car. With practice, many actions will become automatic, and you will have a powerful new tool at your disposal.

Read me First

The QuarkXPress screen.

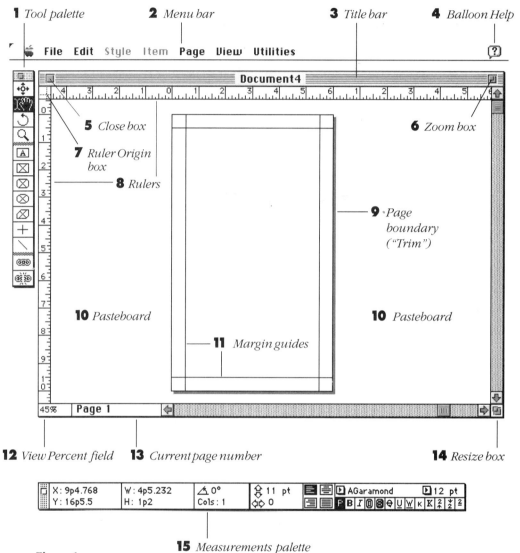

1 *Tool palette*   **2** *Menu bar*   **3** *Title bar*   **4** *Balloon Help*

5 *Close box*   **6** *Zoom box*

7 *Ruler Origin box*

8 *Rulers*

9 *Page boundary ("Trim")*

10 *Pasteboard*   **10** *Pasteboard*

11 *Margin guides*

12 *View Percent field*   **13** *Current page number*   **14** *Resize box*

15 *Measurements palette*

Figure 1.

Key to the QuarkXPress Screen.

1 *Tool palette*

There are seven moveable palettes. The Tools, Measurements, Document Layout, Style Sheets, Colors, and Trap Information palettes are opened from the View menu. Library palettes are opened from the Utilities menu.

2 *Menu bar*

Press any of the menu bar headings to access a list of dialog boxes, pop-up menus, commands and features.

3 *Title bar*

The file name is displayed in the document's title bar. Press and drag the title bar to move the document window.

4 *Balloon Help*

With Balloon Help on, moving the cursor over an item will open a small balloon containing information about that item. Turn Balloon Help on and off from the Help menu.

5 *Close box*

Click the Close box to close the currently active file.

6 *Zoom box*

Click the Zoom box to enlarge the document window; click on it again to return the window to its previous size. Clicking the Zoom box will force the screen to redraw.

7 *Ruler Origin box*

Press and drag from the ruler origin box to reposition the intersection of the horizontal and vertical rulers, also known as the zero point. Click on the ruler origin box to reset

the zero point to the uppermost left corner of the page.

8 *Rulers*

Ruler increments can be displayed in one of seven measurement systems. Select Show Rulers or Hide Rulers from the View menu. Guides can be dragged from the vertical and horizontal rulers to aid in the layout process.

9 *Page boundary*

The edge, or "trim" size, of the page.

10 *Pasteboard*

Items can be created on the pasteboard and then dragged onto any document page, or stored on the pasteboard for later use.

11 *Margin Guides*

Margin guides are displayed for layout purposes only and do not print. Select Show Guides and Hide Guides from the View menu.

12 *View Percent field*

The view size of a document is displayed, and can be modified, in this field.

13 *Current Page number*

The number of the currently displayed page.

14 *Resize box*

Press and drag this box to resize the document window.

15 *Measurements palette*

Many of the commands that are listed under the various menus are accessible in the Measurements palette.

How to use the mouse:

The mouse is used in three basic ways.

Click 🔺	Press and release the mouse button quickly.
	Use to: Select an item, activate a dialog box button, or create an insertion point in text.
Double-click 🔺🔺	Press and release the mouse button twice in quick succession.
	Use to: Launch an application, open or import a file, select a word, or highlight an entry field.
Press and drag ⋯🔺	Press and hold down the mouse button, move the mouse on the mousepad, then release the mouse button.
	Use to: Highlight text, select from a menu or pop-up menu, create or resize a box or line, or move an item, palette, or window.

Other terms used in this book:

Highlight

Select text by pressing and dragging over it or by clicking twice to select a word, three times to select a line, or four times to select a paragraph.
(See Chapter 5, Highlight Text)

Enter

A highlighted field.

A new value entered.

Completely highlight the contents of an entry field (referred to as "field"), on the Measurements palette or in a dialog box and replace with a new value. Double-clicking is sufficient to highlight most, but not all, fields. Press Tab to highlight the next field in succession. Press Shift-Tab to highlight the previous field. If more than one value exists within a selection in the document, the corresponding entry field will be blank. A new value can be entered into a blank box.

Check/Uncheck

Turn an option on or off by clicking the check box. A checked box indicates that an option is turned on.

Press

Quickly press and release a key on the keyboard.
(See Keyboard Shortcuts in this chapter)

Select

Choose from a menu or pop-up menu by pressing and dragging to highlight a selection, then releasing the mouse button, or click once on an item so that it can be modified.
(See Menus on the following page)

How to use a menu.

Press and drag from a menu heading downward and release the mouse button when a selection is highlighted. Select from a pop-up menu by pressing and dragging downward through the main menu and then to the right or left through the pop-up menu. Release the mouse when a selection is highlighted.

About menus:

Each of the seven menu headings provides access to related commands for modifying layouts and page elements and executing various functions. The seven menus are illustrated on the following pages.

Figure 2.

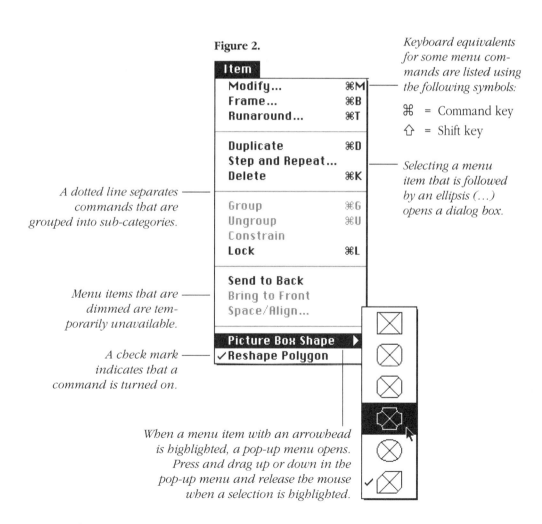

Keyboard equivalents for some menu commands are listed using the following symbols:

⌘ = Command key

⇧ = Shift key

Selecting a menu item that is followed by an ellipsis (…) opens a dialog box.

A dotted line separates commands that are grouped into sub-categories.

Menu items that are dimmed are temporarily unavailable.

A check mark indicates that a command is turned on.

When a menu item with an arrowhead is highlighted, a pop-up menu opens. Press and drag up or down in the pop-up menu and release the mouse when a selection is highlighted.

Menus

The File menu.

Most File menu commands apply to the document as a whole, such as creating, opening, closing, saving, or printing a file. Other File menu commands include exporting text, importing text and pictures, and quitting the application.

The Edit menu.

Edit menu commands include Select All, Clear, Preferences, Clipboard functions, Find/Change, Style Sheets, Colors and H&Js. The Undo command will undo the last modification made.

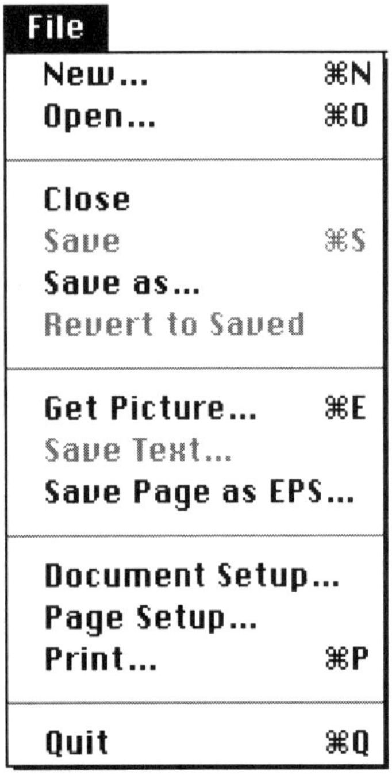

Menus

File	
New...	⌘N
Open...	⌘O
Close	
Save	⌘S
Save as...	
Revert to Saved	
Get Picture...	⌘E
Save Text...	
Save Page as EPS...	
Document Setup...	
Page Setup...	
Print...	⌘P
Quit	⌘Q

Figure 3. *The File menu.*

Edit	
Undo Item Change	⌘Z
Cut	⌘X
Copy	⌘C
Paste	⌘U
Clear	
Select All	⌘A
Subscribe To...	
Subscriber Options...	
Show Clipboard	
Find/Change	⌘F
Preferences	▶
Style Sheets...	
Colors...	
H&Js...	

Figure 4. *The Edit menu.*

The Style menu.

Style menu commands modify the contents of a text box, including typographic specifications and paragraph formatting, when text is selected; they modify the contents of a picture box, such as color, shade or contrast, when a picture is selected; they modify line attributes when a line is selected. The Style menu is available only when the Content tool and an item are selected.

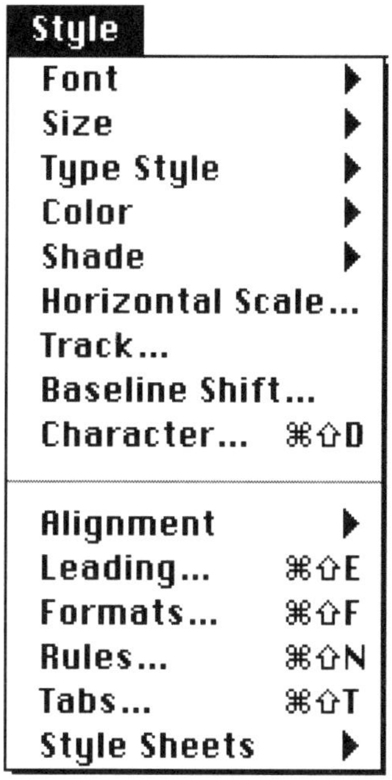

Figure 5. *The Style menu with a **text box** selected.*

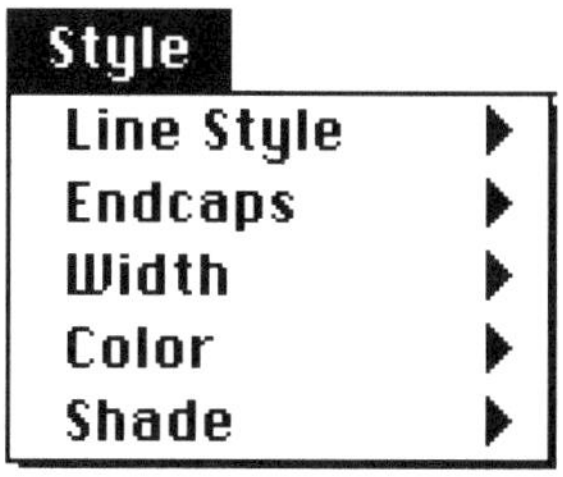

Figure 6. *The Style menu with a **line** selected.*

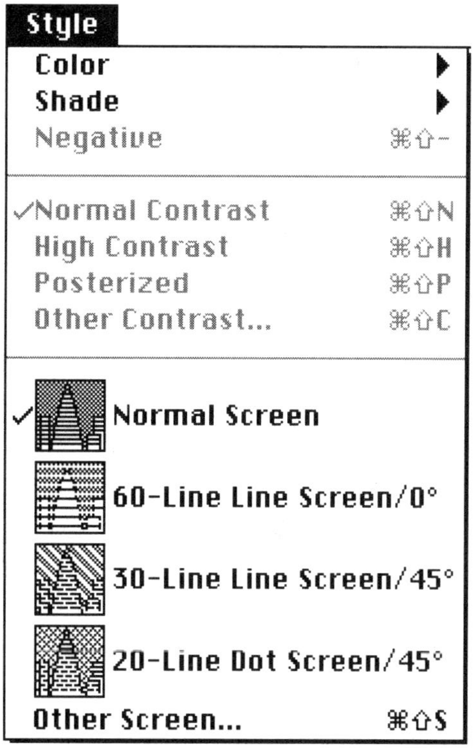

Figure 7. *The Style menu with a **picture box** selected.*

The Item menu.

Item menu commands modify items — text boxes, pictures boxes, and lines. Deleting, framing, grouping, duplicating, locking, aligning and layering are some Item commands. The Item menu is available only when an item is selected.

The Page menu.

Page menu commands are used to add, delete and number pages, move through a document, and modify master guides.

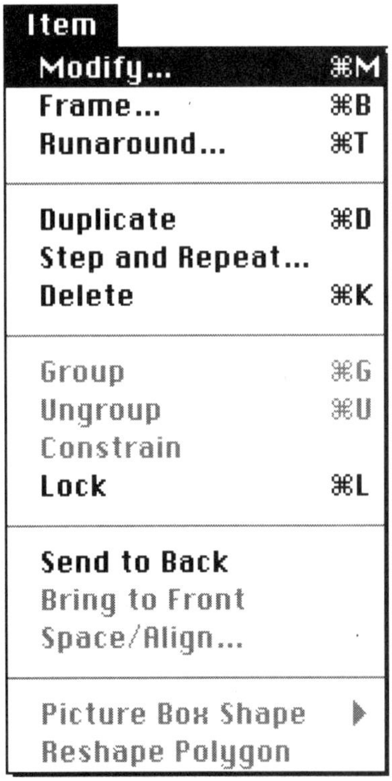

Item	
Modify...	⌘M
Frame...	⌘B
Runaround...	⌘T
Duplicate	⌘D
Step and Repeat...	
Delete	⌘K
Group	⌘G
Ungroup	⌘U
Constrain	
Lock	⌘L
Send to Back	
Bring to Front	
Space/Align...	
Picture Box Shape	▶
Reshape Polygon	

Figure 8. *The Item menu.*

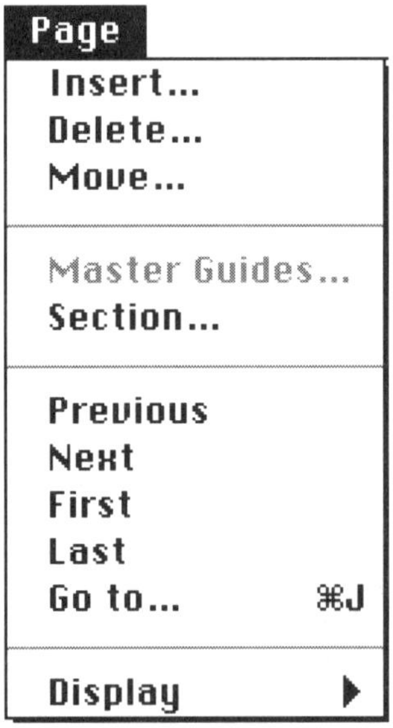

Page	
Insert...	
Delete...	
Move...	
Master Guides...	
Section...	
Previous	
Next	
First	
Last	
Go to...	⌘J
Display	▶

Figure 9. *The Page menu.*

The View menu.

View menu commands control document view sizes and the display of guides, rulers, invisibles and palettes.

The Utilities menu.

Utilities menu commands include miscellaneous functions, such as checking spelling, libraries, picture and font usage, tracking and kerning tables, and optional XTensions.

View

Fit in Window	⌘0
50%	
75%	
Actual Size	⌘1
200%	
Thumbnails	
Hide Guides	
Show Baseline Grid	
Snap to Guides	
Hide Rulers	⌘R
Show Invisibles	⌘I
Hide Tools	
Hide Measurements	
Show Document Layout	
Show Style Sheets	
Show Colors	
Show Trap Information	
Show Value Converter	
Windows	▶

Figure 10. *The View menu.*

Utilities

Check Spelling	▶
Auxiliary Dictionary...	
Edit Auxiliary...	
Suggested Hyphenation...	⌘H
Hyphenation Exceptions...	
Library...	
Font Usage...	
Picture Usage...	
Tracking Edit...	
Kerning Table Edit...	
Remove Manual Kerning	
Alternate Em Spaces	

Figure 11. *The Utilities menu.*

Menus

Dialog boxes:

Dialog boxes are like fill-in forms with multiple choices. The various methods of indicating one's choices are shown in **Figures 12-14**. Click OK or press Return to exit a dialog box and implement the indicated changes.

Dialog boxes can be opened from menus or through keyboard shortcuts. A dialog box will open when any menu item that is followed by an ellipsis (…) is selected.

✔ Tips

■ In any dialog box, press Tab to highlight the next field. Hold down Shift and press Tab to highlight the previous field.

■ Hold down Command (⌘) and press "Z" to undo changes made in a dialog box since it was opened.

*Round **buttons** can be clicked on and off. Only one button can be selected per group.*

*Numbers can be typed into **fields** in any of the seven measurement systems used in QuarkXPress.*

Check box options can be clicked on or off. If there is an "x" in a check box, that option is turned on.

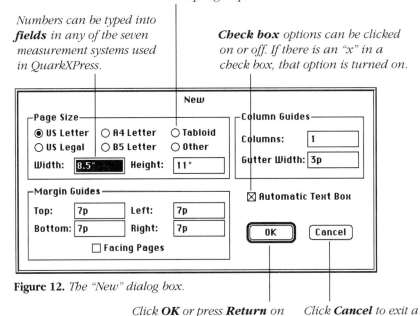

Figure 12. *The "New" dialog box.*

*Click **OK** or press **Return** on the keyboard to exit a box and accept the new settings.*

*Click **Cancel** to exit a box with no modifications taking effect.*

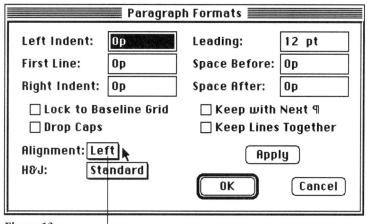

Figure 13.

Boxes with shadows open into pop-up menus.

Some dialog boxes can be moved by pressing and dragging their title bars.

If more than one value exists within a selection in the document, the corresponding field will be blank. For example, if highlighted text includes 8 pt. and 12 pt. leading, the Leading field will be blank.

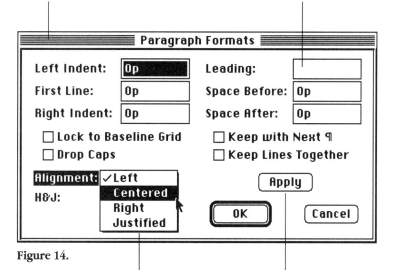

Figure 14.

Press and drag the mouse to make a selection from a pop-up menu.

*Click **Apply** or hold down Command (⌘) and press "A" to preview modifications in the document with the dialog box open. Hold down **Option** and click **Apply** to turn on Continuous Apply mode. Hold down Option and click Apply again to turn off Continuous apply mode.*

The Tool palette.

The Tool palette contains 13 tools for editing, item creation, and linking. Like all palettes, the Tool palette is moved by pressing and dragging the dotted bar, and closed by clicking the Close box. The Tool palette is opened or closed by selecting Show Tools or Hide Tools from the View menu.

✔ Tips

- To select the next tool in the Tool palette using the keyboard, hold down Command (⌘) and press Tab. To select the previous tool, hold down Command (⌘) and Shift and press Tab.

- Hold down Option and select any item creation or linking tool to keep it selected. To deselect a tool, click on another tool.

Figure 15.
The Tool palette.

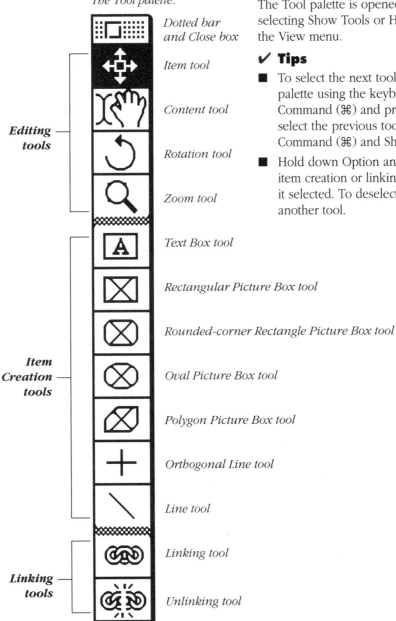

Dotted bar and Close box

Item tool

Content tool

Rotation tool

Zoom tool

Text Box tool

Rectangular Picture Box tool

Rounded-corner Rectangle Picture Box tool

Oval Picture Box tool

Polygon Picture Box tool

Orthogonal Line tool

Line tool

Linking tool

Unlinking tool

Editing tools

Item Creation tools

Linking tools

The Tool Palette

The Measurements palette.

The Measurements palette contains some of the commands and options
that are available under menus. The information on the Measurements
palette changes depending on what kind of item and tool are selected.
The palette is blank when no item is selected. Appendix B lists keyboard
shortcuts for use with the Measurements palette.

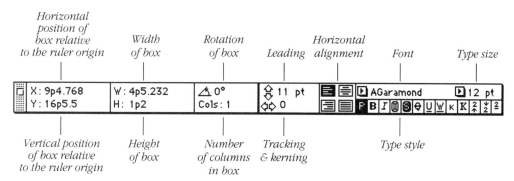

Figure 16. *The Measurements palette with the **Content tool** and a **text box** selected.*

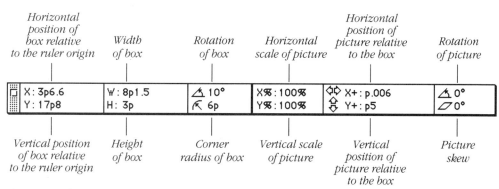

Figure 17. *The Measurements palette with the **Content tool** and a **picture box** selected.*

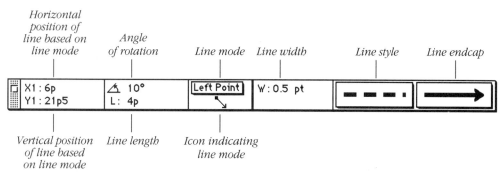

Figure 18. *The Measurements palette with the **Content tool** and a **line** selected.*

The Document Layout palette.

The Document Layout palette is used to rearrange, insert and delete document pages, move through a document, and create, modify and apply master pages.

Blank single-sided and facing-page icons.

Facing master page icon.

Document page icon.

The number of the page currently on display is in outline style.

Display a different page by double-clicking its icon.

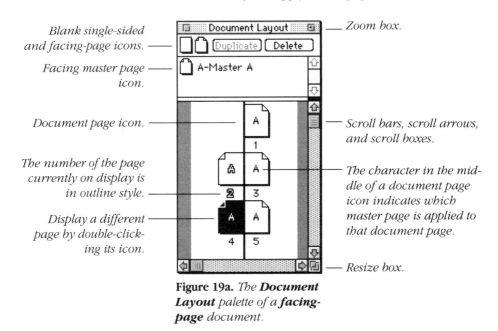

Zoom box.

Scroll bars, scroll arrows, and scroll boxes.

The character in the middle of a document page icon indicates which master page is applied to that document page.

Resize box.

Figure 19a. *The* **Document Layout** *palette of a* **facing-page** *document.*

The Style Sheets palette.

The Style Sheets palette is used to apply style sheets, which are sets of multiple character and paragraph specifications.

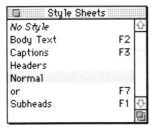

Figure 19b. *The* **Style Sheets** *palette.*

The Colors palette.

The Colors palette is used to apply colors to text, pictures, boxes, and lines, and to create blends.

Figure 19c. *The* **Colors** *palette.*

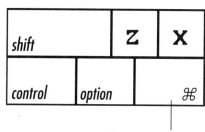

The Command key.

Figure 21. *The **Command** (⌘), **Option, Shift,** and **Control** keys are available on the left side of all Apple keyboards, and on the right side of an Apple extended keyboard.*

About keyboard shortcuts:

There are keyboard equivalents for many of the commands that are used in QuarkXPress. Most keyboard shortcuts are performed by holding down one or more keys on the keyboard, pressing and releasing another key or keys, and then finally releasing the first set of keys. For example, to perform the Save keystroke, hold down Command (⌘), press and release "S", then release Command.

(See Appendix B for a list of shortcuts)

To perform a keyboard shortcut:

1. Hold down the Command (⌘), Shift, Control, Option key or keys **(Figures 21-22)**.

2. Press and release the second key or keys.

3. Release the Command (⌘), Shift, Control, Option key or keys.

In this book, the Shift, Control, and Option keys are referred to by name. The Command name and icon (⌘) are used together to avoid confusion because the word "Command" does not appear on most keyboards.

✔ Tip

■ Do not use Enter in place of Return.

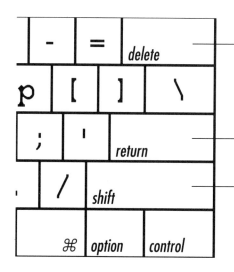

*The **Delete** key is used to delete text as well as text boxes, picture boxes, and lines.*

*The **Return** key is used to create new paragraphs. It is also used in lieu of pressing OK to exit a dialog box, or to accept changes made in the Measurements palette.*

*The **Shift** key is often used in keyboard shortcuts, but also maintains its traditional function for inputting uppercase characters.*

Figure 22. *The right side of an Apple extended keyboard.*

Keyboard Shortcuts

About Balloon Help:

If you are working on a computer that is operating with System 7 or later, a feature called Balloon Help is available. When this option is turned on and the cursor is moved over a screen icon, menu command, or dialog box, a balloon will open containing a brief description of that feature.

To turn Help Balloons on, select Show Balloons from the Help menu **(Figure 23)**.

To turn Help Balloons off, select Hide Balloons from the Help menu **(Figure 24)**.

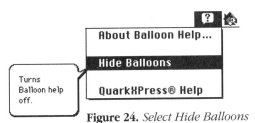

Figure 23. *Select Show Balloons from the Help menu.*

Figure 24. *Select Hide Balloons from the Help menu.*

About QuarkXPress' measurement systems:

Numbers in fields are displayed in the current default measurement system, but numbers can be entered in any of the other measurement systems used in QuarkXPress. The following measurement systems can be selected for a file: inches, inches decimal, picas, points, millimeters, centimeters, and ciceros **(Figures 25-26)**.

(See Chapter 18, Set Defaults)

✔ Tips

■ Do not enter "pts" for points or "in" for inches.

■ Picas and points can be combined. For example, to indicate four picas and six points, enter "4p6."

The seven measurement systems used in QuarkXPress. Use only these abbreviations in entry fields.	
Inches/ *Inches Decimal*	"
Picas	P
Points	pt
	or p followed by a number ("p6")
Centimeters	cm
Millimeters	mm
Ciceros	c

Figure 25. *Enter a number in any measurement system used in QuarkXPress.*

Figure 26. *When the Return key is pressed, the number is converted into the file's current default measurement system.*

Figure 1. *A picture in a picture box. This box has a .25 point frame applied to it.*

Figure 2. *A picture box with no frame applied to it.*

"Beauty! I've starved myself since you forgot about me. Now at least I shall die in peace..."
"Live!" cried Beauty. "And let us marry. How could I live without you, my dearest Beast?"

Figure 3. *A text box with a frame.*

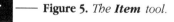

Figure 4. *A 2 point line.*

Like every software application, QuarkXPress has its own unique structure.

■ ***Pictures and text must be placed in picture and text boxes. Lines are drawn independently.***

The border of a text or picture box will print only when a frame is applied to it **(Figures 1-4)**.

■ ***Picture boxes, text boxes, and lines are defined as items.***

■ ***The picture or text that is contained in a box is defined as the contents of the box.***

■ ***To modify an item or its contents, the correct tool must be used.***

As a general rule, the Item tool is used to modify a box (an item), and the Content tool is used to modify the contents of a box (a picture or text). Tool selection is indicated as the first step for most procedures in this book. In some instances, the Item and Content tools can be used interchangeably, and this is also noted.

Click on a tool icon once to select a tool **(Figures 5-6)**.

Figure 5. *The **Item** tool.*

Figure 6. *The **Content** tool.*

■ **An item must be selected before it can be modified (Figures 7-8).**

■ **The information on the Measurements palette varies depending on which kind of tool and item is selected.**

The left side of the Measurements palette will display item information pertaining to a picture box, text box, line, or group, such as its angle of rotation or position on the page, if it is selected with the Item or Content tool **(Figure 9a)**.

The right side of the Measurements palette will display content information about a picture or text, such as point size or leading, only if it is selected with the Content tool **(Figures 9b)**. The right side of the Measurements palette will display information pertaining to the style of a line if it is selected with the Item or Content tool.

The Measurements palette will be blank if no item is selected **(Figure 9c)**.

Figure 7. *A picture box that is not selected.*

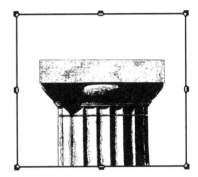

Figure 8. *Eight handles are displayed when a box is selected.*

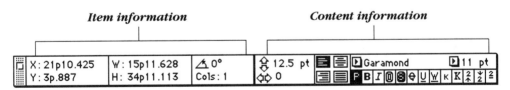

Figure 9a. *The Measurements palette with the **Item tool** and a **text box** selected.*

Item information   **Content information**

Figure 9b. *The Measurements palette with the **Content tool** and **text** selected.*

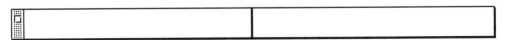

Figure 9c. *The Measurements palette with **no item** selected.*

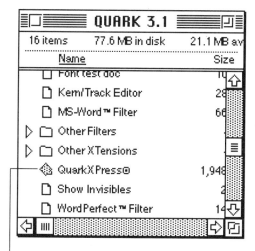

Figure 1. *Double-click the diamond-shaped application icon in the QuarkXPress folder.*

To launch QuarkXPress:

Double-click the QuarkXPress folder icon on the Finder desktop. Then double-click the diamond-shaped QuarkXPress application icon **(Figure 1)**.

or

Double-click any existing QuarkXPress file icon on the Finder desktop **(Figure 2)**.

✔ Tip

■ On a Macintosh with System 7 or later, the Finder desktop is visible at all times. If you activate the Finder desktop by accidentally clicking on it, return to QuarkXPress by clicking anywhere in an open QuarkXPress document window, or select QuarkXPress from the applications menu in the upper right-hand corner of the screen **(Figure 3)**.

Launch QuarkXPress

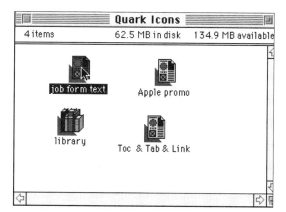

Figure 2. *Double-click any QuarkXPress file icon to launch the application **and** open the file simultaneously.*

Figure 3. *Select any open application from the applications menu.*

To create a new file:

1. Launch QuarkXPress.
   (See instructions on previous page)

2. Select New from the File menu
   (Figure 4).

Steps 3-8 are optional.

3. Click a Page Size button **(Figure 5)**.
   or
   Enter numbers in the Width and Height
   fields to create a custom size document.

4. Check or uncheck the Facing Pages
   box.

5. Modify the numbers in the Margin
   Guides fields.

6. Modify the number in the Columns
   field.

7. Modify the number in the Gutter
   Width field if the number of columns
   is greater than 1.

8. Check the Automatic Text Box box
   to have a text box to appear automatically within the margin guides on
   every document page.

9. Click OK or press Return.

✔ **Tips**

■ Laser printers do not print to the edge
   of the paper. Enter margin guides of
   approximately .5″ (3p) for an 8.5″ x
   11″ document.

■ If the page width of your document
   is greater than the page height and
   the page width is less than 8.5″,
   before printing, choose Page Setup
   from the File menu and click the landscape Orientation icon.
   (See page 174)

■ The New dialog box creates new files.
   The Open dialog box opens existing
   files.

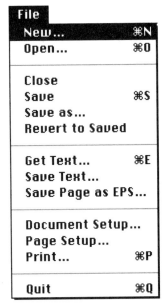

Figure 4. *Select **New** from the **File** menu.*

*Click a preset **Page Size** button or enter numbers between 1" and 48" in the **Width** and **Height** fields. A4 Letter is 210 mm x 297 mm; B5 Letter is 182 mm x 257 mm; Tabloid is 11" x 17". Numbers can be entered in any measurement system used in QuarkXPress.*

*Enter a **Gutter Width** between 3 and 288 points (4").*

*Enter a number between 1 and 30 in the **Columns** field.*

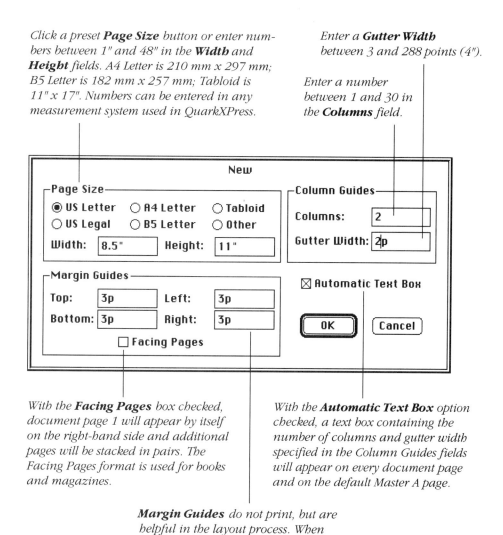

*With the **Facing Pages** box checked, document page 1 will appear by itself on the right-hand side and additional pages will be stacked in pairs. The Facing Pages format is used for books and magazines.*

*With the **Automatic Text Box** option checked, a text box containing the number of columns and gutter width specified in the Column Guides fields will appear on every document page and on the default Master A page.*

***Margin Guides** do not print, but are helpful in the layout process. When the Facing Pages box is checked, the Left and Right Margin Guides fields are labeled **Inside** and **Outside**.*

Figure 5. *The **New** dialog box.*

To save a new file:

1. Select Save from the File menu
   (**Figure 6**).

2. The "Save current document as" field
   will be highlighted automatically.
   Type a document name (**Figure 7a**).

3. If you are working on a Macintosh
   with System 6.07 or earlier, click Drive
   to select a location for the new file.

   If you are working on a Macintosh with
   System 7 or later, click Desktop, select
   a drive from the scroll list, then click
   Open (**Figures 7b**).

4. *Optional:* Select a folder or sub-
   folder in which to save the file, then
   Click Open.

5. Click Save (**Figure 7c**).

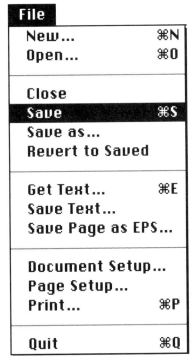

Figure 6. *Select* **Save** *from the* **File** *menu.*

Figure 7a. *The* **Save As** *dialog box with System 7 or later.*

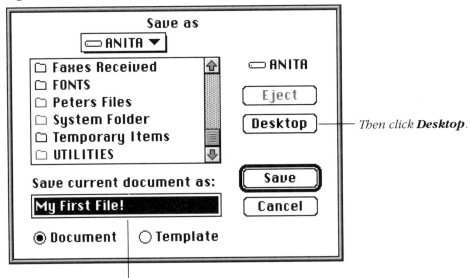

Then click **Desktop***.*

First, type in a name for the new file in the **Save current document as** *field.*

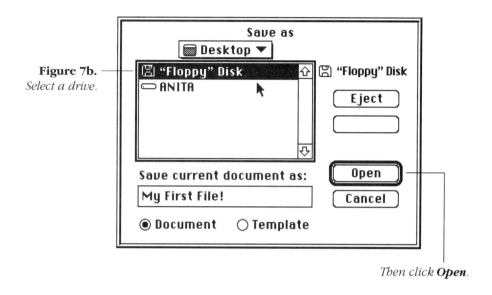

Figure 7b.
Select a drive.

*Then click **Open**.*

Figure 7c. *Make sure the name of the disk or folder you have selected to save in is displayed here.*

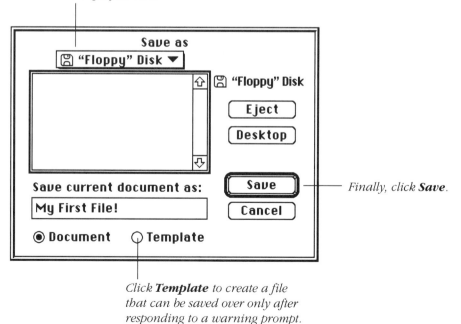

*Finally, click **Save**.*

*Click **Template** to create a file that can be saved over only after responding to a warning prompt.*

To save over an existing file:

Select Save from the File menu **(Figure 8)**.
or
Hold down Command (⌘) and press "S".

✔ Tips

■ **Save frequently!** If your computer freezes, you will be able to take full advantage of the Revert to Saved feature.

■ The Save command under the File menu is dimmed when a file has been saved and no new modifications have been made to it.

To revert to the last saved version:

1. Select Revert to Saved from the File menu.

2. When the prompt "Revert to the last version saved?" appears, click OK or press Return **(Figure 9)**.

✔ Tip

■ You can use the Revert to Saved feature to restore an earlier version of a file while experimenting with multiple design variations, or to restore a file that has been modified by a household pet walking across your keyboard.

File	
New...	⌘N
Open...	⌘O
Close	
Save	⌘S
Save as...	
Revert to Saved	
Get Text...	⌘E
Save Text...	
Save Page as EPS...	
Document Setup...	
Page Setup...	
Print...	⌘P
Quit	⌘Q

Figure 8. *Select **Save** from the **File** menu.*

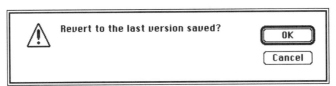

Figure 9. *If you select **Revert to Saved** from the **File** menu, this prompt will appear. Click **OK** to restore the last saved version.*

Figure 10. *Select **Save As** from the **File** menu.*

To duplicate a file:

1. Open a file to be duplicated.

2. Select Save As from the File menu **(Figure 10)**.

3. Enter a new name in the Save current document as field, or modify the existing name **(Figure 11)**.

4. Select a location in which to save the duplicate file.

5. Click Save.

✔ Tip

■ If the title of the active file is **not** altered in the Save as dialog box and you click Save, a warning prompt will appear. Click Replace to save over the original file, or click Cancel. The active file will not be duplicated.

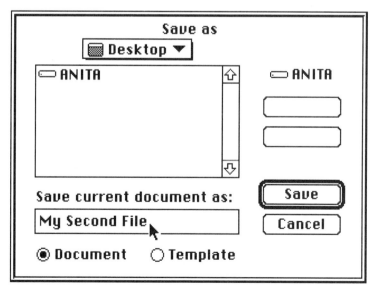

Figure 11. *Enter a new name for the duplicate file or alter the existing name, then click **Save**.*

Modify a Document's Page Size

To modify a document's page size:

1. Select Document Setup from the File menu **(Figure 12)**.

2. Click a preset page size.
or
Enter custom numbers in the Width and Height fields **(Figure 13)**.

3. Click OK or press Return.

✔ Tips

■ A single-sided document can be converted into a facing-page document by checking the Facing Pages box. To convert a facing-page document into a single-sided document, delete all the facing master pages in the document, and then uncheck the Facing Pages box.
(See Chapter 12, About Master Pages)

■ Column and margin guides are modified in the Master Guides dialog box, which can be opened from the Page menu when a master page is displayed.
(See Chapter 12, Modify Guides)

■ Reduced page size values will not be accepted if any items in the current file are too large to fit within the new pasteboard dimensions.

Figure 12. *Select* **Document Setup** *from the* **File** *menu.*

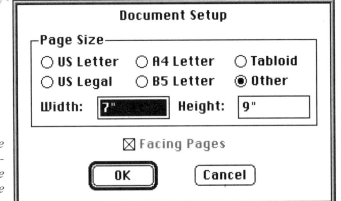

Figure 13. *Change the* **Width** *and* **Height** *of a document and check or uncheck the* **Facing Pages** *option in the Document Setup dialog box.*

Figure 14a. *Select* **Open** *from the* **File** *menu to open an existing file.*

To open a QuarkXPress file from within the application:

1. Select Open from the File menu **(Figure 14a)**.

2. Double-click a file name **(Figure 14b)**.
or
Click a file name once, then click Open. Multiple QuarkXPress files can be open at a time.

✔ Tip

■ Use the Open dialog box to convert a file to Version 3.2.

To open a QuarkXPress file from the Desktop:

Double-click a file icon. If QuarkXPress has not yet been launched, double-clicking a QuarkXPress file will launch the application and open the file **(Figure 15)**.

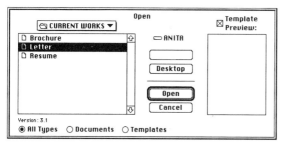

Figure 14b. *Click a file name, then click* **Open**.

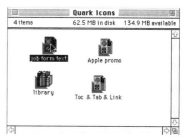

Figure 15. *Open a QuarkXPress file from the desktop by double-clicking its icon.*

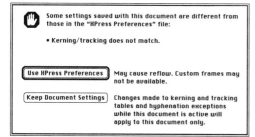

Figure 16. *The XPress Preferences prompt.*

XPress Preferences.

Tracking and kerning table settings, custom frame data, and hyphenation exceptions are stored in individual documents and in the QuarkXPress folder in a file called XPress Preferences. If, upon opening a file, the document settings do not match the XPress Preferences settings, a prompt will appear **(Figure 16)**. Click Use XPress Preferences to apply the Preferences resident on that machine. Click Keep Document Settings to leave the document as is.

To close a file:

Click the Close box in the upper left-hand corner of the document window **(Figure 17)**.

or

Select Close from the File menu.

✔ Tip

■ If you attempt to close a file that has never been saved, a prompt will appear giving you the option to save or discard the file, or cancel the close operation **(Figure 19)**.

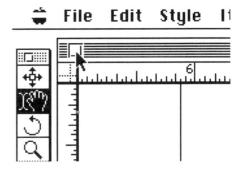

Figure 17. *Click the Close box in the upper left-hand corner of the document window to close a file.*

To quit the application:

Select Quit from the File menu **(Figure 18)**.

or

Hold down Command (⌘) and press "Q".

✔ Tip

■ Quitting the application will close all open QuarkXPress files. If changes have been made to an open file since it was last saved, a prompt will appear giving you the option to save again before quitting or cancel the quit operation **(Figure 20)**.

Figure 18. *Select **Quit** from the **File** menu to close the application and close any open QuarkXPress files.*

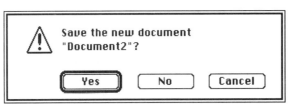

Figure 19. *If you attempt to close a file that has never been saved, this prompt will appear.*

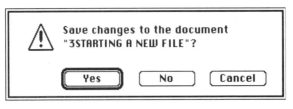

Figure 20. *If you attempt to quit the application and modifications were made to the file since it was last saved, this prompt will appear.*

Close a File; Quit the Application

```
View
  Fit in Window      ⌘0
  50%
  75%
  Actual Size        ⌘1
  200%
  Thumbnails

  Hide Guides
  Show Baseline Grid
  Snap to Guides
  Hide Rulers        ⌘R
  Show Invisibles    ⌘I

  Hide Tools
  Hide Measurements
  Show Document Layout
  Show Style Sheets
  Show Colors
  Show Trap Information
  Show Value Converter
  Windows            ▶
```

Figure 1. *Select from a list of view sizes under the* **View** *menu.*

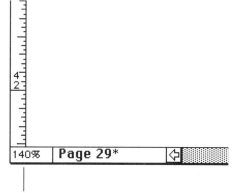

Figure 2. *The* **View Percent field**.

There are many ways to move from page to page and to change from small to large display sizes, or "views." Modifying the view size of a file does not alter the actual page size, only the size at which it is displayed.

To select a view size from the View menu:

Select Fit in Window, 50%, 75%, Actual Size, 200%, or Thumbnails from the View menu **(Figure 1)**.

✔ Tip

■ Page elements cannot be modified in Thumbnails view. Pages within a file can be rearranged in Thumbnails view, and pages can be drag-copied from one file to another if both documents are in Thumbnails view. *(See Chapter 6, Rearrange Pages)*

To change the view size using the View Percent field:

1. Double-click in the View Percent field in the lower left-hand corner of the document window **(Figure 2)**.

2. Enter a number between 10 and 400.

3. Press Return.

✔ Tips

■ If the view size is changed when an item is selected or text is highlighted, the item or text will be centered in the document window in the new view size.

■ It is not necessary to enter the % symbol in the View Percent field.

Change View Sizes

To change the view size using the Zoom tool from the keyboard:

Hold down Control and click on the page to enlarge the view size **(Figure 3)**.

or

Hold down Control and Option and click on the page to reduce the view size **(Figure 4)**.

or

Hold down Control and press and drag a marquee around an area on the page that you wish to enlarge **(Figure 5)**.

✔ Tip

■ Accessing the Zoom tool from the keyboard is faster than selecting and then deselecting the Zoom tool from the Tool palette.

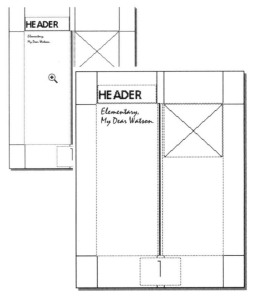

Figure 3. *Hold down **Control** and click on the page to enlarge the view size.*

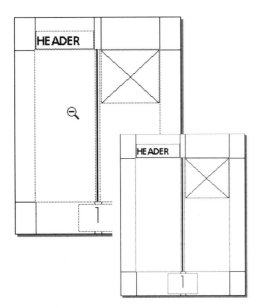

Figure 4. *Hold down **Option** and **Control** and click on a page to reduce the view size.*

Figure 5. *Hold down **Control** and press and drag over a section of a page to magnify that chosen area.*

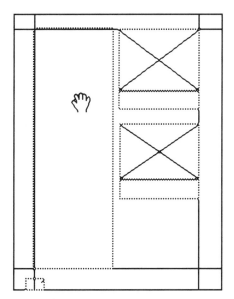

Figure 6. *Hold down **Option** and press and drag with the mouse to move a page in the document window.*

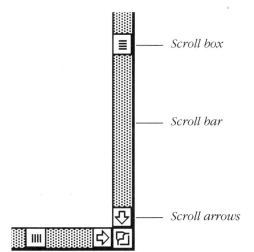

Scroll box

Scroll bar

Scroll arrows

Figure 7. *The standard Macintosh window features: scroll boxes, bars, and arrows.*

To move through a document using the page grabber hand:

Hold down Option and press and drag to move a page in the document window. The cursor will temporarily turn into a hand icon **(Figure 6)**.

✔ Tip

■ The Page Grabber Hand feature is turned on in the Application Preferences dialog box, opened from the Preferences pop-up menu under the Edit menu.

To move through a document using the scroll arrows, bars and boxes:

Click on a **scroll arrow** to move a short distance within a document in the direction the arrow is pointing **(Figure 7)**.
or
Move a **scroll box** to move through a document more quickly.
or
Click on a grey **scroll bar** to move through a document a full screen at a time. Click in the gray area above the scroll box to move a full screen upward, and below the box to move a full screen downward. Click to the left of the scroll box to move a full screen to the left, and to the right of the scroll box to move a full screen to the right.

Move Through a Document

To move through a document using an extended keyboard:

Press Page Up or Page Down to move up or down a full screen **(Figure 8)**.

or

Press Home to move to the beginning of a document or press End to move to the end of a document.

✔ Tip

- Hold down Shift and press Page Up to display the top of the previous page, or Page Down to display the top of the next page.

To move through a document using the Page menu:

Select Previous, Next, First, or Last from the Page menu **(Figure 9)**.

or

Select Go to from the Page menu or hold down Command (⌘) and press "J". Enter the desired page number in the Go to Page field, then click OK or press Return **(Figure 10)**.

✔ Tip

- If a page has a prefix applied using the Section command, be sure to enter the prefix before the number in the Go to dialog box. To display a page based on its position in the document rather than its applied Section number, enter "+" before the number.

(See Chapter 12, Number Sections)

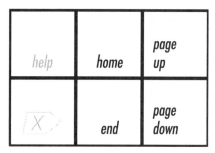

Figure 8. *A section of an extended keyboard.*

Figure 9. *Select **Previous**, **Next**, **First**, **Last**, or **Go to** from the **Page** menu.*

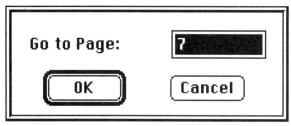

Figure 10. *The **Go to** dialog box can be accessed quickly by holding down Command (⌘) and pressing "J".*

Move Through a Document

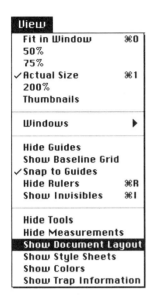

Figure 11. *Select **Show Document Layout** from the **View** menu.*

To move through a document using the Document Layout palette:

1. Select Show Document Layout from the View menu **(Figure 11)**.

2. Double-click a document page icon **(Figure 12)**.

✔ Tip

■ The page icon of the first page in a Section will be marked with an asterisk. Page icons are numbered according to the position of the pages in the document.

(See also page 140)

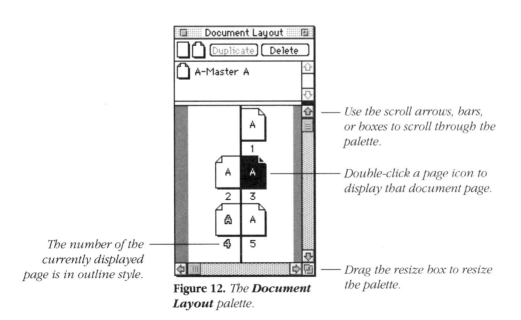

The number of the currently displayed page is in outline style.

— *Use the scroll arrows, bars, or boxes to scroll through the palette.*

— *Double-click a page icon to display that document page.*

— *Drag the resize box to resize the palette.*

Figure 12. *The **Document Layout** palette.*

Move Through a Document

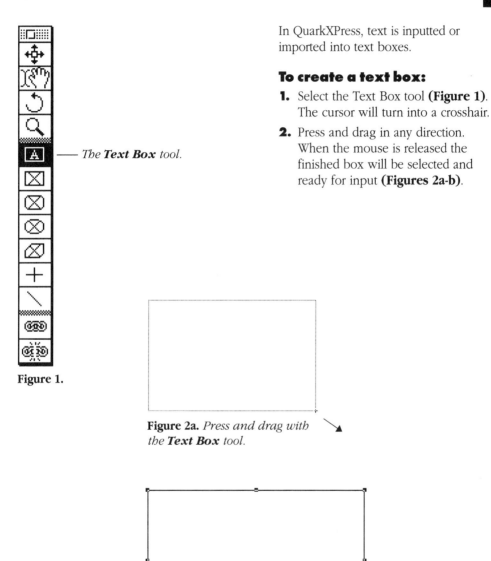

Figure 1.

— *The **Text Box** tool.*

In QuarkXPress, text is inputted or imported into text boxes.

To create a text box:

1. Select the Text Box tool **(Figure 1)**. The cursor will turn into a crosshair.

2. Press and drag in any direction. When the mouse is released the finished box will be selected and ready for input **(Figures 2a-b)**.

Figure 2a. *Press and drag with the **Text Box** tool.*

Figure 2b. *A new text box is created.*

Create a Text Box

To resize a text box manually:

1. Select the Item or Content tool.

2. Click on a box.

3. Press and drag any handle **(Figures 3-4)**.

✔ Tips

■ Make sure the point of the cursor arrow is directly over one of the box handles before pressing the mouse. The cursor will change into a pointing hand icon.

■ To resize a box and preserve its original proportions, hold down Option and Shift while dragging.

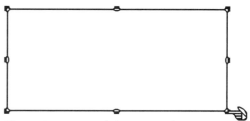

Figure 3. *Press and drag any of the four corner handles of a box.*

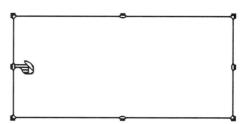

Figure 4 *Press and drag any of the four midpoint handles of a box.*

To resize a text box using the Measurements palette:

1. Select the Item or Content tool.

2. Click on a box.

3. Next to the W in the Measurements palette, enter a number in increments as small as .001 to modify the width of the box **(Figure 5)**.

and/or

Next to the H in the Measurements palette, enter a number to modify the height of the box.

4. Press Return.

✔ Tip

■ Numbers can be entered in any of the measurement systems used in QuarkXPress. Be sure to include the proper abbreviation, such as "p" or "mm," if the number is in a measurement system other than the default measurement system.

(See Chapter 1, Measurement Systems)

The **horizontal position** of the box. The number can be replaced, or a plus or minus sign and a specified amount can be entered to the right of the current number.

The **width** of the box.

```
X: 2p6-3"     W: 11p
Y: 35p        H: 6"
```

The **vertical position** of the box.

The **height** of the box.

Figure 5. *In this illustration of the Measurements palette, numbers in the fields have been entered in different measurement systems.*

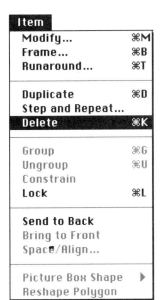

Figure 6. *Select a box, then select* **Delete** *from the* **Item** *menu.*

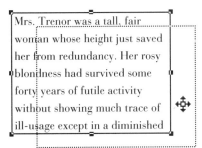

Figure 7a. *Make sure the cursor turns into an Item tool icon before you drag the mouse. A text box, as well as any other item, can be dragged from one page to another.*

Figure 7b. *If you do not pause for the text to redraw, only the outline of the box will be displayed as it is moved.*

To delete a text box:

1. Select the **Item** or **Content** tool.

2. Click on a text box.

3. Select Delete from the Item menu **(Figure 6)**.
or
Hold down Command (⌘) and press "K".

✔ Tip

■ A text box selected with the Item tool can also be deleted by pressing Delete on the keyboard or selecting Clear from the Edit menu.

To move a text box manually:

1. Select the Item tool.

2. Press inside a text box, pause briefly for the text to redraw, then drag **(Figures 7a-b)**.

✔ Tip

■ Hold down Shift as you drag to constrain the movement to a horizontal or vertical axis. Release the mouse before releasing Shift.

To reposition a text box using the Measurements palette:

1. Select the Item or Content tool.

2. Click on a text box.

3. Enter a number next to the X in the Measurements palette to modify the horizontal position of the box relative to the ruler origin **(Figure 5)**.
and/or
Enter a number next to the Y in the Measurements palette to modify the vertical position of the box relative to the ruler origin.

4. Press Return.

(See also Chapter 9, Use a Guide to Position a Box)

Delete a Text Box; Move a Text Box

To input text:

1. Create a new text box.
   (See Create a Text Box in this chapter)
   or
   Click in an already existing box to create an insertion point.

2. Select the Content tool.

3. Make sure the text box is still selected, then begin to type **(Figure 8)**.

✔ Tips

■ Press Return as you are typing to begin a new paragraph.

■ Select Show Invisibles from the View menu to reveal paragraph returns, spaces, and other non-printing characters **(Figure 9)**.

■ To position the first line of text in a box a specified distance from the top of the box, select Modify from the Item menu and enter a number in the First Baseline field.
   (See Text Inset in this chapter)

As soon as they were gone, Elizabeth walked out to recover her spirits; or in other words, to dwell without interruption on those subjects that must deaden them more. Mr. Darcy's behavior astonished

Figure 8. *Text is typed into a text box with the Content tool selected.*

As·soon·as·they·were·gone,·Elizabeth· walked·out·to·recover·her·spirits;·or·in· other·words,·to·dwell·without·interruption· on·those·subjects·that·must·deaden·them· more.·Mr.·Darcy's·behavior·astonished· and·vexed·her.¶
"Why,·if·he·came·only·to·be·silent,·
Jane Austen

Figure 9. *Press Return to begin a new paragraph. Select Show Invisibles from the View menu to display paragraph returns and other non-printing characters.*

What does the text overflow symbol mean?

If a text box is too small to display all the text that it contains, a text overflow symbol will appear in the lower right-hand corner of the box **(Figure 10)**. The text overflow symbol will disappear if the text box is enlarged enough to display all the type that it contains.

✔ Tip

■ The text overflow symbol does not print. It is merely an indicator that there is text in the buffer. Only the text that is visible in the box will print.

As soon as they were gone, Elizabeth walked out to recover her spirits; or in other words, to dwell without interruption on those subjects that must deaden them more. Mr. Darcy's behavior astonished ⊠

Figure 10. *The text overflow symbol appears when a box is too small to display all the text that it contains.*

On an exceptionally hot evening early in July a young man came out of the garret in which he lodged in S. Place and walked slowly, as though in hesitation, towards K. Bridge.

He had successfully avoided meeting his landlady on the staircase. His garret was under the roof of a high, five-storied-

Figure 11. *Double-click to highlight a **word**.*

On an exceptionally hot evening early in July a young man came out of the garret in which he lodged in S. Place and walked slowly, as though in hesitation, towards K. Bridge.

He had successfully avoided meeting his landlady on the staircase. His garret was under the roof of a high, five-storied

Figure 12. *Triple-click to highlight a **line**.*

On an exceptionally hot evening early in July a young man came out of the garret in which he lodged in S. Place and walked slowly, as though in hesitation, towards K. Bridge.

He had successfully avoided meeting his landlady on the staircase. His garret was under the roof of a high, five-storied

Figure 13. *Click four times to highlight a **paragraph**.*

To highlight text:

1. Select the Content tool.

2. Press and drag over the text to be highlighted.

or

Click the following number of times:

1 click	To create an **insertion point**
2 clicks	To highlight a **word and the space following it**
3 clicks	To highlight a **line**
4 clicks	To highlight a **paragraph**
5 clicks	To highlight a **story**

(Figures 11-13)

✔ Tips

■ If a box is deselected and then selected again with the Content tool, the last group of characters highlighted will be highlighted again. To create a new insertion point, click once more in the text box.

■ A story can also be highlighted by selecting the Content tool, clicking in a text box, then choosing **Select All** from the Edit menu. A story consists of text contained in one box or a series of linked boxes.

■ If Select All is chosen with the **Item** tool selected, all items on the currently displayed page or spread and surrounding pasteboard will be selected.

■ Text can also be highlighted by clicking in a text box at the beginning of a desired selection, then holding down Shift and clicking at the end of the selection.

To delete one character:

1. Select the Content tool.

2. Click to the right of a character to be deleted **(Figure 14)**.

3. Press Delete.

✔ Tip

■ Press the left or right pointing arrow key on the keyboard to move the insertion point one character at a time.

CHES|TER

Figure 14. *If the Delete key were pressed with the cursor in this insertion point, the "S" would be deleted.*

To delete more than one character:

1. Select the Content tool.

2. Highlight the text that is to be deleted **(Figure 15)**.

3. Press Delete.

CHESTER

Figure 15. *If the Delete key were pressed with this selection highlighted, the "HES" would be deleted.*

About the Clipboard:

The **Clipboard** is a holding area that stores one cut or copied selection at a time. The current contents of the Clipboard can be retrieved an unlimited number of times with the Paste command. The Cut, Copy and Paste commands are found under the Edit menu **(Figure 16)**. The Clipboard contents are purged when you quit the application and when the computer is shut down or restarted.

Figure 16. *The Clipboard is accessed via the **Cut, Copy** and **Paste** selections under the **Edit** menu.*

Hip. Well shone, moon—Truly, the
moon shines with a good grace.

Dem. Well roared, lion.
The. Well run, Thisbe.
The. Well moused, lion.

Figure 17a. *To move text, highlight it,
then select **Cut** from the **Edit** menu.*

Dem. Well roared, lion.
The. Well run, Thisbe.
The. Well moused, lion.

Figure 17b. *Click to create a new
insertion point.*

Dem. Well roared, lion.
The. Well run, Thisbe.
Hip. Well shone, moon—Truly, the
moon shines with a good grace.
The. Well moused, lion.
                    William Shakespeare

Figure 17c. *Select **Paste** from the **Edit** menu.*

To rearrange text using the Clipboard:

1. Select the Content tool.

2. Highlight the text that is to be moved
(Figure 17a).

3. Select **Cut** from the Edit menu to
place the highlighted text on the
Clipboard and **remove** it from its
current location.

or

Select **Copy** from the Edit menu to
place a copy of the highlighted text on
the Clipboard and **leave** the highlighted text in its current location.

4. Click in the text to create a new insertion point **(Figure 17b)**.

5. Select **Paste** from the Edit menu
(Figure 17c).

✔ Tips

■ The Clipboard can also be used to cut
or copy a text box, picture box, line,
or group with the Item tool selected,
or a picture with the Content tool
selected. Be sure to Paste using the
same tool that was used to Cut or Copy.

■ A text box that is linked to another
text box cannot be cut or copied.

(See Chapter 6, Link Text Boxes)

Accessing the Clipboard using the keyboard.

Cut	Command + **X**
Copy	Command + **C**
Paste	Command + **V**

The Clipboard

To frame a text box:

1. Select the Item or Content tool.

2. Click on a box.

3. Select Frame from the Item menu **(Figure 18)**.
or
Hold down Command (⌘) and press "B".

4. Select a preset width from the Width pop-up menu **(Figure 19)**.
or
Enter a custom width between .001 and 504 points in the Width field.

Steps 5-7 are optional.

5. Select an alternate style from the Style window.

6. Select a color from the Color pop-up menu.

7. Select a shade from the Shade pop-up menu or enter a percentage in the Shade field in increments as small as .1%.

8. Click OK or press Return **(Figure 20)**.

✔ Tip

■ Enter 0 in the Width field to remove a frame.

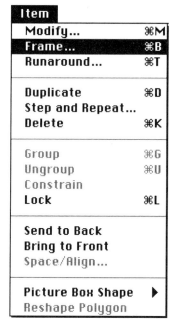

Figure 18. *Select* **Frame** *from the* **Item** *menu.*

Figure 19. *The Frame Specifications dialog box.*

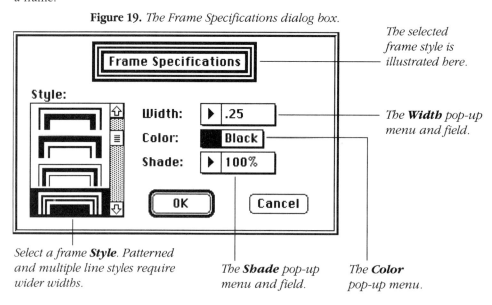

The selected frame style is illustrated here.

The **Width** *pop-up menu and field.*

Select a frame **Style**. *Patterned and multiple line styles require wider widths.*

The **Shade** *pop-up menu and field.*

The **Color** *pop-up menu.*

Figure 20. *Frames of varying styles and widths can be used to embellish boxes.*

SPEAK what you think now in hard words, and to-morrow speak what to-morrow thinks in hard words again, though it contradict every thing you said to-day.—"Ah, so you shall be sure to be misunderstood."—Is it so bad, then, to be misunderstood? Pythagoras was misunderstood, and Socrates, and Jesus, and Luther, and Copernicus, and Galileo, and Newton, and every pure and wise spirit that ever took flesh. To be great is to be misunderstood.

Ralph Waldo Emerson

Fish, like guests, smell after three days.

If you have built castles in the air, your work need not be lost; that is where they should be. Now put the foundations under them.

Henry David Thoreau

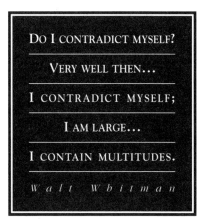

Do I contradict myself?

Very well then…

I contradict myself;

I am large…

I contain multitudes.

W a l t   W h i t m a n

Matzoh-Ball Soup

2 T. chicken fat (schmaltz)
2 large eggs, beaten
1 cup matzoh meal
Freshly ground pepper
Nutmeg
1 T. parsley, minced
1 lb. helium
4 cups chicken broth

1. Place matzoh meal in a bowl. Add 1 cup boiling water and mix well.
2. Add schmaltz, eggs, parsley, and helium and mix well. Season to taste with pepper and nutmeg.
3. Refrigerate for at least a half hour.
4. Bring chicken broth to a boil in a large saucepan.
5. Roll dough into balls about 1" in diameter.
6. Drop matzoh balls into broth one at a time, boil gently for 15 minutes, and serve.

Frame a Text Box

About Text Inset:

The Text Inset feature is used to adjust the space between text and the four edges of the box that contains it. A Text Inset value greater than zero should be applied to a box with a frame.

To modify the Text Inset:

1. Select a text box.

2. Select Modify from the Item menu **(Figure 21)**.

3. Enter an amount in the Text Inset field **(Figure 22)**.

4. Click OK or press Return **(Figures 23-24)**.

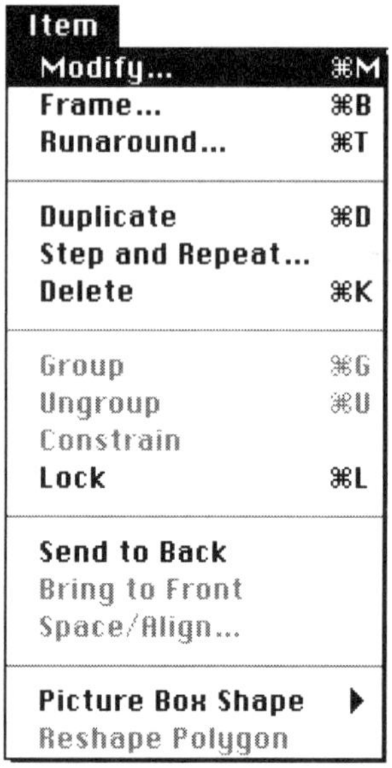

Figure 21. Select ***Modify*** *from the* ***Item*** *menu.*

Item	
Modify...	⌘M
Frame...	⌘B
Runaround...	⌘T
Duplicate	⌘D
Step and Repeat...	
Delete	⌘K
Group	⌘G
Ungroup	⌘U
Constrain	
Lock	⌘L
Send to Back	
Bring to Front	
Space/Align...	
Picture Box Shape	▶
Reshape Polygon	

Text Box Specifications

Origin Across:	22p2.634
Origin Down:	38p7.382
Width:	16p
Height:	10p3.4
Box Angle:	0°
Columns:	1
Gutter:	1p.024
Text Inset:	12 pt

☐ Suppress Printout

First Baseline
Offset: 0p
Minimum: Ascent

Vertical Alignment
Type: Centered

Background
Color: None

OK   Cancel

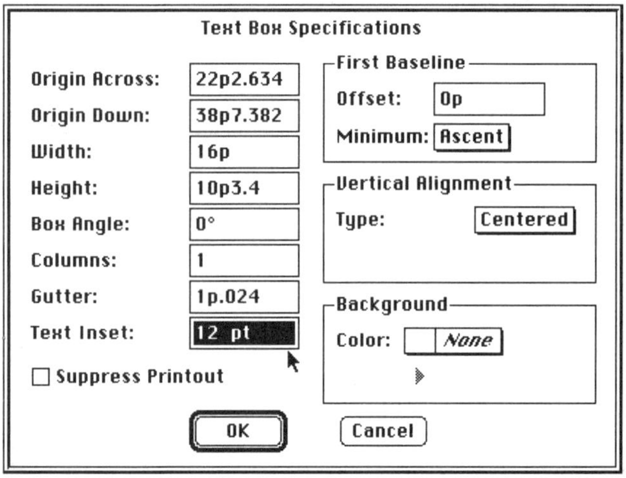

Figure 22. The ***Text Inset*** *field in the* ***Text Box Specifications*** *dialog box.*

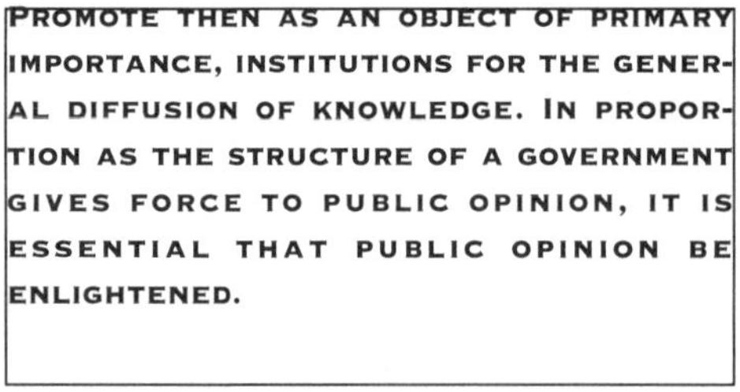

PROMOTE THEN AS AN OBJECT OF PRIMARY IMPORTANCE, INSTITUTIONS FOR THE GENERAL DIFFUSION OF KNOWLEDGE. IN PROPORTION AS THE STRUCTURE OF A GOVERNMENT GIVES FORCE TO PUBLIC OPINION, IT IS ESSENTIAL THAT PUBLIC OPINION BE ENLIGHTENED.

Figure 23. *A text box with a text inset of 0 pt.*

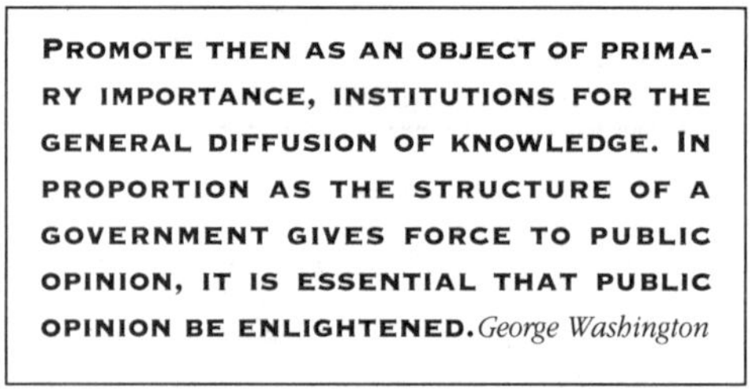

PROMOTE THEN AS AN OBJECT OF PRIMARY IMPORTANCE, INSTITUTIONS FOR THE GENERAL DIFFUSION OF KNOWLEDGE. IN PROPORTION AS THE STRUCTURE OF A GOVERNMENT GIVES FORCE TO PUBLIC OPINION, IT IS ESSENTIAL THAT PUBLIC OPINION BE ENLIGHTENED.*George Washington*

Figure 24. *A text box with a text inset of 8 pt.*

Text Inset

Figure 25. *The **rotation angle** of a text box.*

X : 10p	W : 5p3	⊿ 30°
Y : 12p	H : 2p5	Cols : 1

—— *The **Rotation tool**.*

Figure 26.

To rotate a text box using the Measurements palette:

1. Select the Item or Content tool.

2. Click on a text box.

3. In the rotation field on the Measurements palette, enter a number between -360° and 360° **(Figure 25)**. Enter a positive number to rotate counterclockwise. Enter a negative number to rotate clockwise.

4. Press Return.

✔ Tip

■ Text in a rotated position can be modified.

To rotate a text box using the Rotation tool:

1. Select the Rotation tool **(Figure 26)**.

2. Click on a text box.

3. Press to create an axis point for rotation, then drag the mouse away from the axis to create a "lever" **(Figure 27)**.

4. Drag clockwise or counterclockwise **(Figure 28)**.

✔ Tip

■ Hold down Shift while dragging to rotate in 45° increments.

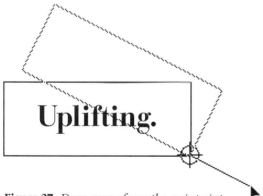

Figure 27. *Drag away from the axis point to create a "lever" before rotating, so the rotation will be easier to control.*

Figure 28. *A text box rotated -90 .°*

Rotate a Text Box

Text boxes can be made "see-through" and layered on top of each other.

To make a box transparent:

1. Select the Item or Content tool.

2. Click on the text box that is to be on the top layer.

3. Select Runaround from the Item menu **(Figure 29)**.

4. Select None from the Mode pop-up menu **(Figure 30)**.

5. Click OK or press Return.

6. Select Show Colors from the View menu.

7. Click the Background icon on the Colors palette **(Figure 31)**.

8. Click None. Selecting Black with a 0% shade will not result in the same effect.

9. If the box is not on the top layer, select Bring to Front from the Item menu **(Figure 29)**.

10. Click in the margin or pasteboard to deselect all items and make the screen redraw **(Figures 32-35)**.

✔ Tip

■ To select an item that is behind another item, hold down Command (⌘), Option, Shift and click. Each click will select the next item behind in succession.
(See "Layer Items" on page 163)

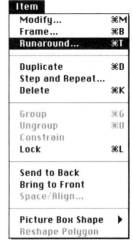

Figure 29. Select **Runaround** *from the* **Item** *menu.*

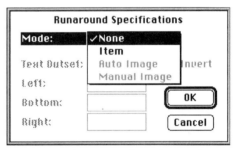

Figure 30. *Select* **None** *from the* **Mode** *pop-up menu.*

Click the **background** *icon.*

Then click **None** *to make the top box transparent.*

Figure 31. *The* **Colors** *palette.*

Layer Text Boxes

Figure 32. *A variety of effects can be created by making boxes see-through. This shadow effect was created using two text boxes. A shade of 30% was applied to the "shadow" type.*

Figure 33. *Boxes can be rotated and made transparent.*

Figure 34. *Boxes can be layered to create an illusion of depth.*

Figure 35. *Text boxes can be layered on top of a picture box.*

To wrap the text of one box around another box:

1. Create a new text box on top of an existing text box.
   (See Create a Text Box in this chapter)
2. With the new box still selected, select Runaround from the Item menu **(Figure 36)**.
3. Select Item from the Mode pop-up menu **(Figure 37)**.
4. Enter a number in the Top, Left, Bottom and Right fields to adjust the space between the text box and the type wrapping around it.
5. Click OK or press Return **(Figures 38-39)**.

✔ Tip

- Text can also be wrapped around an existing box. The box that is to have text wrapped around it must be in front. Select it and choose Bring to Front from the Item menu, if necessary.
  (See Chapter 15, Layer Items)

Item
Modify... ⌘M
Frame... ⌘B
Runaround... ⌘T
Duplicate ⌘D
Step and Repeat...
Delete ⌘K
Group ⌘G
Ungroup ⌘U
Constrain
Lock ⌘L
Send to Back
Bring to Front
Space/Align...
Picture Box Shape
Reshape Polygon

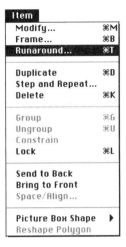

Figure 36. *Select **Runaround** from the **Item** menu.*

Runaround Specifications
Mode: Item
Top: 6 pt
Left: 4
Bottom: 8
Right: 6
OK
Cancel

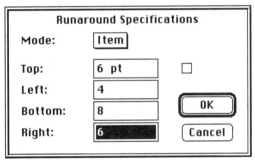

Figure 37. *Select **Item** from the **Mode** pop-up menu.*

We thus learn that man is descended from a hairy, tailed quadruped, probably arboreal in its habits, and an inhabitant of the Old World. This creature, if its whole structure had been examined by a naturalist, would have been classed amongst the Quadrumana, as surely as the still more ancient progenitor of the Old and New World monkeys.
We thus learn that man is descended from a hairy, tailed quadruped, probably arboreal in its habits, and an inhabitant of the Old World.
The Quadrumana and all the higher mammals are probably derived from an ancient marsupial animal, and this through a long series of diversified forms, from some amphibian-like creature, and this again

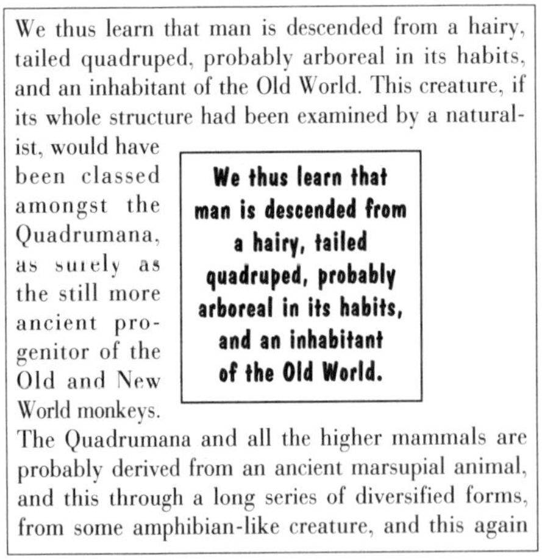

Figure 38. *Text will only wrap around **three** sides of a box that is placed **within a column**.*

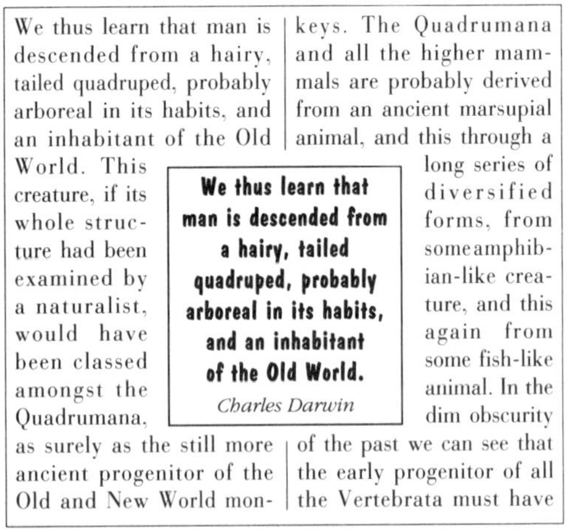

We thus learn that man is descended from a hairy, tailed quadruped, probably arboreal in its habits, and an inhabitant of the Old World. This creature, if its whole structure had been examined by a naturalist, would have been classed amongst the Quadrumana, as surely as the still more ancient progenitor of the Old and New World mon-
keys. The Quadrumana and all the higher mammals are probably derived from an ancient marsupial animal, and this through a long series of diversified forms, from some amphibian-like creature, and this again from some fish-like animal. In the dim obscurity of the past we can see that the early progenitor of all the Vertebrata must have
We thus learn that man is descended from a hairy, tailed quadruped, probably arboreal in its habits, and an inhabitant of the Old World.
Charles Darwin

Figure 39. *Text will wrap around **all four** sides of a box if it **straddles two columns**.*

Follow these instructions to modify the number of columns and gutter width in an individual box. To change the non-printing margin and column guides or to change the number of columns in a box originating from a master page, see Chapter 12, Modify Guides and Modify a Master Page.

To modify columns using the Measurements palette:

1. Select the Item or Content tool.

2. Select a text box.

3. Enter a number in the "Cols" field on the Measurements palette **(Figure 40)**.

4. Press Return.

To modify columns and/or gutter width using the Modify dialog box:

1. Select the Item or Content tool.

2. Select a text box.

3. Select Modify from the Item menu **(Figure 36)**.

4. Enter a number between 1 and 30 in the Columns field **(Figure 41)**.
and/or
Enter a number in the Gutter field.

5. Click OK or press Return.

Figure 40. *The number of columns in a text box can be modified using the Measurements palette.*

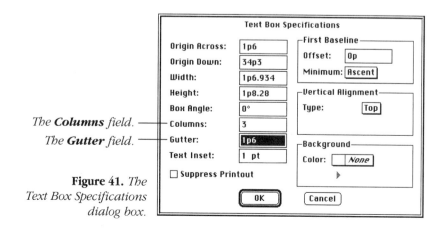

*The **Columns** field.*
*The **Gutter** field.*

Figure 41. *The Text Box Specifications dialog box.*

Modify Columns

About Save Text:

Text in a QuarkXPress file can be saved in a word processing file format. The text in the QuarkXPress file is not affected.

To save text as a word processing file:

1. Select the Content tool.

2. Highlight text to be saved.
   or
   Click in a story.

3. Select Save Text from the File menu **(Figure 42)**.

4. Enter a title in the Save Text as field **(Figure 43)**.

5. If text is highlighted in the document, click Entire Story or Selected Text. If you clicked in a story, only the Entire Story option will be available.

6. Select a file format from the Format pop-up menu.

7. Select a location in which to save the text file.

8. Click Save.

✔ Tips

- The import/export filter for the chosen word processing file format must be in the QuarkXPress folder.

- Text saved in the ASCII format will be stripped of all formatting. Text saved in a word processing application format may be stripped of some formatting. Text saved in the XPress Tags format will retain all formatting, but will be displayed with special codes.

File	
New...	⌘N
Open...	⌘O
Close	
Save	⌘S
Save as...	
Revert to Saved	
Get Text...	⌘E
Save Text...	
Save Page as EPS...	
Document Setup...	
Page Setup...	
Print...	⌘P
Quit	⌘Q

Figure 42. *Select **Save Text** from the **File** menu.*

Figure 43. *The Save Text dialog box.*

*Enter a title in the **Save Text as** field.*

*Click **Entire Story** or **Selected Text** (if available).*

*Select a file **Format**.*

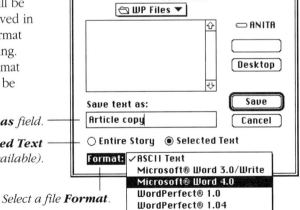

Save Text

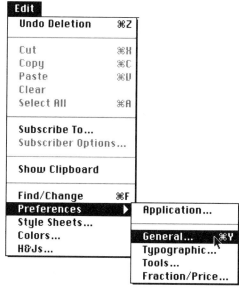

Edit

Undo Deletion	⌘Z
Cut	⌘X
Copy	⌘C
Paste	⌘V
Clear	
Select All	⌘A
Subscribe To...	
Subscriber Options...	
Show Clipboard	
Find/Change	⌘F
Preferences ▶	**Application...**
Style Sheets...	**General...** ⌘Y
Colors...	Typographic...
H&Js...	Tools...
	Fraction/Price...

Figure 1. *Select* **General** *from the* **Preferences** *pop-up menu under the* **Edit** *menu.*

About auto page insertion:

When Auto Page Insertion and Automatic Text Box are both turned on, and text is imported *or* input into an automatic text box, new pages are added, if necessary, to contain any overflow text. Text boxes will be linked from page to page.

To turn on auto page insertion:

1. Select New from the File menu to create a new document.
2. Check the Automatic Text Box box.
3. Define the Page Size, Margin Guides, and Column Guides.
   (See Chapter 3, Create a New File)
4. Click OK or press Return.
5. Select General from the Preferences pop-up menu under the Edit menu **(Figure 1)**.
6. Select End of Story, End of Section, or End of Document from the Auto Page Insertion pop-up menu **(Figure 2)**.
7. Click OK or press Return.

Auto Page Insertion

General Preferences for IMPORTING TEXT

Horizontal Measure:	Picas	Points/Inch:	72
Vertical Measure:	Picas	Ciceros/cm:	2.1967
Auto Page Insertion:	✓Off	Snap Distance:	6
Framing:	End of Story	☐ Render Above:	24 pt
Guides:	End of Section	☒ Greek Below:	5 pt
	End of Document		
Item Coordinates:	Page	☐ Greek Pictures	
Auto Picture Import:	On (verify)		
Master Page Items:	Delete Changes	☒ Accurate Blends	
		☐ Auto Constrain	

[OK]   [Cancel]

Figure 2. *Select* **End of Story, End of Section** *or* **End of Document** *from the* **Auto Page Insertion** *pop-up menu in the General Preferences dialog box.*

About importing text:

Text files created in word processing programs, such as Microsoft Word, can be imported into QuarkXPress. The import filter for the chosen file format must be in the QuarkXPress folder on the same level as the application when it is launched.

To import text:

1. *Optional:* Turn on Auto Page Insertion.
(See instructions on the previous page)

2. Select the Content tool.

3. Click in a text box. Click in an automatic text box for auto page insertion. (If Auto Page Insertion is Off, the imported text will flow into a single box or a series of manually linked boxes, but new pages will not be added.)
(See Link Text Boxes in this chapter)

4. Select Get Text from the File menu **(Figure 3)**.
or
Hold down Command (⌘) and press "E".

5. Make sure the Convert Quotes box is checked **(Figure 4)**.

6. Select a text file and click Open.
or
Double-click a text file **(Figures 5a-6b)**.

Figure 3. *Select **Get Text** from the **File** menu to import a word processing file.*

Figure 4. *The Get Text dialog box.*

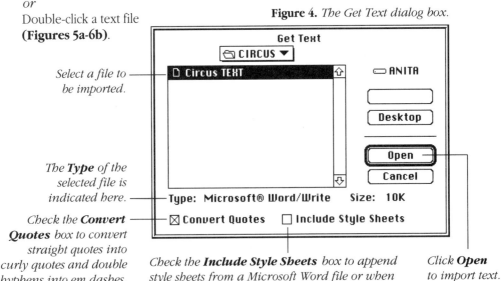

Select a file to be imported.

*The **Type** of the selected file is indicated here.*

*Check the **Convert Quotes** box to convert straight quotes into curly quotes and double hyphens into em dashes.*

*Check the **Include Style Sheets** box to append style sheets from a Microsoft Word file or when importing an ASCII file with style tag codes.*

*Click **Open** to import text.*

Import Text

Auto Page Insertion on:

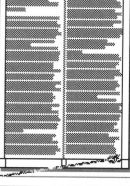

Figure 5b. *New pages are created automatically to accommodate the imported word processing file, and text is linked in a continuous flow.*

Figure 5a. *Auto Page Insertion is **on** and the automatic text box is selected. Then a word processing file is imported.*

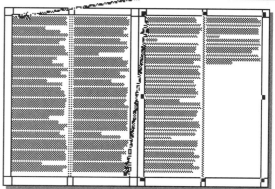

Auto Page Insertion off:

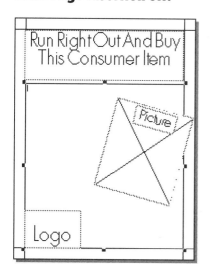

Figure 6a. *Auto Page Insertion is **off**, and a text box is selected.*

Figure 6b. *The text overflow symbol appears after the text is imported.*

Import Text

To insert blank pages using the Page menu:

Steps 1-3 are optional.

1. Select Go to from the Page menu **(Figure 7)**.

2. Enter the number of the page that is to have text inserted before or after it.

3. Click OK.

4. Select Insert from the Page menu **(Figure 7)**.

5. Enter the number of pages to be inserted in the Insert field **(Figure 8)**.

6. Click *before page, after page,* or *at end of document.*

7. Click OK or press Return.

✔ Tip

■ New pages can be based on a Master Page, Blank Single or Blank Facing Page. To link new pages to an automatic text chain, click in an automatic text box before selecting Insert Pages from the Page menu. Select a Master Page containing an automatic text box on which to base the new page(s), and check the Link to Current Text Chain box. *(See pages 51-53 in this chapter, and Chapter 12, About Master Pages)*

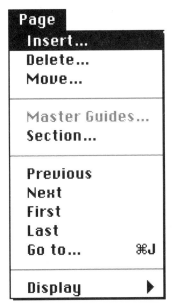

Figure 7. *The **Go to** and **Insert Pages** dialog boxes are opened from the **Page** menu.*

Select a location for the inserted pages.

The number in this field reflects the currently displayed page. A different number can be entered.

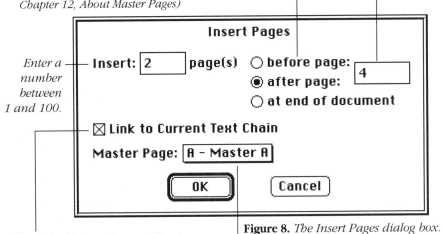

Enter a number between 1 and 100.

Figure 8. *The Insert Pages dialog box.*

*Check the **Link to Current Text Chain** box to link the new pages to a selected automatic text box.*

*New pages can be based on a **Master Page** or a blank page.*

Figure 9. *Select **Show Document Layout** from the **View** menu.*

To insert pages using the Document Layout palette:

1. Select Show Document Layout from the View menu **(Figure 9)**.

2. Press and drag a blank or master page icon into the document icon area **(Figure 10-14b)**.

✔ Tips

- A blank page will have no master page applied to it. You can apply a master page to it later. *(See page 138)*

- Changes made using the Document Layout palette, such as adding, deleting, or rearranging pages, cannot be undone with the Undo command. Use the Revert to Saved command, if necessary.

- A page cannot be placed to the left of the first page in a facing-page document.

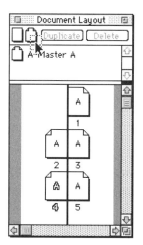

Figure 10. *Press and drag a **blank** page icon to insert a new page.*

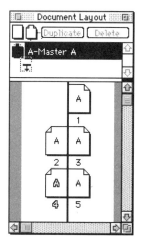

Figure 11. *Or press and drag a **master** page icon.*

(Continued on the following page)

Insert Pages Manually

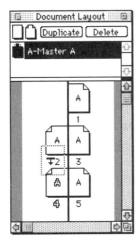

Figure 12. *To place a page between spreads in a facing-page document, release the mouse when the **Force Down** pointer is displayed.*

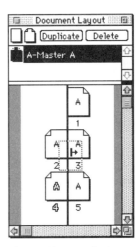

Figure 13. *In a facing-page document, if you release the mouse when the **Force Right** pointer is displayed, subsequent pages may reshuffle. Pages will not reshuffle in a single-sided document.*

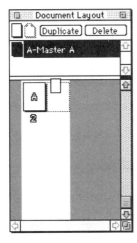

Figure 14a. *To create a **spread** in a single-sided document, place a new page next to an existing page.*

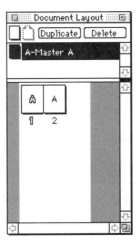

Figure 14b. *Pages 1 and 2 will display side-by-side on the screen. 48" is the maximum width.*

Insert Pages Manually

Figure 15. *Select **Delete** from the **Page** menu.*

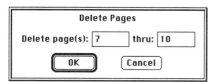

Figure 16. *Enter starting and ending page numbers to delete a series of pages.*

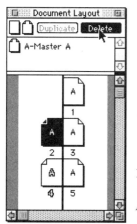

Figure 17a. *Click on a document page icon, then click **Delete**.*

Figure 17b. *Click **OK** when this prompt appears.*

To delete pages using the Page menu:

1. Select Delete from the Page menu **(Figure 15)**.

2. Enter a number in the first field to delete a single page.
   or
   Enter numbers in both fields to delete a series of pages **(Figure 16)**.

3. Click OK or press Return.

✔ Tip

■ If Auto Page Insertion is on and all the text in a linked chain does not fit on the remaining pages, new pages will be added automatically to accommodate the text.

To delete pages using the Document Layout palette:

1. Select Show Document Layout from the View menu **(Figure 9)**.

2. Click on a document page icon **(Figures 17a)**.
   or
   Click on the icon of the first page in a series to be deleted, hold down Shift and click on the icon of the last page in the series, then release Shift.
   or
   Hold down Command (⌘) and click on non-consecutive page icons. (Hold down Command (⌘) and click a selected page icon to deselect it.)

3. Click Delete.

4. When the prompt "Are you sure you want to remove these pages?" appears, click OK or press Return **(Figure 17b)**.

✔ Tip

■ Hold down Option and click Delete to delete pages without the prompt appearing.

To rearrange pages in Thumbnails view:

1. Select Thumbnails from the View menu.

2. Select the Item or Content tool.

3. Press and drag a page icon to a new location **(Figure 18)**.

✔ Tip

■ Pages can be **drag-copied** from one document to another in Thumbnails view. Open two files and select Thumbnails view for both. Drag a page icon from one file to the other. A copy will be made automatically. A page cannot be copied to a document whose page size is smaller than than that of the document it is copied from. A page to which a facing-page master has been applied cannot be copied to a single-sided document.

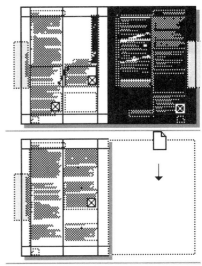

Figure 18. *Press and drag a page to a new location.*

To rearrange pages using the Document Layout palette:

1. Select Show Document Layout from the View menu **(Figure 9)**.

2. Press and drag a document page icon to a new location **(Figure 19)**.
   or
   Click on the icon of the first page in a series to be moved, hold down Shift and click on the icon of last page in the series, release Shift, then drag the pages to a new location.
   (See also the figures on page 56)

✔ Tip

■ You can also rearrange pages using the Move dialog box, opened from the Page menu.

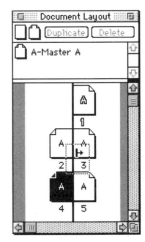

Figure 19. *If you force a page between two pages in a facing-page document, the remaining pages may reshuffle. Note the **Force Right** pointer.*

About Linking:

Boxes can be linked manually so that if text is added or deleted, it will move up or down in a continuous flow from box to box. Text contained in one box or a series of linked boxes is called a story. Manual linking can be used in addition, or as an alternative to, automatic page insertion.

Figure 20. *Select the Linking tool. To keep the Linking tool selected so as to link multiple boxes, hold down Option and click the Linking tool. A moving marquee will appear around the tool in the palette. Deselect it by clicking another tool.*

To link one text box to another:

1. Select the Linking tool **(Figure 20)**.
2. Click on a text box. A moving marquee will appear **(Figure 21)**.
3. Click on an **empty** text box. An arrow will briefly appear, showing the new link **(Figure 22)**.

Link Text Boxes

> Again I see you're about to pounce,
> alas, my poor computer mouse.
>
> And losing this page I cannot afford,
> but there you march across the keyboard.
>
> You can't be hungry again so fast
> Why the time's just barely passed.
>
> Oh maybe I'll give you just a nibble,
> just so you'll stay out of trib'l.

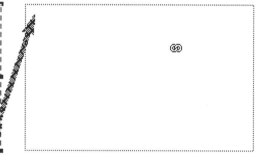

Figure 21. *Click on a text box.*

*Then click on an **empty** text box.*

Again I see you're about to pounce,
alas, my poor computer mouse.

And losing this page I cannot afford,
but there you march across the keyboard.

You can't be hungry again so fast
Why the time's just barely passed.

Oh maybe I'll give you just a nibble,
just so you'll stay out of trib'l.

I know it's warmer than my lap,
but the printer's not the place to nap.

And I don't need your claws to catch,
the printer's pages as they hatch.

To keep you from my papers chew'n
I guess I shouldn't leave them strew'n.

I just wish you wouldn't eat'm
before I've had a chance to read'm.

Figure 22. *These boxes are linked.*

To unlink text boxes:

1. Select the Unlinking tool **(Figure 23)**.

2. Click on one of the two text boxes that are to be unlinked.

3. Click on the point or tail of the arrow between the two boxes **(Figures 24-25)**. Links preceding the break will remain intact; the link to succeeding boxes will be broken.

✔ Tip

■ If you are unable to unlink with the Unlinking tool, make sure there are no other boxes obstructing the one that you are trying to click on.

Figure 23. *Select the **Unlinking tool**.* ——

Ah, what can ever be more stately and admirable to me than mast-hemm'd Manhattan?

River and sunset and scallop-edg'd waves of flood-tide?

The sea-gulls oscillating their bodies, the hay-boat in the twilight, and the belated lighter?

What gods can exceed these that clasp me by the hand, and with voices I love call me promptly and loudly by my nighest name as I approach?

What is more subtle than this which ties me to the woman or man that looks in my face?

Which fuses me into you now, and pours my meaning into you?   *Walt Whitman*

Figure 24. *Click on one of the two text boxes, and then on the point or tail of the arrow between them.*

Ah, what can ever be more stately and admirable to me than mast-hemm'd Manhattan?

River and sunset and scallop-edg'd waves of flood-tide?

The sea-gulls oscillating their bodies, the hay-boat in the twilight, and the belated lighter?

Figure 25. *The link is broken.*

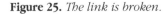

Unlink Text Boxes

Oronte. Do you find anything to object to in my sonnet?

Alceste. I do not say that. But, to keep him from writing, I set before his eyes how, in our days, that desire had spoiled a great many very worthy people.

Oronte. Do I write badly? Am I like them in any way?

Alceste. I do not say that. But, in short, I said to him: What pressing need is there for you to rhyme, and what the deuce drives you into print? If we can pardon the sending into the world of a

badly-written book, it will only be in those unfortunate men who write for their livelihood. Believe me, resist your temptations, keep these effusions from the public, and do not, how much soever you may be asked, forfeit the reputation which you enjoy at

Molière

Figure 26. *Select the Unlinking tool, hold down **Shift** and click inside the box to be unlinked from the chain.*

To delete a box from a text chain and preserve the chain:

1. Select the Item or Content tool.

2. Select the box to be deleted.

3. Select Delete from the Item menu.

To unlink a box from a text chain and preserve the box and the chain:

1. Select the Unlinking tool **(Figure 23)**.

2. Hold down Shift and click **inside** the text box to be removed from the link chain **(Figures 26-27)**.

Oronte. Do you find anything to object to in my sonnet?

Alceste. I do not say that. But, to keep him from writing, I set before his eyes how, in our days, that desire had spoiled a great many very worthy people.

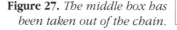

Oronte. Do I write badly? Am I like them in any way?

Alceste. I do not say that. But, in short, I said to him: What pressing need is there for you to rhyme, and what the deuce drives you into print? If we can pardon the sending into the world of a

Figure 27. *The middle box has been taken out of the chain.*

About jump lines:

When text is linked between non-consecutive pages, as in a newsletter or magazine, there is usually an indicator to guide the reader to the continuation of the story or article. These "Continued on" and "Continued from" indicators are referred to as "jump lines." When the Next Box Page Number command is inserted, it is instantly converted into the page number of the next linked box in the chain. If the text is re-linked to a different page, this number is automatically updated.

To insert a "Continued on" command:

1. Select the Text Box tool.

2. Create a separate small box that overlaps the main text box of a story.

3. With the box still selected, choose Runaround from the Item menu and choose Item from the Mode sub-menu.

4. Click OK.

5. Select the Content tool.

6. Type any desired text into the small box, such as "Continued on page."

7. Hold down Command (⌘) and press "4" to insert the Next Box Page Number command **(Figure 28)**.

To insert a "Continued from" command:

Follow the above instructions. For step 7, hold down Command (⌘) and press "2" to insert a Previous Box Page Number command **(Figures 29-30)**.

Elizabeth here felt herself called on to say something in vindication of his behaviour to Wickham; and therefore gave them to understand, in as guarded a manner as she could, that by what she had heard from his relations in Kent, his actions were capable of a very different construction; and that his

Continued on page 3

Figure 28. *The text box containing the* ***Next Box Page Number*** *command is placed so that it overlaps the main text box.*

Figure 29. *The* ***Previous Box Page Number*** *command is inserted here.*

Continued from page 1

character was by no means so faulty, nor Wickham's so amiable, as they had been considered in Hertfordshire. In confirmation of this, she related the particulars of all the pecuniary transactions in which they had been connected, without actually naming her authority, but stating it to be such as might be relied on.

Jane Austen

Continued from page <None>

Figure 30. *If the characters <None> appear instead of a page number, either the text box containing the Previous or Next Box Page Number command is not overlapping a linked text box, or the text box it rests in is not linked to a box on another page.*

PARAGRAPH FORMATTING

Style

Font	▶
Size	▶
Type Style	▶
Color	▶
Shade	▶
Horizontal Scale...	
Kern...	
Baseline Shift...	
Character...	⌘⇧D
Alignment	▶
Leading...	⌘⇧E
Formats...	**⌘⇧F**
Rules...	⌘⇧N
Tabs...	⌘⇧T
Style Sheets	▶

Figure 1. *The paragraph formatting features are grouped together below the dotted line under the **Style** menu.*

About paragraph formatting:

All the commands described in this chapter affect entire paragraphs rather than individual characters. These commands are grouped together under the Style menu **(Figure 1)**. A paragraph is defined as any number of characters or words followed by a Return (¶). The paragraph formatting commands can be applied to text manually or using style sheets (see Chapter 11).

To indent a paragraph:

1. Select the Content tool.

2. Click in a paragraph or press and drag through a series of paragraphs.

3. Select Formats from the Style menu **(Figure 1)**.
or
Hold down Command (⌘) and Shift and press "F".

4. Enter a number in the Left Indent and/or Right Indent fields **(Figure 2)**.

5. Click Apply to preview.

6. Click OK or press Return **(Figures 3-5)**.
(See also Figure 39a in this chapter)

Paragraph Indents

Paragraph Formats

Figure 2. *Enter numbers in the **Left Indent** and/or **Right Indent** fields in the Paragraph Formats dialog box.*

Left Indent:	4 p	Leading:	14 pt
First Line:	0p	Space Before:	0p
Right Indent:	0p	Space After:	0p

☐ Lock to Baseline Grid ☐ Keep with Next ¶
☐ Drop Caps ☐ Keep Lines Together

Alignment: Left
H&J: Standard

Apply
OK   Cancel

*Click **Apply** to preview changes.*

THE MAIN CONCLUSION ARRIVED AT IN THIS WORK, NAMELY, THAT MAN IS DESCENDED FROM SOME LOWLY ORGAN-ISED FORM, WILL, I REGRET TO THINK, BE HIGHLY DISTASTEFUL TO MANY. BUT THERE CAN HARDLY BE A DOUBT THAT WE ARE DESCENDED FROM BARBARIANS.

Figure 3. *A paragraph with 0 indents.*

THE MAIN CONCLUSION ARRIVED AT IN THIS WORK, NAMELY, THAT MAN IS DESCENDED FROM SOME LOWLY ORGANISED FORM, WILL, I REGRET TO THINK, BE HIGHLY DISTASTEFUL TO MANY. BUT THERE CAN HARDLY BE A DOUBT THAT WE ARE DESCENDED FROM BARBARIANS.

Figure 4. *A paragraph with a left indent of 2p.*

THE MAIN CONCLUSION ARRIVED AT IN THIS WORK, NAMELY, THAT MAN IS DESCENDED FROM SOME LOWLY ORGANISED FORM, WILL, I REGRET TO THINK, BE HIGHLY DISTASTEFUL TO MANY. BUT THERE CAN HARDLY BE A DOUBT THAT WE ARE DESCENDED FROM BARBARIANS.

Charles Darwin

Figure 5. *A paragraph with a right indent of 2p.*

Paragraph Indents

Oronte. [To Alceste] But for you, you know our agreement. Speak to me, I pray, in all sincerity.

Alceste. These matters, sir, are always more or less delicate, and every one is fond of being praised for his wit.

But I was saying one day to a certain person, who shall be nameless, when he showed me some of his verses, that a gentleman ought at all times to exercise a great control over that itch for writing which sometimes attacks us, and should keep a tight rein over the strong propensity which one has to display such amusements; and that, in the frequent anxiety to show their productions, people are frequently exposed to act a very foolish part.

Molière

Figure 6. *A first line indent enhances readability.*

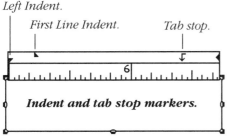

Left Indent.

First Line Indent. *Tab stop.*

Indent and tab stop markers.

Figure 7a. *The special Paragraph Formats ruler is the width of the selected text box.*

Figure 7b. *The **First Line** indent field in the Paragraph Formats dialog box.*

To indent the first line of a paragraph:

1. Select the Content tool.

2. Click in a paragraph or press and drag through a series of paragraphs.

3. Select Formats from the Style menu **(Figure 1)**.
or
Hold down Command (⌘) and Shift and press "F".

4. Enter a number in the First Line field **(Figure 7b)**.

5. Click Apply to preview.

6. Click OK or press Return **(Figure 6)**.

✔ Tips

■ Indents and tab stops can be adjusted by pressing and dragging the indent and tab stop markers in the special ruler that is displayed when the Paragraph Formats dialog box is open. Insert a new tab stop by clicking in the ruler **(Figure 7a)**.
(See Set Tabs in this chapter)

■ The first paragraph after a headline or subhead is usually not indented.

■ Paragraph indent values are in addition to any Text Inset value applied to the text box.
(See Chapter 5, Text Inset)

Paragraph Indents

Paragraph Formats

Left Indent:	0p	**Leading:** 14 pt
First Line:	p10	**Space Before:** 0p
Right Indent:	0p	**Space After:** 0p

☐ **Lock to Baseline Grid**   ☐ **Keep with Next ¶**
☐ **Drop Caps**   ☐ **Keep Lines Together**

Alignment: Left
H&J: Standard

[**Apply**]

[**OK**]   [**Cancel**]

About Leading:

Leading is the distance from baseline to baseline between lines of type, and is measured in points. Three types of leading are used in QuarkXPress.

Absolute leading is an amount that remains fixed regardless of the point size of the type to which it is applied **(Figure 8)**.

Auto leading is a percentage above the point size of the largest character on each line **(Figure 9)**.

Incremental leading is equal to the type size of the largest character on each line plus or minus a specified number of points, such as +2 or -2. Both auto and incremental leading can be problematic.

To modify paragraph leading using the Measurements palette:

1. Select the Content tool.
2. Click in a paragraph or press and drag through a series of paragraphs.
3. Enter a number in the Leading field on the Measurements palette **(Figure 10)**.
   or
   Click the up arrow on the Measurements palette to increase the leading or the down arrow to reduce the leading in 1 point increments. Hold down Option while clicking an arrow to increase or reduce leading in .1 point increments.

But the moment that she moved again he recognized her. The effect upon her old lover was electric, far stronger than the effect of his presence upon her. His fire, the tumultuous ring of his eloquence, seemed to go out of him. His lip struggled and trembled under the words that lay upon it; but deliver them it could not as long as she faced him. His eyes, after their first glance...

Thomas Hardy

Figure 8. *A paragraph with 11 pt.* ***absolute leading****. Note that the leading is consistent regardless of the differences in point size.*

But the moment that she moved again he recognized her. The effect upon her old lover was electric, far stronger than the effect of his presence upon her. His fire, the tumultuous ring of his eloquence, seemed

Figure 9. *The same paragraph with* ***auto leading****.*

Absolute leading.

Incremental leading.

Auto leading.

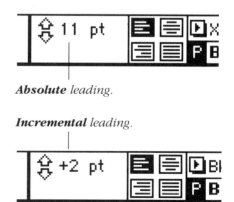

Figure 10. *The **leading** section of the Measurements palette.*

To modify paragraph leading using the keyboard:

1. Select the Content tool.

2. Click in a paragraph or press and drag through a series of paragraphs.

3. Hold down Command (⌘) and Shift and press **'** to increase leading or **;** to decrease leading in 1 point increments.

✔ Tip

■ Add Option to the above keystroke to modify leading in .1 increments.

To modify paragraph leading using the Leading dialog box:

1. Select the Content tool.

2. Click in a paragraph or press and drag through a series of paragraphs.

3. Select Leading from the Style menu **(Figure 11)**.

or

Hold down Command (⌘) and Shift and press "E".

4. Enter an amount in an increment as small as .001 **(Figure 12)**. You don't need to enter "pt".

5. Click OK or press Return.

✔ Tips

■ Use spacious leading for text in wide columns or in a sans serif font. Use tight leading for headlines and sub-heads.

■ Leading values can also be modified using the Formats dialog box, opened from the Style menu.

■ Leading does not affect the position of first line of text in a box. To lower text from the top of its box, select the box, select Modify from the Item menu, then modify the number in the First Baseline field.

Figure 11. *Select* **Leading** *from the* **Style** *menu.*

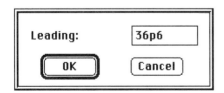

Figure 12. *The* **Leading** *dialog box.*

To add space between paragraphs:

1. Select the Content tool.
2. Click in a paragraph or press and drag through a series of paragraphs.
3. Select Formats from the Style menu **(Figure 13)**.
4. Enter a number in the Space Before and/or Space After fields **(Figure 14)**.
5. Click Apply to preview.
6. Click OK or press Return **(Figure 15)**.

✔ Tip

■ The numbers entered into the Space Before and Space After fields are added together, so it is advisable to use Space After for most paragraphs, and use Space Before for special instances, such as to separate a subhead from the paragraph that precedes it.

Figure 13. *Select* **Formats** *from the* **Style** *menu.*

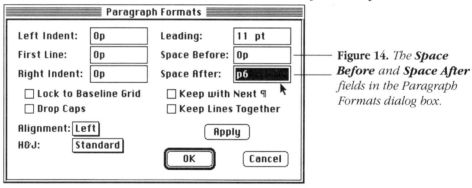

Figure 14. *The* **Space Before** *and* **Space After** *fields in the Paragraph Formats dialog box.*

O to be a Virginian where I grew up! O to be a Carolinian!
O longings irrepressible! O I will go back to old Tennessee
    and never wander more.

Mannahatta

I was asking for something specific and perfect for my city,
Whereupon lo! upsprang the aboriginal name.

Now I see what there is in a name, a word, liquid, sane, unruly,
    musical, self-sufficient,
I see that the word of my city is that word from of old,
Because I see that word nested in nests of water-bays, superb...

Walt Whitman

Figure 15. *The Space Before and Space After commands offer a finer degree of control over spacing between paragraphs than does inserting extra returns.*

About the Keep With Next ¶ command:

When this command is applied to a paragraph, the last line of the paragraph will remain attached to at least the first line of the next paragraph if it falls at the end of a column. This command can be applied to a subhead to keep it attached to the paragraph that follows it, but should not be applied to body text.

To apply the Keep With Next ¶ command:

1. Select the Content tool.
2. Click in a paragraph.
3. Select Formats from the Style menu.
4. Check the Keep With Next ¶ box **(Figure 16)**.
5. Click OK or press Return.

To apply the Keep Lines Together command:

1. Select the Content tool.
2. Click in a paragraph.
3. Select Formats from the Style menu.
4. Check the Keep Lines Together box **(Figure 16)**.
5. Click the All Lines in ¶ button to keep all lines of a paragraph, such as a subhead, together.
   or
   Click the Start button to turn on "orphan and widow control." Enter "2" in the Start and End fields to ensure that no less than two lines of a paragraph are left at the bottom or top of a column.
6. Click OK or press Return.

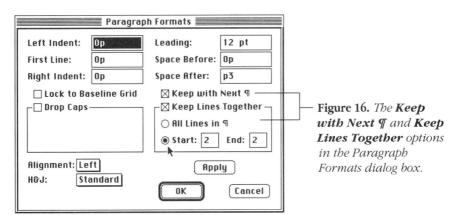

Figure 16. *The* **Keep with Next ¶** *and* **Keep Lines Together** *options in the Paragraph Formats dialog box.*

Keep Lines Together

To align text to the Baseline Grid:

For each paragraph you wish to align to the grid, check the Lock to Baseline Grid box in the Paragraph Formats dialog box. You can do this via a style sheet *(see Chapter 11)*. In the Typographic Preferences dialog box, opened from the Edit menu, enter a Baseline Increment that is the same as or a multiple of the text leading. To display the non-printing grid lines, choose Show Baseline Grid from the View menu.

To "break" a line without creating a new paragraph:

1. Select the Content tool.

2. Click in the text where a line break is to occur.

3. Hold down Shift and press Return. With Invisibles on, a Shift-Return is displayed as a left-pointing arrow icon **(Figures 17-19)**.

✔ Tips

■ To remove a line break command, or "soft return," click at the beginning of the next line and press Delete.

■ This command can be used to adjust headlines or fix awkward breaks in ragged right copy.

Figure 17. *This is an awkward break.*

The night so luminous on the spar-deck, but otherwise on the cavernous ones below — levels so very like the tiered galleries in a coal-mine — the luminous night passed away. Like the prophet in the chariot disappearing in heaven and dropping his mantle to Elisha, the withdrawing night transferred its pale robe to the peeping day.

The night so luminous on the spar-deck, but otherwise on the cavernous ones below — levels so very like the tiered¶

galleries in a coal-mine — the luminous night passed away. Like the prophet in the chariot disappearing in heaven and dropping his mantle to Elisha, the withdrawing night transferred its pale robe to the peeping day.

Figure 18. *A paragraph return creates a new paragraph.*

The night so luminous on the spar-deck, but otherwise on the cavernous ones below — levels so very like the tiered ← galleries in a coal-mine — the luminous night passed away. Like the prophet in the chariot disappearing in heaven and dropping his mantle to Elisha, the withdrawing night transferred its pale robe to the peeping day.

Herman Melville

Figure 19. *A **Shift-Return** creates a new line within a paragraph.*

A quick way to copy paragraph formats from one paragraph to another within a story.

Click in a paragraph or press and drag through a series of paragraphs that are to be modified. Hold down Option and Shift and click in the paragraph whose formats you would like to copy.

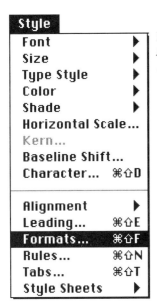

Figure 20. *Select* **Formats** *from the* **Style** *menu.*

About hanging indents:

A format in which the first line of a paragraph is aligned flush left and the remaining lines are indented is referred to as a hanging indent. Hanging indents can be used to make subheads, bullets, or other special text prominent **(Figure 22)**.

To create a hanging indent using the Formats dialog box:

1. Select the Content tool.
2. Click in a paragraph or press and drag through a series of paragraphs.
3. Select Formats from the Style menu **(Figure 20)**.
4. Enter a number in the Left Indent field **(Figure 21)**.
5. Enter the same number in the First Line field preceded by a minus (-) sign.
6. Click OK or press Return.

A positive number is entered in the **Left Indent** *field.*

A negative number is entered in the **First Line Indent** *field.*

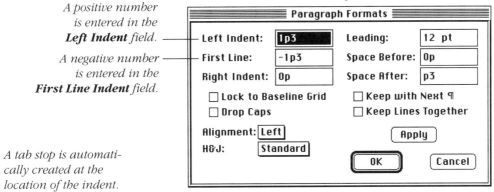

Figure 21. *The Paragraph Formats dialog box.*

A tab stop is automatically created at the location of the indent.

D. Pedro. He is in earnest.

Claud. In most profound earnest; and I'll warrant you for the love of Beatrice.

D. Pedro. And hath challenged thee?

Claud. Most sincerely.

D. Pedro. What a pretty thing man is when he goes in his doublet and hose, and leaves off his wit!

Claud. He is then a giant to an ape: but then is an ape a doctor to such a man?

William Shakespeare

Figure 22. *Hanging indents.*

About the Indent Here character:

The Indent Here character is used to create hanging indents. It is useful for formatting small amounts of text. However, it can be applied to only one paragraph at a time, and cannot be incorporated into a style sheet. To format more than one paragraph at a time, create hanging indents using positive and negative indents in the Formats dialog box.

(See instructions on the previous page)

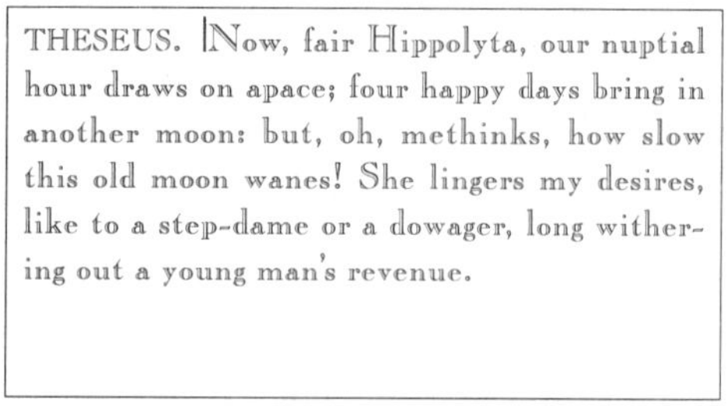

Figure 23. *To insert the Indent Here command, click in the text, hold down Command (⌘) and press "\".*

To create a hanging indent using the Indent Here character:

1. Select the Content tool.

2. Click in a paragraph where the indent is to be inserted **(Figures 23-24)**.

3. Hold down Command (⌘) and press backslash (\).

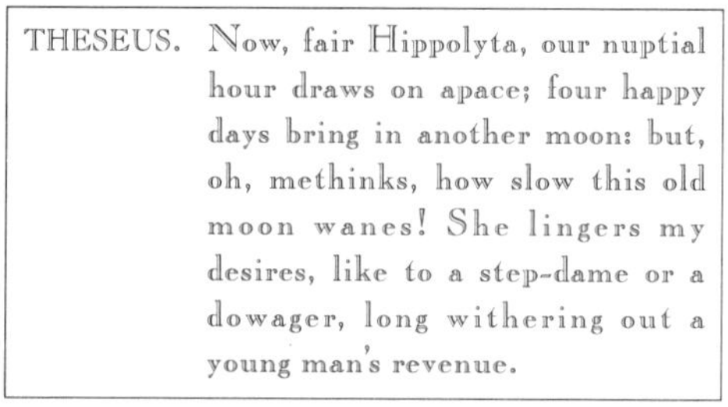

Figure 24. *A hanging indent is created.*

To remove an Indent Here character:

1. Select the Content tool.

2. Click just to the right of the Indent Here character **(Figure 25)**.

3. Press Delete.

Figure 25. *The Indent Here character displays as a vertical dotted line when Show Invisibles is selected from the View menu. Select a large view size to see it.*

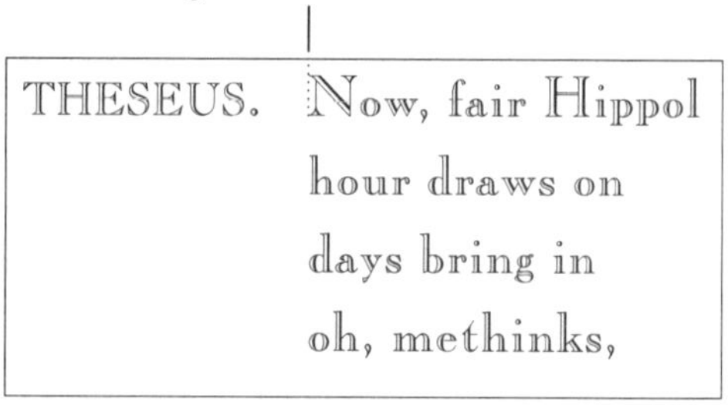

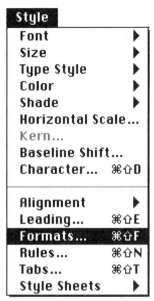

Style

Font	▶
Size	▶
Type Style	▶
Color	▶
Shade	▶
Horizontal Scale...	
Kern...	
Baseline Shift...	
Character...	⌘⇧D
Alignment	▶
Leading...	⌘⇧E
Formats...	⌘⇧F
Rules...	⌘⇧N
Tabs...	⌘⇧T
Style Sheets	▶

Figure 26. *Select* ***Formats*** *from the* ***Style*** *menu.*

To insert an automatic drop cap:

1. Select the Content tool.

2. Click in a paragraph.

3. Select Formats from the Style menu **(Figure 26)**.

4. Check the "Drop Caps" box **(Figure 27)**.

   Steps 5-7 are optional.

5. Enter a number in the Character Count field to modify the number of characters to be enlarged to form the drop cap.

6. Enter a number in the Line Count field to modify the height of the drop cap. The drop cap adjusts to fit the line count; the maximum line count is 8.

7. Click Apply to preview.

8. Click OK or press Return **(Figures 28-29)**.

Figure 27. *Check the* ***Drop Caps*** *box in the Paragraph Formats dialog box.*

The number of characters to be "dropped."

The number of lines of text the drop cap will fit into.

Paragraph Formats

Left Indent:	0p	Leading:	11 pt
First Line:	0p	Space Before:	0p
Right Indent:	0p	Space After:	0p

☐ Lock to Baseline Grid   ☐ Keep with Next ¶

☒ Drop Caps — ┌ ☐ Keep Lines Together ┐
  Character Count: 1   ○
  Line Count: 3   ○

Alignment: Left   [Apply]
H&J: Standard

[OK]   [Cancel]

Automatic Drop Caps

ot only was her first-floor flat invaded at all hours by throngs of singular and often undesirable characters but her remarkable lodger showed an eccentricity and irregularity in his life which must have sorely tried her patience. His incredible untidiness, his addiction to music at strange hours, his occasional revolver practice within doors, his weird and often malodorous scientific experiments, and the atmosphere of violence and danger which hung around him made him the very worst tenant in London. On the other hand, his payments were princely...

Figure 28. *A drop cap with a character count of 1 and a line count of 5.*

NOT only was her first-floor flat invaded at all hours by throngs of singular and often undesirable characters but her remarkable lodger showed an eccentricity and irregularity in his life which must have sorely tried her patience. His incredible untidiness, his addiction to music at strange hours, his occasional revolver practice within doors, his weird and often malodorous scientific experiments, and the atmosphere of violence and danger which hung around him made him the very worst tenant in London. On the other hand, his payments were princely...

Figure 29. *A drop cap with a character count of 3 and a line count of 2.*

To resize an automatic drop cap manually:

1. Select the Content tool.

2. Press and drag to highlight a drop cap character or characters **(Figure 30)**.

3. In the point size field of the Measurements palette, enter a number greater than 100% to enlarge the drop cap, or a number less than 100% to reduce the drop cap. The minimum is 10% and the maximum is 400% **(Figure 31)**.

4. Press Return **(Figure 32)**.

To kern next to a drop cap:

1. Select the Content tool.

2. Click in the first line of the paragraph between the drop cap and the character to the right of it. A long blinking I-beam will appear when the cursor has been inserted correctly **(Figure 33)**.

3. In the Tracking & Kerning section of the Measurements palette, click the left arrow to delete space or the right arrow to add space **(Figure 34)**.

✔ Tip

■ Hold down Option while clicking on the left or right arrow to kern in finer increments.

To remove an automatic drop cap:

1. Select the Content tool.

2. Click in a paragraph containing a drop cap.

3. Select Formats from the Style menu.

4. Uncheck the "Drop Caps" box.

5. Click OK or press Return.

An anomaly which often struck me in the character of my friend Sherlock Holmes was that, although in his methods of thought he was the neatest and most methodical of mankind, and although also he affected a certain quiet primness of dress, he was none the less in his personal habits one of the most intidy

Figure 30. *Highlight a drop cap.*

Figure 31. *Modify the size percentage in the Measurements palette.*

An anomaly which often struck me in the character of my friend Sherlock Holmes was that, although in his methods of thought he was the neatest and most methodical of mankind, and although also he affected a certain quiet primness of dress, he was none the less in his per-

Figure 32. *A drop cap enlarged to 125%.*

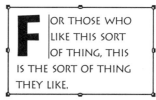

FOR THOSE WHO LIKE THIS SORT OF THING, THIS IS THE SORT OF THING THEY LIKE.

Figure 33. *The cursor positioned for kerning next to a drop cap.*

Figure 34. *The Tracking & Kerning section of the Measurements palette.*

Non-printing characters and the keystrokes used to produce them.		
Tab	→	Tab
Word Space	.	Space bar
New Paragraph	¶	Return
New Line	↵	Shift-Return
New Column	↓	Enter
New Box	↯	Shift-Enter
Indent Here	⋮	Command \

About Tabs:

Tabs are commands that are used to align columns of text or figures. Using spaces to create columns will result in uneven spacing due to variable character widths. If no custom tabs have been set, text will jump to the nearest default tab stop. Default tab stops are ½ inch apart. Up to 20 custom tab stops can be applied to a paragraph **(Figures 35-36)**.

To insert tabs into text:

1. Select the Content tool.
2. Press Tab as you input copy before typing each new column. The cursor will jump to the next tab stop.
   or
   To add a tab to already inputted text, click to the left of the text that is to start each new column and press Tab.
   or
   Hold down Option and press Tab to set a right indent tab flush with the right indent of the box.

Endangered vs. non-Endangered Bears			
	1930	*1992*	*2000* (Projected)
Pandas	1 million	4 thousand	0
Koalas	6 million	3 thousand	7
Poohs	1 million	2 billion	3 billion

Figure 35. *Use tabs to align columns of text.*

Endangered·vs.·non-Endangered·Bears¶			
→	*1930* →	*1992* →	*2000*·(Projected)

Figure 36. *Select **Show Invisibles** from the **View** menu to display tab symbols and other non-printing characters.*

To set a custom tab stop:

1. Select the Content tool.

2. Highlight **all** the copy for which the tab stop is to be set.

3. Select Tabs from the Style menu **(Figure 37)**.

or

Hold down Command (⌘) and Shift and press "T".

4. Select Left, Center, Right, Decimal, or Comma from the Alignment pop-up menu **(Figure 38)**.

5. *Optional:* To create a leader, enter any keyboard character in the Fill Character field. Enter a period (.) to create a dot leader **(Figure 39b)**.

6. Click in the tabs ruler where the tab stop is to occur **(Figure 39a)**.

or

Enter a position number in the Position field using any measurement system, then click Apply **(Figure 39b)**.

7. *Optional:* Repeat step 6 to create additional tab stops. If you use the Position field, click Apply after enter–ing each position number.

8. Click OK or press Return **(Figures 41-42)**.

✔ Tip

■ To move a tab stop, drag the tab marker to the left or right.

(See also the first Tip on page 65)

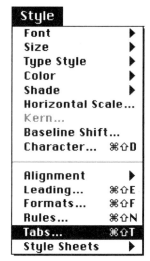

Figure 37. *Select **Tabs** from the **Style** menu.*

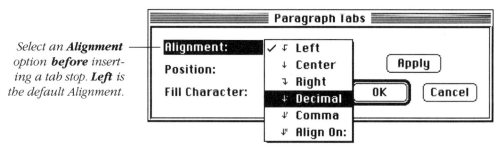

*Select an **Alignment** option **before** insert-ing a tab stop. **Left** is the default Alignment.*

Figure 38. *The **Paragraph Tabs** dialog box.*

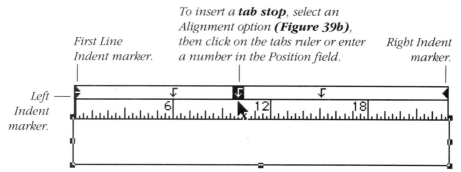

To insert a **tab stop**, select an
Alignment option **(Figure 39b)**,
then click on the tabs ruler or enter
a number in the Position field.

First Line
Indent marker.

Right Indent
marker.

Left —
Indent
marker.

Figure 39a. *You can move the indent markers on the Tabs ruler to modify paragraph indents, but more precise indent values can be applied using the Paragraph Formats dialog box (see pages 63-65).*

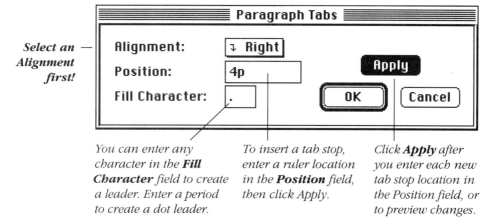

Select an —
Alignment
first!

You can enter any
character in the **Fill
Character** field to create
a leader. Enter a period
to create a dot leader.

To insert a tab stop,
enter a ruler location
in the **Position** field,
then click Apply.

Click **Apply** after
you enter each new
tab stop location in
the Position field, or
to preview changes.

Figure 39b. *The **Paragraph Tabs** dialog box. Up to 20 tab stops can be inserted per paragraph. A right indent tab created using the Option-Tab keystroke will not have a corresponding marker on the ruler.*

Figure 40. *To align tab stops to a custom character, select **Align On** from the **Alignment** pop-up menu, then type a character in the **Align On** field.*

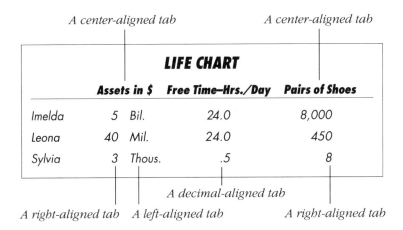

Figure 41. *Center, Left, Right and Decimal-aligned tabs were used to create this chart.*

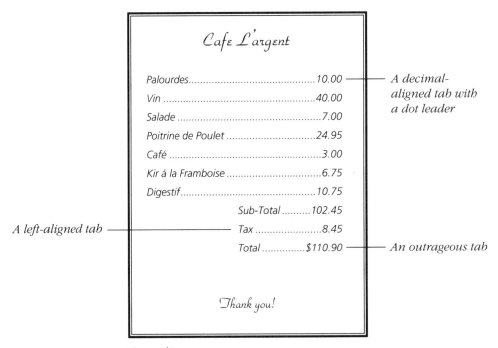

Figure 42.

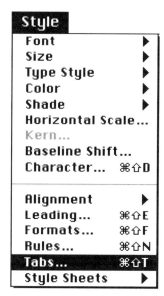

Style

Font	▶
Size	▶
Type Style	▶
Color	▶
Shade	▶
Horizontal Scale...	
Kern...	
Baseline Shift...	
Character...	⌘⇧D
Alignment	▶
Leading...	⌘⇧E
Formats...	⌘⇧F
Rules...	⌘⇧N
Tabs...	⌘⇧T
Style Sheets	▶

Figure 43. *Select* **Tabs** *from the* **Style** *menu.*

To remove custom tab stops:

1. Select the Content tool.

2. Highlight the text from which the tab stops are to be removed.

3. Select Tabs from the Style menu **(Figure 43)**.

4. Hold down Option and click on the tabs ruler to remove **all** the tab stops.
or
Press and drag a tab stop marker up or down out of the ruler **(Figure 44)**.

5. Click OK or press Return.

✔ Tip

■ If you highlighted two or more paragraphs and the highlighted text contains more than one set of tab stops, only the tab stops for the first paragraph will be displayed, but new tab settings will affect all the highlighted text.

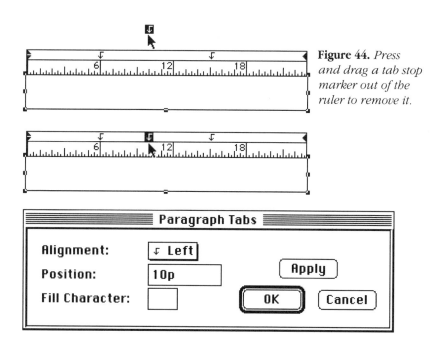

Figure 44. *Press and drag a tab stop marker out of the ruler to remove it.*

Paragraph Tabs

Alignment:	⌴ Left
Position:	10p
Fill Character:	

Apply

OK Cancel

About paragraph rules:

A rule inserted using the Paragraph Rules feature remains anchored to the paragraph even if the paragraph is moved, which is not the case for lines created with the Line tools. And paragraph rules can be modified in their appearance and position, unlike the Underline style.

To insert a paragraph rule:

1. Select the Content tool.

2. Click in a paragraph or press and drag through a series of paragraphs.

3. Select Rules from the Style menu **(Figure 45)**.

   or

   Hold down Command (⌘) and Shift and press "N."

4. Check the Rule Above or Rule Below box. The dialog box will expand **(Figure 46)**.

5. Select a width from the Width pop-up menu or enter a custom width in the Width field **(Figure 47)**.

6. Select Indents or Text from the Length pop-up menu.

7. Highlight the entire Offset field, and enter a number in any measurement system to Offset a Rule Above from the baseline of the first line of the paragraph or Offset a Rule Below from the baseline of the last line of the paragraph.

Steps 8-11 are optional.

8. Modify the number in the From Left or From Right fields to indent the rule.

9. Select a style from the Style pop-up menu.

10. Select a color from the Color pop-up menu.

(Continued on the following page)

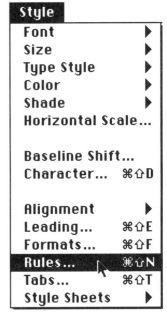

Figure 45. *Select **Rules** from the **Style** menu.*

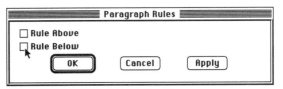

Figure 46. *The Paragraph Rules dialog box expands when the **Rule Above** or **Rule Below** box is checked (see Figure 47).*

11. Select a shade from the Shade pop-up menu or enter a custom shade in the Shade field.

12. Click Apply to preview.

13. Click OK or press Return **(Figures 48-51)**.

✔ Tips

■ Be sure to enter an Offset for a Rule Above that is at least as large as the point size of the type. The Offset for both a Rule Above and Rule Below originates from the baseline.

■ Setting an absolute number for the Offset is preferable to using a percentage.

(Continued on the following page)

Figure 47. *The Paragraph Rules dialog box.*

*The amount a rule is indented is determined by the number in the **From Left** and/or **From Right** fields as well as any existing paragraph indents and text inset values.*

*Select **Indents** or **Text** from the Length pop-up menu.*

*Select from eleven **Styles**.*

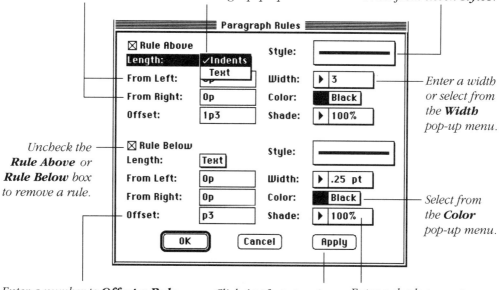

*Uncheck the **Rule Above** or **Rule Below** box to remove a rule.*

*Enter a width or select from the **Width** pop-up menu.*

*Select from the **Color** pop-up menu.*

*Enter a number to **Offset** a **Rule Above** from the baseline of the first line of the paragraph or **Offset** a **Rule Below** from the baseline of the last line of the paragraph.*

*Click **Apply** to preview.*

*Enter a shade percentage or select from the **Shade** pop-up menu.*

Paragraph Rules

Figure 48. *A "reverse" rule effect can be created by coloring text white, selecting a wide width for the rule, and using a negative Offset. A negative value of up to half the width of the rule can be entered. This is a 16 point black Rule Above, with the Indents option selected from the Length pop-up menu, Left and Right Indents of 0, and an Offset of -p4.*

ETHAN FROME

By Edith Wharton

I had the story, bit by bit, from various people, and, as generally happens in such cases, each time it was a different story.

If you know Starkfield, Massachusetts, you know the post-office. If you know the post-office you must have seen Ethan Frome drive up to it, drop the reins on his hollow-backed bay and

Rules can be used to jazz up subheads.

Rules can be used to jazz up subheads.

Figure 49. *In this example, rules of varying lengths and weights have been combined.*

Paragraph Rules

Norton Thorpe clapped the young Frenchman on the shoulder and, with a hearty smile, shook his hand. "My dear chap! How could I possibly object to my daughter becoming not only the new Countess d'Auvergne but also the wife of an up-and-coming electronics genius!" Lisa, her

"How could I possibly object to my daughter becoming not only the new Countess d'Auvergne but also the wife of an up-and-coming electronics genius..."

eyes moist with tears of joy, not only because of her future marriage but also because of her restored relationship with her father, threw her arms around Nancy in a warm embrace exclaiming: "Oh, Nancy, none of this could ever have happened if you hadn't worked so hard to solve

Figure 50. *Paragraph rules can be used to separate a pull quote from body text.*

Figure 51. *Rules can be used to emphasize headlines. In this example, a Return was inserted after every line, making every line a separate paragraph.*

ALL

THE

REALLY GOOD

IDEAS

I EVER HAD

CAME

TO ME

WHILE I WAS

MILKING

A COW.

Grant Wood

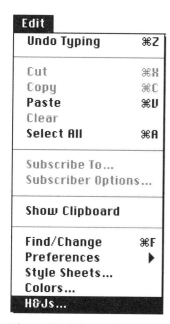

Figure 52. *Select **H&Js** from the **Edit** menu.*

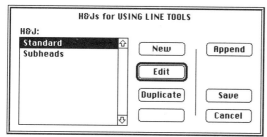

Figure 53. *Click **New** or select an H&J and click **Edit**.*

Figure 54. *The Edit Hyphenation & Justification dialog box.*

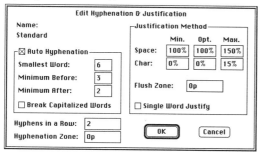

About hyphenation:

Hyphenation lessens gaps between words in justified type and smooths ragged edges in non-justified type.

Hyphenation (and Justification) specifications are stored in H&Js. A document can have several H&Js, and they are applied to paragraphs using the Paragraphs Formats dialog box.

To turn on hyphenation:

1. Select H&Js from the Edit menu **(Figure 52)**.

2. Click New to create a new H&J **(Figure 53)**.
   or
   Select an H&J and click Edit. The Standard H&J can be modified.

3. Enter a name if the H&J is new.

4. Check the Auto Hyphenation box **(Figure 54)**.

Steps 5-10 are optional.

5. In the Smallest Word field, modify the minimum number of characters a word must contain to be hyphenated.

6. In the Minimum Before field, modify the minimum number (1-6) of a word's characters that must precede a hyphen.

7. In the Minimum After field, modify the minimum number (2-8) of a word's characters to follow a hyphen.

8. Check or uncheck the Break Capitalized Words box.

9. Modify the number of consecutive lines that can end with a hyphen in the Hyphens in a Row field.

10. Enter a number larger than zero in the Hyphenation Zone field to create a more ragged edge (less hyphenation).

11. Click OK or press Return.

12. Click Save **(Figure 53)**.

   (See Apply an H&J on the following page)

Hyphenation

To apply an H&J:

1. Select the Content tool.

2. Click in a paragraph or press and drag through a series of paragraphs.

3. Select Formats from the Style menu **(Figure 55)**.

or

Hold down Command (⌘) and Shift and press "F".

4. Select an H&J from the H&Js pop-up menu **(Figure 57)**.

5. Click OK or Press Return.

✔ Tips

■ The Normal style sheet will have the Standard H&J associated with it unless a different H&J is selected for it. *(See Chapter 11, Edit a Style Sheet)*

■ The new Enhanced Hyphenation Method creates better word breaks when Auto Hyphenation is turned on. Select Enhanced Hyphenation from the Hyphenation Method pop-up menu in the Typographic Preferences dialog box, opened from the Edit menu. Select Standard to use the method built into earlier versions of QuarkXPress **(Figure 56)**.

Figure 55. *Select **Formats** from the **Style** menu.*

Figure 56. *Select Enhanced or Standard Hyphenation Method in the Typographic Preferences dialog box.*

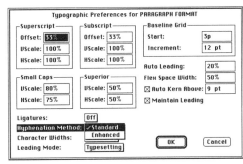

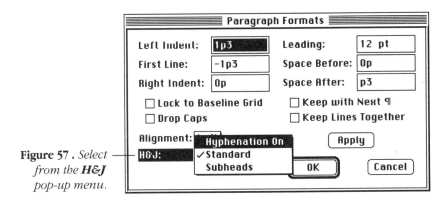

Figure 57. *Select from the **H&J** pop-up menu.*

*Enter a point size between 2 to 720 in the **Size** field.*

*Select a preset point size from the **Size** pop-up menu.*

Figure 1. *The Measurements palette.*

To resize type using the Measurements palette:

1. Select the Content tool.
2. Highlight the text to be resized.
3. Select a preset size from the Size pop-up menu on the right side of the Measurements palette **(Figure 1)**.
   or
   In the Size field on the Measurements palette, enter a number between 2 and 720 in increments as small as .001 point, then press Return. It is not necessary to enter "pt" **(Figure 2)**.

✔ Tips

■ You can also select a preset point size from the Size pop-up menu under the Style menu. You can enter a custom point size in the "Other" dialog box, opened from the Size pop-up menu.

■ Use style sheets to apply paragraph-wide typographic attributes quickly. *(See Chapter 11, Style Sheets)*

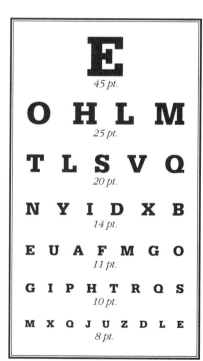

Figure 2.

To resize type using the keyboard:

1. Select the Content tool.
2. Highlight the text to be resized.
3. Hold down Command (⌘) and Shift and press "<" to reduce the text or ">" to enlarge the text to preset sizes.
   or
   Hold down Command (⌘), Option, Shift and press "<" to reduce the text or ">" to enlarge the text in 1 point increments.

To change a font:

1. Select the Content tool.

2. Highlight the text to be modified.

3. Select a font from the Font pop-up menu in the Measurements palette **(Figure 3)**.

or

Click in the font field to the left of the current font name, type the new font name, then press Return. Entering the first few characters of the font name is usually sufficient **(Figure 4)**.

✔ Tips

■ Hold down Command (⌘), Option, Shift and press "M" to highlight the Font field on the Measurements palette.

■ Fonts can also be selected from the Font pop-up menu under the Style menu.

■ Font, Size, Color, Shade, Style, Horizontal Scale, Track Amount, and Baseline Shift modifications can be made using the Character dialog box, opened from the Style menu.

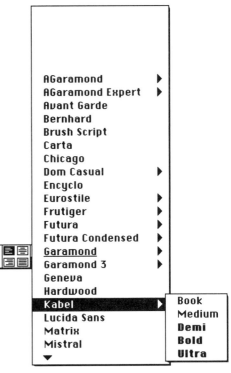

Figure 3. *Fonts are grouped by families in this Font pop-up menu with a utility called Adobe Type Reunion.*

Press this arrowhead to open the Font pop-up menu.

Or click just to the left of the current font name and type a new font name.

Figure 4. *The Font field on the Measurements palette.*

Change Fonts

To style type:

1. Select the Content tool.

2. Highlight the text to be styled.

3. Click one or more of the style icons on the Measurements palette **(Figure 6)**.

✔ Tips

■ Click the "P" on the Measurements palette to remove **all** styling from highlighted type.

■ To remove **one** style at a time, click any highlighted style icon on the Measurements palette.

■ It is not advisable to input text with the Caps key locked. Lowercase characters can easily be converted into caps or small caps, but characters input with the Caps key locked cannot be converted to lowercase.

■ When the small caps style is applied to type, uppercase characters remain uppercase and lowercase characters are converted to small caps **(Figure 5)**.

■ Superscript type sits above the baseline; subscript type rests below the baseline; superior type is aligned with the cap height of the font and reduced in point size.

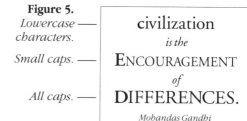

To style type using the keyboard.

Hold down **Command** and **Shift** and press any of the following keys:

Plain	**P**
Bold	**B**
Italic	**I**
Underline	**U**
Word Underline	**W**
Strike Thru	**/**
Outline	**O**
Shadow	**S**
All Caps	**K**
Small Caps	**H**
Superscript	**+**
Subscript	**-**
Superior	**V**

Figure 5.
Lowercase characters. —

Small caps. —

All caps. —

civilization
is the
Encouragement
of
DIFFERENCES.
Mohandas Gandhi

Style Type

Figure 6. *The style icons on the Measurements palette.*

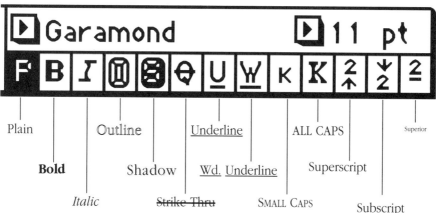

To modify horizontal alignment:

1. Select the Content tool.

2. Click in a paragraph or press and drag through a series of paragraphs.

3. Click one of the four Horizontal Alignment icons on the Measurements palette **(Figure 7-8)**.

✔ Tips

■ Only one alignment option can be applied per paragraph.

■ The horizontal alignment options can also be applied using the Alignment pop-up menu under the Style menu, or using the Formats dialog box, opened from the Style menu.

Flush left, ragged right *Centered*

Flush right, ragged left *Justified*

Figure 7. *The four alignment icons on the Measurements palette.*

To change the horizontal alignment of type using the keyboard.

Hold down **Command** and **Shift**, and press any of the following keys:

Flush left, ragged right	**L**
Centered	**C**
Flush right, ragged left	**R**
Justified	**J**

Flush left, ragged right —

So we was all right now, as to the shirt and the sheet and the spoon and the candles, by the help of the calf and rats and the mixed-up counting; and as to the candlestick, it warn't no consequence, it would blow over by and by....

So we was all right now, as to the shirt and the sheet and the spoon and the candles, by the help of the calf and rats and the mixed-up counting; and as to the candlestick, it warn't no consequence, it would blow over by and by....

— *Centered*

Flush right, ragged left —

So we was all right now, as to the shirt and the sheet and the spoon and the candles, by the help of the calf and rats and the mixed-up counting; and as to the candlestick, it warn't no consequence, it would blow over by and by....

So we was all right now, as to the shirt and the sheet and the spoon and the candles, by the help of the calf and rats and the mixed-up counting; and as to the candlestick, it warn't no consequence, it would blow over by and by....

Mark Twain

— *Justified*

Figure 8. *The four horizontal alignment options.*

Horizontal Alignment

Item

Modify...	⌘M
Frame...	⌘B
Runaround...	⌘T
Duplicate	⌘D
Step and Repeat...	
Delete	⌘K
Group	⌘G
Ungroup	⌘U
Constrain	
Lock	⌘L
Send to Back	
Bring to Front	
Space/Align...	
Picture Box Shape	▶
Reshape Polygon	

Figure 9. *Select* **Modify** *from the* **Item** *menu.*

To modify vertical alignment:

1. Select the Item or Content tool.
2. Click on a text box.
3. Select Modify from the Item menu **(Figure 9)**.
4. Select one of the four Vertical Alignment options from the Type pop-up menu **(Figure 11)**.
5. Click OK or press Return **(Figure 10)**.

✔ Tips

- In vertically justified text with an Inter ¶ Max value of 0, space is added evenly between lines and paragraphs. An Inter ¶ Max value greater than 0 represents the maximum space added between paragraphs before leading is affected.
- Make sure there is no return at the end of the last line in a box with bottom, centered, or justified Vertical Alignment.

Figure 10.

Never put off
till tomorrow
what you can
do the day
after tomorrow.

Top Alignment.

Never put off
till tomorrow
what you can
do the day
after tomorrow.

Bottom Alignment.

Never put off
till tomorrow
what you can
do the day
after tomorrow.

Centered Alignment.

Never put off

till tomorrow

what you can

do the day

after tomorrow.

Mark Twain

Justified Alignment.

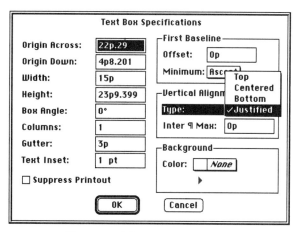

Figure 11. *The* **Vertical Alignment** *options.*

About tracking and kerning:

Kerning is the adjustment of space between a pair of characters when the cursor is inserted between them. **Tracking** is the adjustment of the space to the right of one or more highlighted characters. The same section of the Measurements palette is used for Tracking and Kerning.

To kern type using the Measurements palette:

1. Select the Content tool.

2. Click between two characters **(Figure 12)**.

3. Click the right arrow to add space or the left arrow to delete space **(Figure 13-14)**.

or

Enter a number between -500% and 500% in increments as small as .01 in the Tracking & Kerning field, then press Return.

To track type using the Measurements palette:

1. Select the Content tool.

2. Highlight any number of characters.

3. Click the right arrow to add space or the left arrow to delete space **(Figures 13, 15a-b)**.

or

Enter a number between -500% and 500% in increments as small as .01 in the Tracking & Kerning field, then press Return.

✔ Tips

■ To kern or track in finer increments, hold down Option while clicking the right or left arrow.

■ Tracking or kerning values can also be applied using the Kern or Track dialog box opened from the Style menu.

Tomorrow

Figure 12. *Click between two characters to kern.*

Figure 13. *The Tracking & Kerning arrows and field on the Measurements palette.*

Tomorrow

Figure 14. *The space between the "T" and the "o" has been reduced.*

C I V I L I Z A T I O N
is the
E N C O U R A G E M E N T
of
D I F F E R E N C E S.
Mohandas Gandhi

Figure 15a. *A phrase with positive tracking values.*

Nothing great was ever achieved without enthusiasm.
Emerson

Figure 15b. *A phrase with a negative tracking value of -6. Positive and negative tracking values can be used to create a variety of typographic effects.*

Tracking and Kerning

To Tr Ta Yo Ya Wo Wa We Va Vo

Figure 16. *These are some of the character pairs that often need extra kerning, particularly in large point sizes.*

Style is self-plagiarism.

Figure 17a. *A phrase with a normal word space value.*

Style is self-plagiarism.

Alfred Hitchcock

Figure 17b. *The same phrase with a word space value of -10. Negative Word Space Tracking can improve the appearance of headlines and other phrases set in large point sizes.*

Utilities
Check Spelling ▶
Auxiliary Dictionary...
Edit Auxiliary...
Suggested Hyphenation... ⌘H
Hyphenation Exceptions...
Library...
Font Usage...
Picture Usage...
Tracking Edit...
Kerning Table Edit...
Remove Manual Kerning
Alternate Em Spaces

Figure 18. *Select **Remove Manual Kerning** from the **Utilities** menu to restore normal kerning values to highlighted text.*

To kern or track using the keyboard:

1. Select the Content tool.
2. Click between two characters or highlight any number of characters.
3. Hold down Command (⌘) and Shift and press left bracket ([) to delete space, or right bracket (]) to add space.

✔ Tip

- To kern or track in finer increments, add the Option key to the above keyboard shortcut.

Note: The Word Space Tracking and Remove Manual Kerning commands are included in the FeaturesPlus XTension. They are not part of the QuarkXPress application.

To adjust the space between words only:

1. Select the Content tool.
2. Highlight one or more words.
3. Hold down Command (⌘), Control, Shift and press left bracket ([) to delete space, or right bracket (]) to add space **(Figures 17a-b)**.

✔ Tips

- Word space tracking can be applied only via the keyboard.
- To adjust word spacing in finer increments, add the Option key to the above keyboard shortcut.

To remove kerning and Word Space Tracking:

1. Select the Content tool.
2. Highlight the kerned text.
3. Select "Remove Manual Kerning" from the Utilities menu **(Figure 18)**.

✔ Tip

- The Remove Manual Kerning command does not restore tracking values.

Tracking and Kerning

About horizontal scaling:

Normal text has a horizontal scale value of 100%. Horizontal scaling is the extending (widening) or condensing (narrowing) of type. The height of the characters is not affected when horizontal scale values are modified.

To horizontally scale text using the Style menu:

1. Select the Content tool.

2. Highlight the text to be scaled.

3. Select Horizontal Scale from the Style menu **(Figure 19)**.

4. Enter a number between 25% and 99% to condense type (make narrower than normal) or a number between 101% and 400% to expand type (make wider than normal) **(Figures 20-22)**.

5. Click OK or press Return.

To horizontally scale text using the keyboard:

1. Select the Content tool.

2. Highlight the text to be scaled.

3. Hold down Command (⌘) and press left bracket ([) to condense in 5% increments, or right bracket (]) to expand in 5% increments.

Figure 19. *Select **Horizontal Scale** from the **Style** menu.*

Figure 20. *The Horizontal Scale feature can be used to stylize type or facilitate copy fitting.*

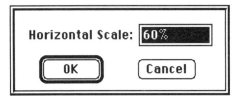

Figure 21. *A value of 60% in the Horizontal Scale dialog box will condense type 40%.*

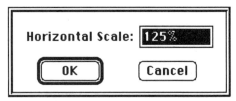

Figure 22. *A value of 125% in the Horizontal Scale dialog box will expand type 25%.*

Horizontal Scaling

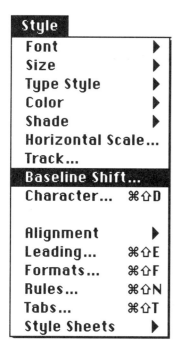

Figure 23. *Select* **Baseline Shift** *from the* **Style** *menu.*

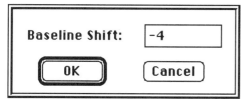

Figure 24. *A negative number in the Baseline Shift dialog box will shift the characters below the baseline; a positive number will shift the characters above the baseline.*

About Baseline Shift:

Using the Baseline Shift command, the position of one or more characters can be raised above or lowered below the baseline.

To shift type using the Baseline Shift dialog box:

1. Select the Content tool.
2. Highlight the characters to be shifted.
3. Select Baseline Shift from the Style menu **(Figure 23)**.
4. Enter a number up to three times the point size of the type to be shifted. Insert a minus sign (-) followed by a number to shift the type below the baseline **(Figures 24-26)**.
5. Click OK or press Return.

To shift type using the keyboard:

1. Select the Content tool.
2. Highlight the characters to be shifted.
3. Hold down Command (⌘), Option, Shift and press hyphen (-) to lower the type below the baseline, or plus sign (+) to raise the type above the baseline in 1 point increments.

Oce^an V_oy^age.

Figure 25. *In this example, some characters have been shifted above the baseline and some have been shifted below the baseline.*

Figure 26. *The Baseline Shift feature is useful for creating logos and other special type configurations.*

Baseline Shift

About Key Caps:

Key Caps is an Apple Menu item that displays keystroke combinations for producing special characters.

To use Key Caps:

1. Select Key Caps from the Apple menu.

2. Select a font from the Key Caps menu.

3. Look at the keyboard diagram as you hold down Option or Option and Shift together. Make a note of the keystroke combination that produces the desired special character **(Figure 27)**.

4. Select Quit from the File menu.

5. If not already selected, select the correct font for the special character keystroke combination.

6. Enter the keystroke combination into your text.

A few special characters and their corresponding keystroke combinations.

"	Option [
"	Option Shift [
'	Option]
'	Option Shift]
•	Option 8
©	Option g
®	Option r
é	Option e, e again
¢	Option 4
—	Option Shift hyphen (em dash)
–	Option hyphen (en dash)
⁄	Option Shift 1
°	Option Shift 8

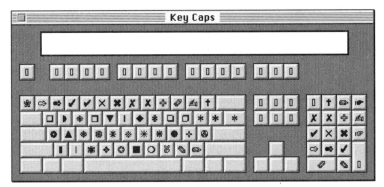

Figure 27. *The Key Caps utility displays special character sets.*

To insert one Zapf Dingbat character:

1. Select the Content tool.

2. Click in a line of text to create an insertion point.

3. Hold down Command (⌘) and Shift and press "Z."

4. Press any key or keyboard combination to produce the desired Zapf Dingbat character **(Figure 28)**.

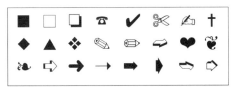

Figure 28. *A few Zapf Dingbats characters.*

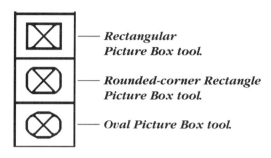

Rectangular
Picture Box tool.

Rounded-corner Rectangle
Picture Box tool.

Oval Picture Box tool.

Figure 1. *Three of the Picture Box tools.*

About Pictures:

In QuarkXPress, pictures can be imported into various-shaped picture boxes. File formats that can be imported include TIFF, RIFF, PAINT, PICT, and EPS.

To create a picture box:

1. Select any of the first three Picture Box tools. The cursor will temporarily turn into a crosshair icon **(Figure 1)**.

2. Press and drag in any direction **(Figures 2a-b)**.

(See Create a Polygon in this chapter)

✔ Tip

■ Hold down Shift and press and drag a handle to reshape a rectangular picture box into a square or an oval picture box into a circle. This tip also applies to text boxes.

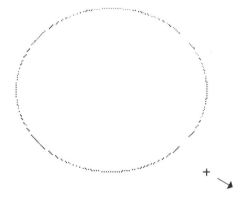

Figure 2a. *Press and drag to create a picture box.*

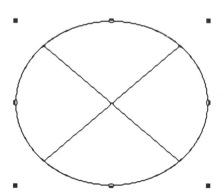

Figure 2b. *An empty picture box has an "x" through its center.*

Create a Picture Box

To resize a picture box manually:

1. Select the Item or Content tool.

2. Click on a picture box.

3. Press and drag any handle **(Figures 3-4)**.

✔ Tip

- Hold down Option and Shift while dragging to preserve the original proportions of the box.

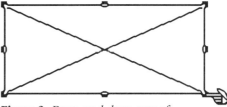

Figure 3. *Press and drag any of the four corner handles of a box.*

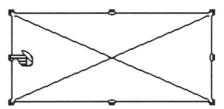

Figure 4. *Press and drag any of the four midpoint handles of a box.*

To resize a picture box using the Measurements palette:

1. Select the Item or Content tool.

2. Click on a picture box.

3. Next to the W in the Measurements palette, enter a number in increments as small as .001 to modify the width of the box **(Figure 5)**.

   and/or

   Next to the H in the Measurements palette, enter a number to modify the height of the box.

4. Press Return.

✔ Tip

- To enlarge or reduce the dimensions of a box by a specified amount, insert the cursor after the current value in the W or H field, enter a plus (+) or minus (-) sign, then enter an additional value in any measurement system used in QuarkXPress.

*The **Width** field with two inches added to the existing four pica width of a box.*

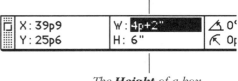

*The **Height** of a box.*

Figure 5. *The Width and Height can be entered in any of the measurement systems used in QuarkXPress.*

Item

Modify...	⌘M
Frame...	⌘B
Runaround...	⌘T
Duplicate	⌘D
Step and Repeat...	
Delete	⌘K
Group	⌘G
Ungroup	⌘U
Constrain	
Lock	⌘L
Send to Back	
Bring to Front	
Space/Align...	
Picture Box Shape	▶
Reshape Polygon	

Figure 6. *Click on a picture box, then select* **Delete** *from the* **Item** *menu.*

To delete a picture box:

1. Select the Item or Content tool.

2. Click on a picture box.

3. Select Delete from the Item menu **(Figure 6)**.

   or

   Hold down Command (⌘) and press "K".

✔ Tip

■ A picture box selected with the Item tool can also be deleted by pressing Delete on the keyboard or selecting Clear from the Edit menu.

To move a picture box manually:

1. Select the Item tool.

2. Press on the inside of a picture box, then drag in any direction **(Figure 7)**.

✔ Tips

■ You can drag a picture box or any other item from one page to another.

■ Pause before dragging to display the picture as it is moved (a clock icon will appear while the picture first redraws). Or, drag immediately to display only the outline of the box as it is moved.

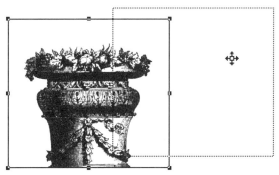

Figure 7. *To move a box, press and drag inside it with the Item tool (note the Item tool icon).*

To reposition a picture box using the Measurements palette:

1. Select the Item or Content tool.

2. Click on a picture box.

3. Enter a number in the X field on the Measurements palette to modify the horizontal position of the box relative to the ruler origin **(Figure 8)**.
and/or
Enter a number in the Y field to modify the vertical position.

4. Press Return.

✔ Tip

■ To move a box a specified amount horizontally or vertically, insert the cursor after the number in the X or Y field, enter a plus (+) or minus (-) sign, and then enter a number in any measurements system used in QuarkXPress **(Figures 9a-b)**.

*The **horizontal** position of a picture box.*

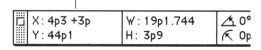

*The **vertical** position of a picture box.*

Figure 8. *The Measurements palette.*

Figure 9a. *Add a positive or negative number to the right of the number in the X or Y field, then press Return.*

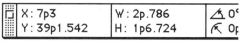

Figure 9b. *The two numbers are added together, causing the box to be repositioned.*

To create a bleed:

To create a bleed, position any item (picture box, text box, or line) so that part of the item is on the page and part of the item is on the pasteboard **(Figure 10)**. An item that is completely on the pasteboard will not print.

✔ Tip

■ Check the Registration Marks box in the Print dialog box to increase the print area around the page.

(See Chapter 17, Printing)

Figure 10. *Items positioned to create a "bleed."*

Figure 11a. *Press and drag from a ruler to place a ruler guide on a document page.*

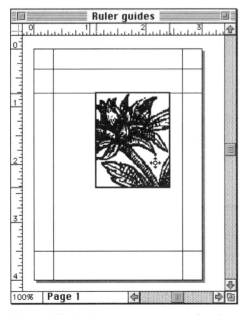

Figure 11b. *An item snaps to a guide when dragged within the specified Snap Distance of the guide.*

About Ruler Guides:

Ruler guides can be dragged from the horizontal or vertical ruler onto the document page to aid in the layout process. If Snap to Guides is turned on from the View menu, an item that is moved near a guide will "snap" to the guide if it is within the distance specified in the Snap Distance field in the General Preferences dialog box. The default Snap Distance is 6 pixels.

To position a box using a ruler guide:

1. Press and drag a guide from the horizontal or vertical ruler onto the document page. As you drag, the position of the guide will be indicated by a marker on the ruler and in the X or Y field on the Measurements palette **(Figure 11a)**.

2. Press and drag an item to the guide. The item will "snap" to the guide if Snap to Guides is on **(Figure 11b)**.

✔ Tips

■ To remove a ruler guide from a page, select the Item tool and drag the guide back onto the ruler.

■ To remove all the horizontal or vertical guides at one time, make sure there is no pasteboard showing between the edge of the page and the corresponding ruler, then hold down Option and click on the horizontal ruler to remove all the horizontal guides, or the vertical ruler to remove all the vertical guides.

■ Ruler guides are displayed in front of page elements or behind page elements depending on whether In Front or Behind is selected from the Guides pop-up menu in the General Preferences dialog box, opened from the Edit menu. Ruler guides do not print.

About importing pictures:

When a picture is imported into a picture box, a screen version of it is saved with the QuarkXPress file for display purposes. Also saved with the QuarkXPress file is information about changes made within the QuarkXPress file, such as cropping, rotating, or scaling. The original picture file is not modified by such changes. A path is created to the original picture file, which the QuarkXPress file accesses when the document is printed.

(See Update a Picture in this chapter)

To import a picture:

1. Select the Content tool.

2. Click on a picture box.

3. Select Get Picture from the File menu **(Figure 12)**.
or
Hold down Command (⌘) and press "E".

4. Select a picture file and click Open **(Figure 13)**
or
Double-click a picture file.

Figure 12. *Select **Get Picture** from the **File** menu.*

Select a picture file.

Figure 13. *The Get Picture dialog box.*

*With the **Picture Preview** box checked, a preview of the currently selected file is displayed.*

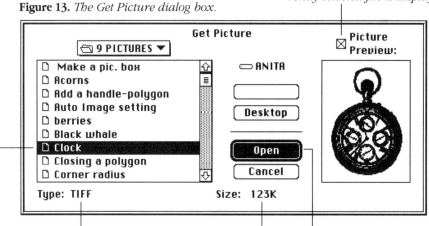

*The picture file **Type**. Quark imports PAINT, PICT, EPS, TIFF and RIFF pictures.*

*The picture **Size**. Click **Open** to import.*

Import a Picture

Horizontal scale of a picture.

X% : 50%	◁▷ X+ : 0p
Y% : 100%	⬔ Y+ : 0p

Vertical scale of a picture.

Figure 14. *When the X and Y percentages differ from each other, a picture's proportions have been altered relative to the original.*

X% : 75%	◁▷ X+ : p5.438
Y% : 75%	⬔ Y+ : p2.472

Figure 15. *When the X and Y percentages match, a picture's proportions have been preserved relative to the original.*

Figure 16. *A picture with an X coordinate of 55% and a Y coordinate of 55%.*

Figure 17. *A picture with an X coordinate of 70% and a Y coordinate of 50%.*

To resize a picture:

1. Select the Content tool.
2. Click on a picture.
3. Hold down Command (⌘), Option, Shift and press the > key to enlarge the picture or the < key to reduce the picture in 5% increments.

   or

   Enter numbers in the X% and/or Y% picture size fields in the Measurements palette, then press Return (**Figures 14-18**).

✔ Tip

■ The percentages in the size fields in the Measurements palette can be supplied as "For Position Only" information to a printer for traditional stripping. These numbers can be used for a scanned picture only if the original was scanned at 100%.

Figure 18. *A picture with an X coordinate of 50% and a Y coordinate of 70%.*

Resize a Picture

Additional keystrokes for resizing pictures.

To fit a picture into its box:

1. Select the Content tool.

2. Click on a picture.

3. Hold down Command (⌘), Option, Shift and press "F" **(Figures 19a-b)**.

✔ Tip

■ If the Option key is not included in the above keystroke, the picture will fit into its box, but its proportions will be altered relative to the original **(Figure 19c)**.

Figure 19a. *A picture before being resized.*

To resize a picture and its box simultaneously:

1. Select the Content tool.

2. Hold down Command (⌘), Option, Shift, pause briefly for the picture to redraw, then press and drag any handle **(Figure 20)**.

Figure 19b. *A picture after the **Command, Option, Shift/F** keystroke has been applied.*

Figure 20. *Hold down **Command, Option, Shift** and press and drag a handle to resize a picture and its box simultaneously.*

Figure 19c. *A picture after the **Command, Shift/F** keystroke has been applied.*

Figure 21. *A picture being moved within its box. Note the hand icon.*

To crop a picture by moving it within its box:

1. Select the Content tool.

2. Press on a picture, pause briefly until the hand icon appears, then drag **(Figure 21)**.

✔ Tip

■ Click on a picture and press any of the four arrow keys on the keyboard to move a picture in 1 point increments. Hold down Option and press any of the arrow keys to move a picture in .1 point increments.

To crop a picture by resizing its box:

1. Select the Item or Content tool.

2. Press and drag any handle of a picture box **(Figures 22a-b)**.

To delete a picture:

1. Select the Content tool.

2. Click on a picture.

3. Press Delete.

Figure 22a. *Press and drag any handle to crop a picture.*

Figure 22b. *After cropping.*

To convert a picture box shape:

1. Select the Item or Content tool.

2. Click on a picture box.

3. Select any shape from the six selections in the Picture Box Shape pop-up menu under the Item menu **(Figures 23-24b)**.

Figure 23. *A picture box can be converted into any of the other shapes found under the **Picture Box Shape** pop-up menu.*

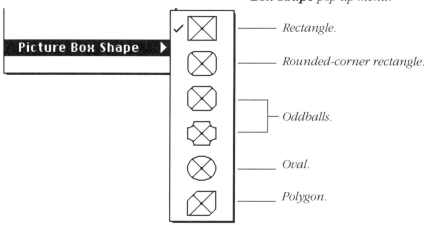

——— *Rectangle.*

——— *Rounded-corner rectangle.*

——— *Oddballs.*

——— *Oval.*

——— *Polygon.*

Convert a Picture Box Shape

Figure 24a. *A rectangular picture box...*

Figure 24b. *...converted into an "oddball."*

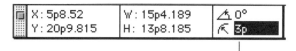

To modify the corners of a picture box:

Enter a number in the corner radius field in the Measurements palette to modify the amount of curve of the corners of a rectangle, rounded-corner rectangle or "oddball" shape **(Figure 25)**.

Figure 25. *In the corner radius field on the Measurements palette, enter a number between 0" and 2" in any measurement system used in QuarkXPress.*

To rotate a picture and its box using the Measurements palette:

1. Select the Item or Content tool.

2. Click on a picture box.

3. In the picture and box angle field on the left side of the Measurements palette, enter a positive number to rotate counterclockwise or a negative number to rotate clockwise between 360° and 360° in increments as small as .001° **(Figure 26)**.

4. Press Return.

*The **picture and box angle** field.*

| X: 4p7.731 | W: 33p4.269 | ⊿ 0° | X%: 100% | ⇔ X+: 0p | ⊿ 20° |
| Y: 22p.531 | H: 3p2.114 | ⋔ 0p | Y%: 100% | ⇕ Y+: 0p | ⟋ 0° |

Figure 26. *The Measurements palette.*

Figure 27.
*The **Rotation tool**.*

To rotate a picture and its box using the Rotation tool:

1. Select the Rotation tool **(Figure 27)**.

2. Click on a picture box.

3. Press to create an anchor point, pause briefly for the picture to redraw, then drag away from the anchor point to create a "lever" **(Figure 28)**.

4. Drag the "lever" clockwise or counterclockwise **(Figure 29)**.

✔ Tip

■ Hold down Shift while dragging with the Rotation tool to rotate an item in 45° increments.

Figure 28. *If you drag away from the axis point before rotating, you will create a "lever," and the rotation will be easier to control. If you do not pause before dragging, only the outline of the box will be displayed as it is being rotated.*

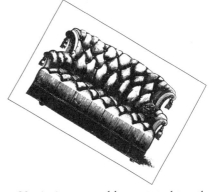

Figure 29. *A picture and box rotated together.*

To rotate a picture alone:

1. Select the Content tool.

2. Click on a picture.

3. In the picture angle field on the right side of the Measurements palette, enter a positive number to rotate counterclockwise or a negative number to rotate clockwise **(Figure 30)**.

4. Press Return **(Figures 31-34)**.

✔ Tip

■ To rotate the picture box and **not** the picture, first rotate the box with the picture, then rotate the picture alone the negative amount. For example, if the picture with its box is rotated 20°, rotate the picture back -20°.

Figure 30. *The* **picture angle** *field.*

| X: 4p7.731 | W: 33p4.269 | △ 0° | X%: 100% | ◁▷ X+: 0p | △ 20° |
| Y: 22p.531 | H: 3p2.114 | ◸ 0p | Y%: 100% | Y+: 0p | ◿ 0° |

Figure 31. *0° rotation.*

Figure 32. *180° rotation.*

Figure 33. *90° rotation.*

Figure 34. *40° rotation.*

Rotate a Picture

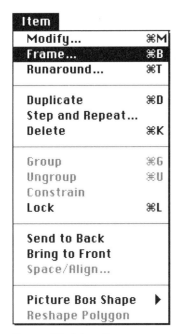

Figure 35. *Select **Frame** from the **Item** menu.*

To frame a picture box:

1. Select the Item or Content tool.

2. Click on a box.

3. Select Frame from the Item menu **(Figure 35)**.
or
Hold down Command (⌘) and press "B".

4. Select a preset width from the Width pop-up menu **(Figure 36)**.
or
Enter a custom width between .001 and 504 points in the Width field.

Steps 5-7 are optional.

5. Select an alternate frame Style. The non-straight line styles can only be applied to a rectangular box.

6. Select a color from the Color pop-up menu.

7. Select a shade from the Shade pop-up menu, or enter a percentage in the Shade field.

8. Click OK or press Return.
(See page 43 for an illustration of various frames)

Figure 36. *The Frame Specifications dialog box.*

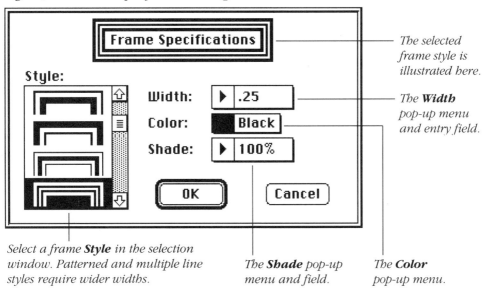

The selected frame style is illustrated here.

*The **Width** pop-up menu and entry field.*

*Select a frame **Style** in the selection window. Patterned and multiple line styles require wider widths.*

*The **Shade** pop-up menu and field.*

*The **Color** pop-up menu.*

Frame a Picture Box

To convert any picture box into a polygon picture box:

1. Click on a picture box of any shape.

2. Select the polygon icon from the Picture Box Shape pop-up menu under the Item menu **(Figure 37)**.

To create a polygon picture box using the Polygon tool:

1. Select the Polygon tool from the tool palette **(Figure 38)**.

2. Click once to establish a starting point.

3. Move the mouse and click to create a second handle. Repeat to create at least one more handle.

4. Close the polygon by clicking on the starting point.

or

Double-click anywhere **(Figures 39a-d)**.

✔ Tips

■ Hold down Command (⌘) and press Period (.) to delete an unfinished polygon.

■ A polygon or oval picture box with a Background of None may not print.

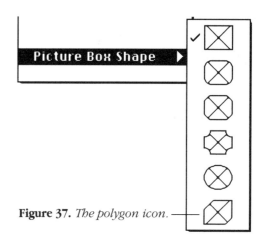

Figure 37. *The polygon icon.*

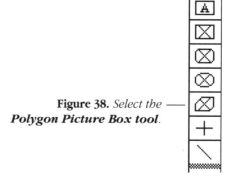

Figure 38. *Select the* ***Polygon Picture Box tool***.

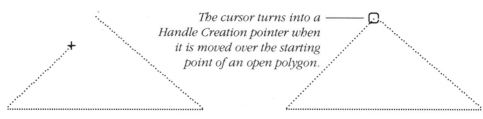

The cursor turns into a Handle Creation pointer when it is moved over the starting point of an open polygon.

Figure 39a. *Click to create handles.*

Figure 39b. *Be sure to close up the polygon, or it will run wild!*

Figure 39c. *The completed polygon.*

Figure 39d. *A polygon with a picture.*

Create a Polygon

Item	
Modify...	⌘M
Frame...	⌘B
Runaround...	⌘T
Duplicate	⌘D
Step and Repeat...	
Delete	⌘K
Group	⌘G
Ungroup	⌘U
Constrain	
Lock	⌘L
Send to Back	
Bring to Front	
Space/Align...	
Picture Box Shape	▶
Reshape Polygon	

Figure 40.
*To modify a polygon, first select **Reshape Polygon** from the **Item** menu.*

Before reshaping a polygon:

1. Select the Item or Content tool.

2. Click on a polygon.

3. Select Reshape Polygon from the Item menu **(Figure 40)**.

To reshape a polygon:

1. Select the Item or Content tool.

2. Click on a polygon.

3. Press and drag a handle or line segment **(Figure 41)**.
or
Add a handle by holding down Command (⌘), moving the cursor over a line segment, then clicking when the cursor turns into a Handle Creation pointer **(Figure 42)**.
or
Delete a handle by holding down Command (⌘), moving the cursor over a handle, then clicking when the cursor turns into a Handle Deletion pointer **(Figure 43)**.

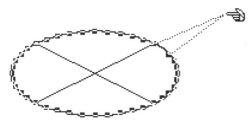

Figure 41. *Press and drag a handle or line segment to reshape a polygon.*

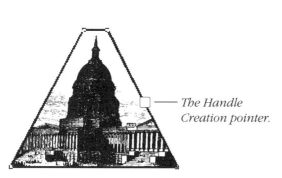

— *The Handle Creation pointer.*

Figure 42. *To add a handle, hold down **Command** (⌘) and click on a line segment.*

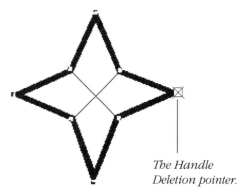

The Handle Deletion pointer.

Figure 43. *To delete a handle, hold down **Command** (⌘) and click on it.*

Reshape a Polygon

About picture styling:

A few of the basic picture modifications, such as posterization or contrast modification, that can be accomplished within QuarkXPress are outlined here. An application solely dedicated to image manipulation should be used for elaborate masking, filtering, or retouching. Keep in mind that modifications made to a picture in QuarkXPress do not affect the original picture file. *(See also Chapter 13, Apply Color)*

To posterize a picture:

1. Select the Content tool.

2. Click on a color bitmap, color or grayscale TIFF, or grayscale RIFF picture.

3. Select Posterized from the Style menu **(Figure 44-46)**.

✔ Tip

■ To restore a picture's contrast values, select the Content tool and click on the picture, then select Normal Contrast from the Style menu.

To apply a shade to a picture:

1. Select the Content tool.

2. Click on a black & white bitmap or a TIFF or RIFF line art picture.

3. Select a preset shade from the Shade pop-up menu under the Style menu.
or
Select Other from the same menu, enter a custom percentage, then click OK **(Figures 44 and 47)**.

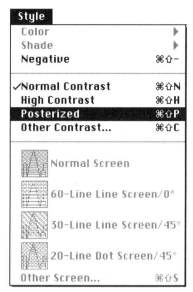

Figure 44. *Select a contrast option from the **Style** menu.*

Figure 45.
Normal Contrast.

Figure 47. *A TIFF line art picture with a 30% shade.*

Figure 46. *Posterization reduces the number of grays in a picture to black, white and four gray levels in between.*

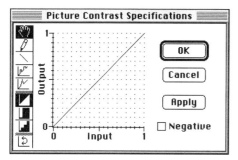

Figure 48a. *The normal contrast setting for a grayscale picture.*

To apply a custom contrast setting to a grayscale picture:

1. Select the Content tool.

2. Click on a grayscale TIFF or RIFF picture.

3. Select Other Contrast from the Style menu **(Figure 44)**.

4. Select the hand tool in the Picture Contrast Specifications dialog box and drag the contrast curve in any direction. Move it downward and to the right to lighten the picture **(Figures 48a-c)**.

or

Select the pencil tool in the Picture Contrast Specifications dialog box and draw a custom curve **(Figures 49a-b)**.

6. Click Apply to preview.

7. Click OK or press Return.

✔ Tip

■ The contrast setting can also be adjusted for a color bitmap or TIFF picture.

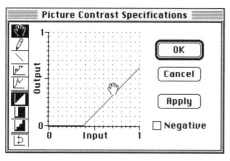

Figure 48b. *The contrast curve moved with the hand tool.*

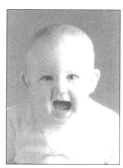

Figure 48c. *A picture with the contrast curve shown in Figure 48b.*

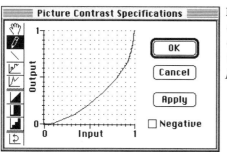

Figure 49a. *A custom contrast curve drawn with the pencil tool.*

Figure 49b. *A picture with the contrast curve shown in Figure 49a.*

Style a Picture

The Save Page as EPS command converts a QuarkXPress page into a picture file. You can use this feature to create special effects — a drop cap to which Auto or Manual Image Runaround can be applied *(see pages 115-117)*, a word that can be cropped, or a page within a page. Or, your service provider may ask you to save a page as an EPS file to color separate it.

Note: An EPS file cannot be edited, so be sure to save the file from which it is generated so you will have the option to generate another EPS file from it later.

To save a page as an EPS file:

1. Create or open a file that contains a page that you would like to save as an EPS file.

2. Select Save Page as EPS from the File menu **(Figure 50)**.

3. Enter a name for the EPS file in the "Save page as" field **(Figure 51)**.

4. Enter the number of the page to be saved as EPS in the Page field.

5. Enter a percentage between 10% and 100% in the Scale field.

6. Click Color or Black & White.

7. Select a location in which to save the file.

8. Click Save. To place the EPS into a document, create a picture box and use the Get Picture command (the way a picture is normally imported) **(Figures 52-55)**.

✔ Tip

■ If you import an EPS file containing text into a QuarkXPress file, the corresponding printer fonts must be available in your system for the EPS to print properly.

(For Save Page as EPS options in Version 3.2, see pages 189 and 217)

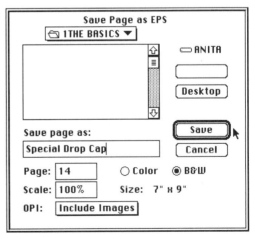

Figure 50. *Select **Save Page as EPS** from the **File** menu.*

Figure 51. *The **Save Page as EPS** dialog box.*

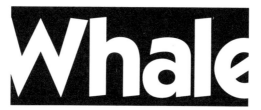

Figure 52. *A file containing this word was saved as an EPS file and then imported into a picture box so that it could be cropped.*

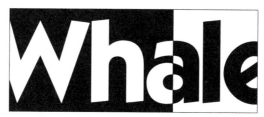

Figure 53. *This compound word was created by placing two picture boxes, each containing an EPS file, side-by-side.*

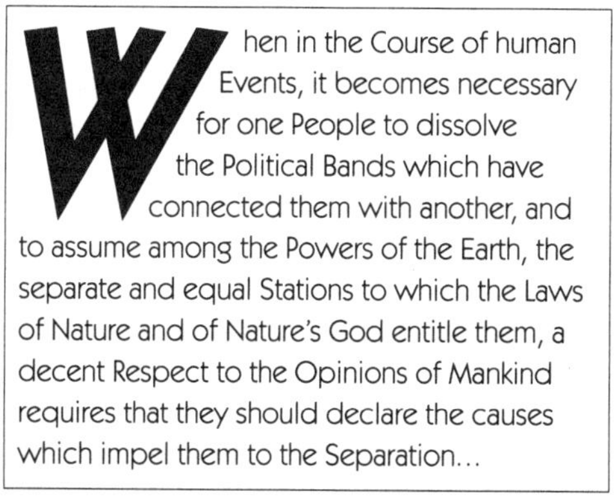

When in the Course of human Events, it becomes necessary for one People to dissolve the Political Bands which have connected them with another, and to assume among the Powers of the Earth, the separate and equal Stations to which the Laws of Nature and of Nature's God entitle them, a decent Respect to the Opinions of Mankind requires that they should declare the causes which impel them to the Separation...

Figure 54. *A small-sized page with a "W" in a text box was saved as an EPS file and then imported into a picture box. The Auto Image Runaround option was applied to the picture to cause the surrounding text to wrap around the contour of the "W."*

Chapter 7 Paragraph Formatting

To "break" a line without creating a new paragraph:

1. Select the Content tool.
2. Click in the text where a line break is to occur.
3. Hold down Shift and press Return. With Invisibles on, a Shift-Return is displayed as a left-pointing arrow icon **(Figures 17-19)**.

✓ **Tips**

- To remove a line break command, or "soft return," click at the beginning of the next line and press Delete.
- This command can be used to adjust headlines or fix awkward breaks in ragged right copy.

Figure 17. *This is an awkward break.*

The night so luminous on the spar-deck, but otherwise on the cavernous ones below — levels so very like the tiered galleries in a coal-mine — the luminous night passed away. Like the prophet in the chariot disappearing in heaven and dropping his mantle to Elisha, the withdrawing night transferred its pale robe to the peeping day.

The night so luminous on the spar-deck, but otherwise on the cavernous ones below — levels so very like the tiered¶

galleries in a coal-mine — the luminous night passed away. Like the prophet in the chariot disappearing in heaven and dropping his mantle to Elisha, the withdrawing night transferred its pale robe to the peeping day.

Figure 18. *A paragraph return creates a new paragraph.*

The night so luminous on the spar-deck, but otherwise on the cavernous ones below — levels so very like the tiered ↩
galleries in a coal-mine — the luminous night passed away. Like the prophet in the chariot disappearing in heaven and dropping his mantle to Elisha, the withdrawing night transferred its pale robe to the peeping day.

Herman Melville

Figure 19. *A **Shift-Return** creates a new line within a paragraph.*

Insert a Line Break

A quick way to copy paragraph formats from one paragraph to another within a story.

Click in a paragraph or press and drag through a series of paragraphs that are to be modified. Hold down Option and Shift and click in the paragraph whose formats you would like to copy.

70

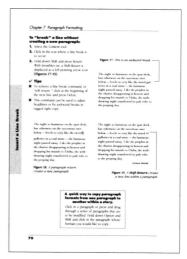

Figure 55. *A page-within-a-page. This is page 70 of this book, saved as an EPS file, then imported into a picture box.*

Save a Page as an EPS

About the Runaround feature:

There are several ways to combine text and pictures. For example, text can wrap around the irregular contours of a picture or around a picture box, or a picture can be placed behind a transparent text box.

To wrap text around a picture box:

1. Select the Item or Content tool.

2. Select a picture box.

3. Select Runaround from the Item menu **(Figure 56)**.

4. Select Item from the Mode pop-up menu **(Figure 57)**.

5. To adjust the space between each side of a rectangular picture box and the text wrapping around it, enter numbers in the Top, Left, Bottom, and Right fields. If any other picture box shape is selected, enter a single number in the Text Outset field.

6. Click OK or press Return **(Figure 58)**.

✔ Tip

■ The picture box must be on top of the text box for Runaround to work. If necessary, select the picture box and select Bring to Front from the Item menu.

Figure 56. *Select **Runaround** from the **Item** menu.*

Item	
Modify...	⌘M
Frame...	⌘B
Runaround...	**⌘T**
Duplicate	⌘D
Step and Repeat...	
Delete	⌘K
Group	⌘G
Ungroup	⌘U
Constrain	
Lock	⌘L
Send to Back	
Bring to Front	
Space/Align...	
Picture Box Shape	▶
Reshape Polygon	

Runaround Specifications

Mode: [Item]

Top: [12 pt] □

Left: [8 pt]

Bottom: [10 pt] [OK]

Right: [12 pt] [Cancel]

Figure 57. *Select **Item** from the **Mode** pop-up menu.*

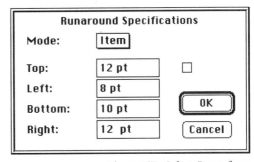

With my aversion to this cat, however, its partiality for myself seemed to increase. It followed my footsteps with a pertinacity which it would be difficult to make the reader comprehend. Whenever I sat, it would crouch beneath my chair, or spring upon my knees, covering me with its loathsome caresses. If I arose to walk it would get between my feet and thus nearly throw me down, or, fastening its long and sharp claws in my dress, clamber, in this manner to, to my breast. At such times, although I longed to destroy it with a blow, I was yet withheld from so doing, partly by a memory of my former crime, but chiefly—let me confess it at once—by absolute *dread of the beast...*

Edgar Allan Poe

Figure 58. *Text will only wrap around three sides of a box that is placed within a column. Text will wrap around all four sides of a box if it straddles two columns, as in this example.*

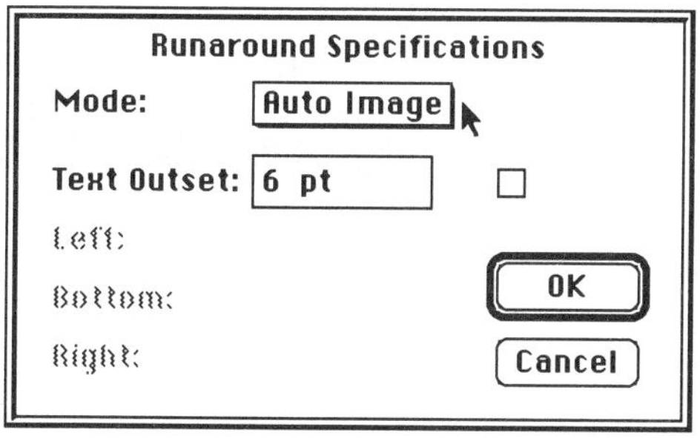

Figure 59. *Select **Auto Image** from the **Mode** pop-up menu.*

To wrap text around a picture:

1. Select the Item or Content tool.

2. Select a picture box.

3. Select Runaround from the Item menu **(Figure 56)**.

4. Select Auto Image from the Mode pop-up menu **(Figure 59)**.

5. Enter a number in points in the Text Outset field to adjust the space between the picture and the surrounding text.

6. Click OK or press Return.

7. Deselect the picture and text box by clicking in the margin or pasteboard to make the screen redraw **(Figure 60)**.

✔ Tip

■ For Auto Image to work properly, as in Figure 60, a picture with an irregular contour silhouetted on a white background should be chosen.

"Then, pray tell me what it is that you can infer from this hat?"

He picked it up and gazed at it in the peculiar introspective fashion which was characteristic of him. "It is perhaps less suggestive than it might have been," he remarked, "and yet there are a few inferences which are very distinct, and a few others which represent at least a strong balance of probability. That the man was highly intellectual is of course obvious upon the face of it, and also that he was fairly well-to-do within the last three years, although he has now fallen upon evil days. He had foresight, but has less now than formerly, pointing to a moral retrogression, which, when taken with the decline of his fortunes, seems to indicate some evil influence, probably drink, at work upon him. This may account also for the obvious fact that his wife has ceased to love him..."   *Sir Arthur Conan Doyle*

Figure 60. *Auto Image Runaround.*

About Manual Image:

When Manual Image Runaround mode is selected for a picture, a second set of handles called the Runaround polygon appears around it. The text wrap around a picture can be customized by modifying the Runaround polygon.

To create a Runaround polygon:

1. Select the Item or Content tool.

2. Select a picture box.

3. Select Runaround from the Item menu **(Figure 61)**.

4. Select Manual Image from the Mode pop-up menu **(Figure 62)**.

5. Enter a number in the Text Outset field to adjust the space between the Runaround polygon and the surrounding text.

6. Click OK or press Return **(Figure 64)**.

7. Deselect the picture and text box by clicking in the margin or pasteboard to make the screen redraw.

To reshape a Runaround polygon:

Press and drag a handle or line segment **(Figure 65)**.

or

Add a handle by holding down Command (⌘), moving the cursor over a line segment, and clicking when the cursor turns into a Handle Creation pointer **(Figure 66)**.

or

Delete a handle by holding down Command (⌘), moving the cursor over a handle, and clicking when the cursor turns into a Handle Deletion pointer **(Figure 67)**.

✔ Tip

■ Hold down the Space bar while reshaping a polygon to prevent the surrounding text from reflowing. The text will reflow when the Space bar is released.

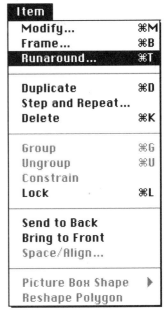

Figure 61. *Select **Runaround** from the **Item** menu.*

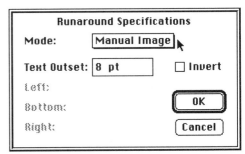

Figure 62. *Select **Manual Image** from the **Mode** pop-up menu.*

Figure 63. *To change the Runaround setting of a picture from Manual Image to None quickly, hold down Command (⌘) and Shift and click on a handle or line segment when the Polygon Deletion pointer is displayed.*

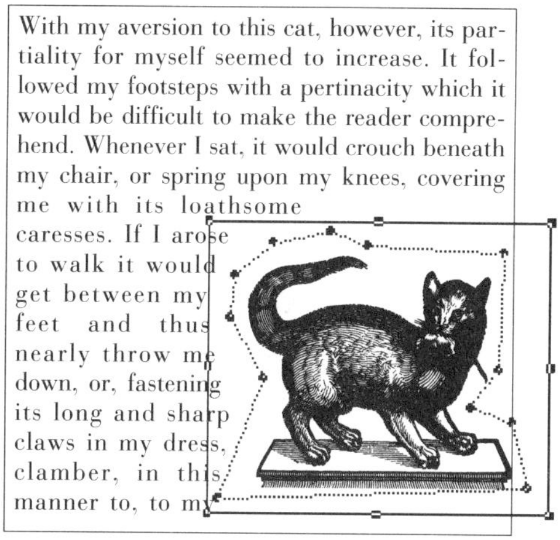

With my aversion to this cat, however, its partiality for myself seemed to increase. It followed my footsteps with a pertinacity which it would be difficult to make the reader comprehend. Whenever I sat, it would crouch beneath my chair, or spring upon my knees, covering me with its loathsome caresses. If I arose to walk it would get between my feet and thus nearly throw me down, or, fastening its long and sharp claws in my dress, clamber, in this manner to, to m

Figure 64. *When the Manual Image option is selected for a picture, a second set of handles called the Runaround polygon appears.*

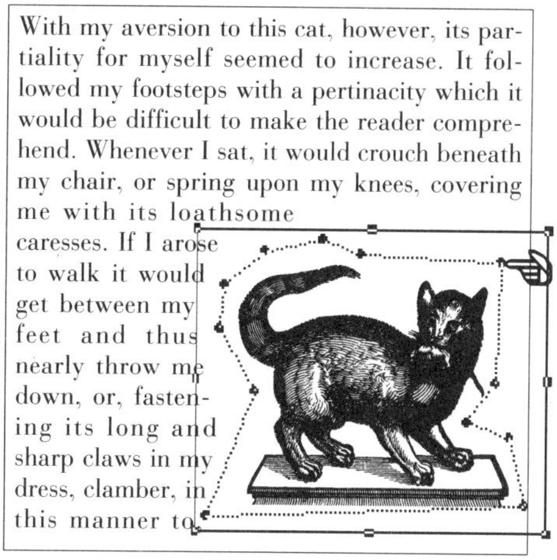

With my aversion to this cat, however, its partiality for myself seemed to increase. It followed my footsteps with a pertinacity which it would be difficult to make the reader comprehend. Whenever I sat, it would crouch beneath my chair, or spring upon my knees, covering me with its loathsome caresses. If I arose to walk it would get between my feet and thus nearly throw me down, or, fastening its long and sharp claws in my dress, clamber, in this manner to

Figure 65. *Press and drag a line segment or handle to reshape a Runaround polygon.*

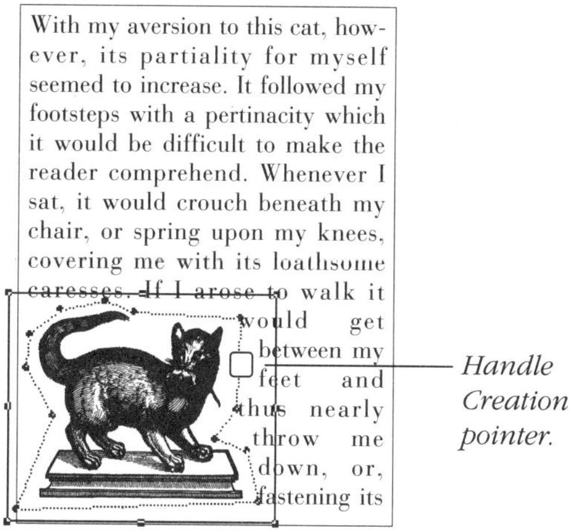

With my aversion to this cat, however, its partiality for myself seemed to increase. It followed my footsteps with a pertinacity which it would be difficult to make the reader comprehend. Whenever I sat, it would crouch beneath my chair, or spring upon my knees, covering me with its loathsome caresses. If I arose to walk it would get between my feet and thus nearly throw me down, or, fastening its

Handle Creation pointer.

Figure 66. *Hold down Command (⌘) and click on a line segment to add a handle.*

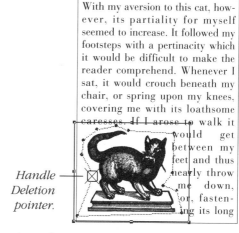

With my aversion to this cat, however, its partiality for myself seemed to increase. It followed my footsteps with a pertinacity which it would be difficult to make the reader comprehend. Whenever I sat, it would crouch beneath my chair, or spring upon my knees, covering me with its loathsome caresses. If I arose to walk it would get between my feet and thus nearly throw me down, or, fastening its long

Handle Deletion pointer.

Figure 67. *Hold down Command (⌘) and click on a handle to delete it.*

You can layer a text box over a picture box (or layer multiple picture boxes or text boxes). For a picture to be visible behind a text box, the background of the text box must be transparent.

To layer pictures and text:

1. Select the Item or Content tool.

2. Click on the box that is to be in front.

3. Select Show Colors from the View menu **(Figure 68)**.

4. Click the Background icon on the Colors palette **(Figure 69)**.

5. Click None. Do not select Black with a shade of 0%.

6. Select Bring to Front from the Item menu.

7. Click in the margin or pasteboard to deselect all items and make the screen redraw **(Figure 70)**.

✔ Tip

■ Apply a light tint to the picture so the text on top of it will be legible.
   (See "Apply color to a picture" on page 146)

   (See also "Layer Items" on page 163)

View

Fit in Window	⌘0
50%	
75%	
Actual Size	⌘1
200%	
Thumbnails	
Hide Guides	
Show Baseline Grid	
Snap to Guides	
Hide Rulers	⌘R
Show Invisibles	⌘I
Hide Tools	
Hide Measurements	
Show Document Layout	
Show Style Sheets	
Show Colors	
Show Trap Information	
Show Value Converter	
Windows	▶

Figure 68. *Select Show Colors from the View menu.*

*Click the **Background** icon.*

```
        Colors
  [□] [⊠] [■] [▸0%]
  [Solid]
  ○#1  ○#2  [0°]
  ─ None   ▲
    Black
    Blue
    Cyan
    Green
    Magenta
```

*Then click **None** to make the background of the top box transparent.*

Figure 69.

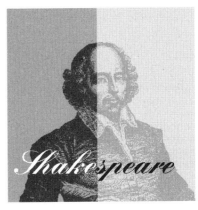

Figure 70. *To create this illustration, two picture boxes, each containing a cropped picture, were placed side-by-side. The picture on the left is 80% black with a 40% black Background; the picture on the right is 40% black with a 20% black Background. The text box has a Background of None and is in front of both picture boxes.*

Layer a Picture Behind Text

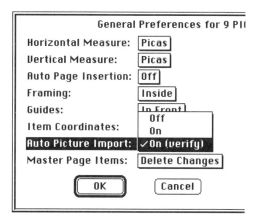

Figure 71. *Select **Off, On,** or **On (verify)** from the **Auto Picture Import** pop-up menu in the **General Preferences** dialog box.*

Figure 72. *Click on a picture file, then click **Update**.*

Figure 73. *Click OK or press Return.*

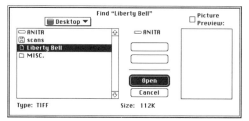

Figure 74. *Select the picture file, then click **Open**.*

The Auto Picture Import options:

When a picture is imported into a Quark-XPress file, the original picture file's name and location information is stored in the QuarkXPress file. If the original picture file is modified, renamed or moved, its path to the QuarkXPress file must be up-dated for it to print properly.
(See "About importing pictures" on page 100)

To update the path to a picture when opening a file:

There are three default settings for updating Modified and Missing picture files when you open a document. These settings are selected from the Auto Picture Import pop-up menu in the General Preferences dialog box, opened from the Edit menu.

If you open a document that was last saved with Auto Picture Import **Off**, the path to a Missing or Modified picture will not be updated; if you selected **On**, the path will be updated automatically; if you selected **On (verify)**, a prompt will appear **(Figure 71)**.

If **On (verify)** is selected, do as follows:

1. Click OK if the prompt appears.

2. Click on a picture name in the Missing/Modified Pictures dialog box **(Figure 72)**. A picture that was modified in another application will be listed as Modified. A picture that was moved or renamed will be listed as Missing.

3. Click Update.

4. For a Modified picture, click OK when the prompt appears **(Figure 73)**.
or
For a Missing picture, locate and select the picture in the "Find..." dialog box, then click Open **(Figure 74)**.

5. Click the Close box to exit the Missing/Modified Pictures dialog box.

Update a Picture

The path to a picture file can be updated at any time using the Picture Usage dialog box.

To update the path to a picture using Picture Usage:

1. Select Picture Usage from the Utilities menu **(Figure 75)**.

2. Select any file with a Status listed as Missing **(Figure 76)**.

3. *Optional:* Click Show Me to see the picture selected in the active document.

4. Click Update to search for the missing picture file.

5. Select the correct picture file in the "Find..." dialog box.

6. Click Open **(Figure 77)**.

Figure 75. *Select **Picture Usage** from the **Utilities** menu.*

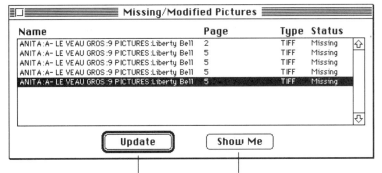

Figure 76. *Click **Update** to search for a missing picture file.*

*Click **Show Me** to see a picture selected in the document.*

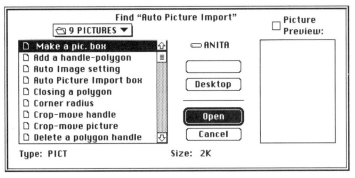

Figure 77. *Select a picture file, then click **Open** to update it.*

Update a Picture

Figure 1. *The Line tools in the Tool palette.*

The ***Orthogonal Line tool*** *draws only vertical and horizontal lines.*

The ***Line tool*** *draws lines at any angle.*

About Lines:

The line creation tools are used to create horizontal, vertical, and diagonal lines and arrows to which a variety of styles and endcaps can be applied. To place rules under type, use the Paragraph Rules feature. *(See Chapter 7, Paragraph Rules)*

To draw a line using the Orthogonal Line tool:

1. Select the Orthogonal Line tool **(Figure 1)**.

2. Press and drag the crosshair icon horizontally or vertically **(Figure 2)**.

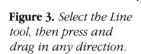

Figure 2. *Select the Orthogonal Line tool, then press and drag.*

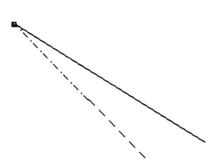

Figure 3. *Select the Line tool, then press and drag in any direction.*

To draw a line using the Line tool:

1. Select the Line tool **(Figure 1)**.

2. Press and drag the crosshair icon in any direction **(Figure 3)**.

✔ Tips

■ Hold down Shift while drawing a line to constrain the line to a 45° angle. An existing line can be reset to a 45° angle by dragging on a handle with Shift held down **(Figure 4)**.

■ To keep a Line tool selected, hold down Option and select it. Deselect it by selecting another tool.

Figure 4. *To snap a line to a 45° angle, drag a handle with Shift held down.*

Draw a Line

To style a line using the Measurements palette:

1. Select the Item or Content tool.

2. Click on a line **(Figure 5)**.

3. In the Width field, enter up to 504 pt in increments as small as .001, then press Return **(Figures 6-7)**.

and/or

Select from the eleven line styles in the Style pop-up menu.

and/or

Select from the six endcap styles in the Endcap pop-up menu.

✔ Tip

■ You can also style a line using the Line Style, Endcaps, Width, Color or Shade pop-up menu under the Style menu, or using the Line Specifications dialog box, opened by selecting Modify from the Item menu. *(Instructions for applying color to a line are on page 146)*

To modify the width of a line using the keyboard:

1. Select the Item or Content tool.

2. Click on a line.

3. Hold down Command (⌘), Option, Shift and press the > key to enlarge or the < key to reduce the width of the line in 1 point increments.

Figure 5. *A line is selected.*

The width is increased.

A new style is applied.

A new endcap is applied.

*The line **Style** pop-up menu.*

*The line **Width** field.*

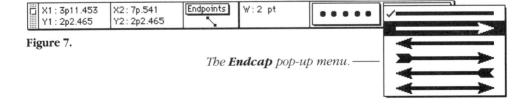

	X1 : 3p11.453	X2 : 7p.541	Endpoints	W : 2 pt
	Y1 : 2p2.465	Y2 : 2p2.465		

Figure 6. *The Measurements palette with a line selected.*

	X1 : 3p11.453	X2 : 7p.541	Endpoints	W : 2 pt
	Y1 : 2p2.465	Y2 : 2p2.465		

Figure 7.

*The **Endcap** pop-up menu.* ——

Style a Line

Figure 8. *Press and drag an endpoint to resize a line.*

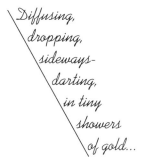

Figure 9. *Non-printing lines can create interesting text shapes. Select a line and then check the Suppress Printout box in the Line Specifications dialog box opened by selecting Modify from the Item menu.*

To resize a line manually:

1. Select the Item or Content tool.

2. Select a line.

3. Press and drag an endpoint to lengthen or shorten the line **(Figure 8)**.

To resize a line using the Measurements palette:

1. Select the Item or Content tool.

2. Select a line.

3. Select Left Point, Midpoint or Right Point from the Mode pop-up menu in the Measurements palette. The line will be measured from the chosen point **(Figure 10)**.

4. Enter a number in the Length field next to the "L" **(Figure 11)**.

5. Press Return.

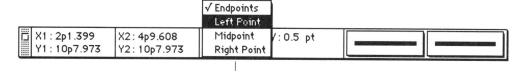

Figure 10. *Select **Left Point**, **Midpoint**, or **Right Point** mode from the Measurements palette.*

The angle of a line can be modified in the rotation angle field. This field is not available when Endpoints mode is selected.

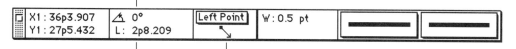

Figure 11. *The **Length** field.*

This icon illustrates the selected mode by indicating the beginning and ending points of the line.

Resize a Line

To move a line manually:

1. Select the Item or Content tool.

2. Drag any part of a line other than an endpoint **(Figure 12)**.

Figure 12. *A line being moved.*

To reposition a line using the Measurements palette:

1. Select the Item or Content tool.

2. Click on a line.

3. Select from the Mode pop-up menu on the Measurements palette **(Figure 10)**.

4. Enter numbers in the X and/or Y fields **(Figures 13-14)**.

5. Press Return.

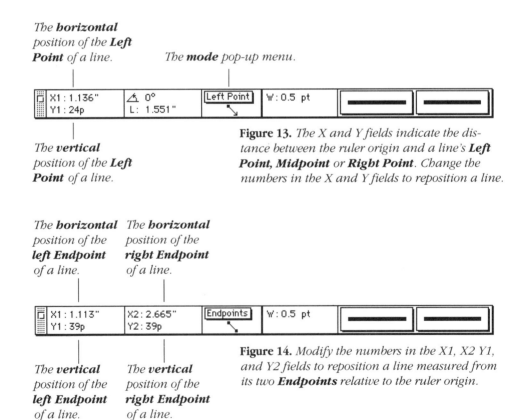

The **horizontal** position of the **Left Point** of a line.

The **mode** pop-up menu.

The **vertical** position of the **Left Point** of a line.

Figure 13. *The X and Y fields indicate the distance between the ruler origin and a line's **Left Point, Midpoint** or **Right Point**. Change the numbers in the X and Y fields to reposition a line.*

The **horizontal** position of the **left Endpoint** of a line.

The **horizontal** position of the **right Endpoint** of a line.

The **vertical** position of the **left Endpoint** of a line.

The **vertical** position of the **right Endpoint** of a line.

Figure 14. *Modify the numbers in the X1, X2 Y1, and Y2 fields to reposition a line measured from its two **Endpoints** relative to the ruler origin.*

Move a Line

STYLE SHEETS

About style sheets:

A style sheet is a set of paragraph and character formatting specifications that can be applied to one or more selected paragraphs with a quick keystroke or by clicking in the Style Sheets palette. If a style sheet is modified, all paragraphs to which it has been applied will be reformatted automatically.

A document can contain up to 127 Style Sheets **(Figure 1)**.

THE BILL OF RIGHTS

A Headline style.

AMENDMENT I.

A Subhead style.

Religious establishment prohibited.
Freedom of speech, of the press, and right to petition.
Congress shall make no law respecting an establishment of religion, or prohibiting the free exercise thereof; or abridging the freedom of speech, or of the press; or the right of the people peaceably to assemble, and to petition the Government for a redress of grievances.

A Body Text style.

AMENDMENT II.

Right to keep and bear arms.
A well-regulated militia, being necessary to the security of a free State, the right of the people to keep and bear arms, shall not be infringed.

A Small Subhead style.

AMENDMENT III.

Conditions for quarters for soldiers.
No soldier shall, in time of peace be quartered in any house, without the consent of the owner, nor in time of war, but in a manner to be prescribed by law.

AMENDMENT IV.

Right of search and seizure regulated.
The right of the people to be secure in their persons, houses, papers, and effects, against unreasonable searches and seizures, shall not be violated, and no warrants shall issue, but upon probable cause, supported by oath or affirmation, and particularly describing the place to be searched, and the persons or things to be seized.

Figure 1. *Use style sheets to apply repeated paragraph specifications quickly.*

To create a new style sheet:

1. Highlight a paragraph and apply any character or paragraph attributes, such as font, point size, type style, color, horizontal scaling, tracking, indents leading, space after, horizontal alignment, tabs, rules, etc. This will be referred to as a "sample" paragraph.

2. With the cursor in the sample paragraph, select Style Sheets from the Edit menu **(Figure 2)**.

3. Click New **(Figure 3)**.

4. Enter a name for the new style sheet in the Name field **(Figure 4)**.

5. *Optional:* Press Tab to move the cursor to the Keyboard Equivalent field, then press any keypad key, with or without Command (⌘), Option, Shift, or Control held down.

6. Click OK or press Return.

7. Click Save **(Figure 5)**.

✔ Tips

■ Apply the new style sheet to the sample paragraph, in addition to any other paragraphs.

■ The style sheet can be edited later, if desired.
(See "Edit a Style Sheet" on pages 130-131)

■ You can also create a new style sheet by selecting Style Sheets from the Edit menu without clicking in a sample paragraph. Click New in the Style Sheets dialog box, enter a name for the new style sheet, then follow steps 3-6 on page 130.

■ In Version 3.2, each Function (F) key has a pre-assigned command. If you choose an F key as a style sheet Keyboard Equivalent, the style sheet shortcut will override the pre-assigned command.

Figure 2. *With the cursor in a "sample" paragraph, select* **Style Sheets** *from the* **Edit** *menu.*

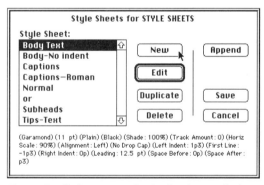

Figure 3. *Click* **New** *in the* **Style Sheets** *dialog box.*

Enter a **Name** for the style sheet. (Assign a descriptive name, such as "Body Text," or "Headlines.")

Enter a **Keyboard Equivalent** for the style sheet.

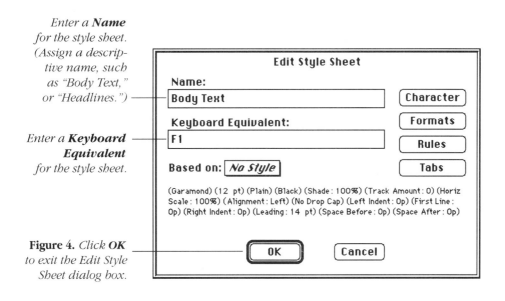

Figure 4. *Click **OK** to exit the Edit Style Sheet dialog box.*

Style sheets are listed in the **Style Sheet** scroll list.

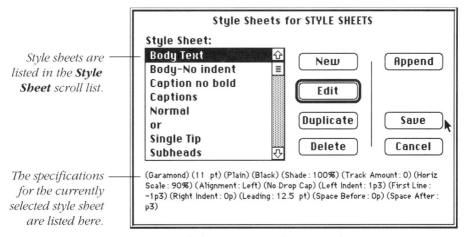

The specifications for the currently selected style sheet are listed here.

Figure 5. *Click **Save** to save the new style sheet and exit the Style Sheets dialog box.*

Create a Style Sheet

To apply a style sheet using the Style Sheets palette:

1. Select Show Style Sheets from the View menu **(Figure 6)**.

2. Select the Content tool.

3. Click in a paragraph or press and drag through a series of paragraphs.

4. Click a style sheet name on the Style Sheets palette **(Figure 7)**. The paragraph or paragraphs will be instantly reformatted.

✔ Tips

■ Text formatted using a style sheet can still be locally formatted using the Measurements palette, keyboard, or Style menu.

■ To clear a style sheet and all local formatting from a paragraph and apply a new style sheet in one keystroke, click in the paragraph, then hold down Option and click on the name of the new style sheet on the Style Sheets palette.

■ Style sheets can also be applied using the Style Sheets pop-up menu under the Style menu.

(To assign a Keyboard Equivalent to a style sheet, see step 5 on page 126)

To apply a style sheet using the keyboard:

1. Select the Content tool.

2. Click in a paragraph or press and drag through a series of paragraphs.

3. Perform the keyboard equivalent assigned to the chosen style sheet.

✔ Tip

■ The keyboard equivalent for each style sheet is listed next to its name on the Style Sheets palette **(Figure 7)** and on the Style Sheets pop-up menu under the Style menu.

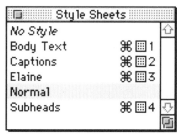

Figure 6. *Select **Show Style Sheets** from the **View** menu.*

Figure 7. *To apply a style sheet, click any name on the **Style Sheets** palette or perform the keyboard equivalent listed next to the style sheet name.*

Apply a Style Sheet

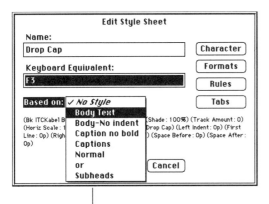

Figure 8. *To base one style sheet on another, select a style sheet from the **Based on** pop-up menu in the Edit Style Sheet dialog box.*

About Based On style sheets:

A new style sheet can be created based on an existing style sheet. The new style sheet is linked to the original style sheet on which it is based. If the original style sheet is modified, any style sheets that are based on it will also change.

For example, a "Drop Cap" style sheet can be created based on a "Body Text" style sheet, adding an automatic drop cap. Modifications made to the "Body Text" style sheet will automatically be made to the "Drop Cap" style sheet.

To base one style sheet on another style sheet:

1. Select Style Sheets from the Edit menu.

2. Click New.

3. Enter a name for the new style sheet **(Figure 9)**.

4. *Optional:* Enter a Keyboard Equivalent.

5. Select a style sheet from the Based on pop-up menu **(Figure 8)**.

6. Edit the style sheet by following steps 3 and 4 on the following page.

7. Click OK to exit the Edit Style Sheet dialog box.

8. Click Save.

Figure 9. *The Edit Style Sheet dialog box of a "Based On" style.*

*The name of the style sheet that the current style sheet is **Based on** is displayed here.*

The specifications listed in the Edit Style Sheet dialog box indicate that this "Drop Cap" style is based on the "Body Text" style, with the Drop Cap option added.

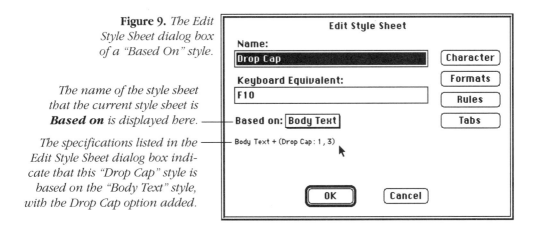

To edit a style sheet:

1. Select Style Sheets from the Edit menu and select a style sheet name **(Figure 10)**.

or

If the Style Sheets palette is open, click in a text box to activate it, hold down Command (⌘), and click on a style sheet name in the palette.

2. Click Edit **(Figure 11)**.

3. Click Character, Formats, Rules or Tabs to open the corresponding dialog box or boxes. Modify text attributes in the Character dialog box; modify paragraph formatting in the Paragraph Formats dialog box; add, delete or edit a rule in the Paragraph Rules dialog box; or add, delete or modify tabs in the Paragraph Tabs dialog box **(Figure 12)**.

4. Click OK or press Return to exit the Character, Formats, Rules, or Tabs dialog box.

5. Click OK to exit the Edit Style Sheet dialog box.

6. Click Save to exit the Style Sheets dialog box. Paragraphs to which the style sheet has already been applied will be instantly reformatted.

▫ Style Sheets	
No Style	⬆
Body Text	F2
Body–No indent	F8
Caption no bold	F5
Captions	F3
Normal	
or	F7 ⬇
Subheads	F1

Figure 10. *Hold down* **Command** *(⌘) and click on a style sheet name to open the Style Sheets dialog box.*

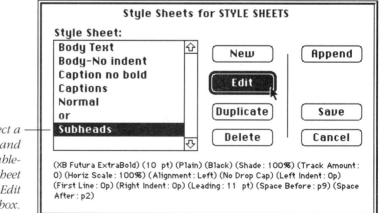

Style Sheets for STYLE SHEETS

Style Sheet:

Body Text	⬆
Body–No indent	
Caption no bold	
Captions	
Normal	
or	
Subheads	⬇

New ⬜ Append

Edit

Duplicate ⬜ Save

Delete ⬜ Cancel

(XB Futura ExtraBold) (10 pt) (Plain) (Black) (Shade: 100%) (Track Amount: 0) (Horiz Scale: 100%) (Alignment: Left) (No Drop Cap) (Left Indent: 0p) (First Line: 0p) (Right Indent: 0p) (Leading: 11 pt) (Space Before: p9) (Space After: p2)

Figure 11. *Select a style sheet name and click* **Edit** *or double-click a style sheet name to open the Edit Style Sheet dialog box.*

Edit a Style Sheet

*The **Name** and **Keyboard Equivalent**
for a style sheet can be changed here.*

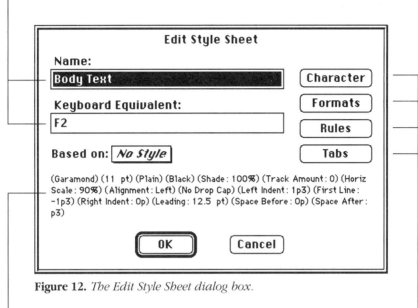

Figure 12. *The Edit Style Sheet dialog box.*

*The current specifications for
the style sheet are listed here.*

*Click **Character, Formats,
Rules** or **Tabs** to open
the corresponding dialog
box or boxes.*

Edit a Style Sheet

About Default Style Sheets.

The Normal style sheet is the default style sheet for all newly created text boxes. If the Normal style sheet is modified with a file open, text entered in any newly created text boxes or text to which the Normal style sheet is already applied will be affected within the active file only. If the Normal style sheet is modified with no file open, the Normal style sheet will be modified for all subsequently created files. Any style sheet created with no file open will be added to the Style Sheets palette of all subsequently created files.

To append style sheets from one file to another:

1. Select Style Sheets from the Edit menu.

2. Click Append **(Figure 13)**.

3. Select the file containing the style sheet or sheets to be appended **(Figure 14)**.

4. Click Open. The appended style sheets will be listed in the Style Sheet scroll list **(Figure 15)**.

5. For each appended style sheet that you **don't** want to save, select it and click Delete.

6. Click Save to exit the Style Sheets dialog box.

✔ Tips

■ If a style sheet that you are attempting to append has the **same name** as a style sheet in the active file you are appending to, the style sheet will not be appended.

■ If a style sheet that you are attempting to append has the **same keyboard equivalent** as a style sheet in the active file you are appending to, the style sheet will be appended, but the keyboard equivalent will not be appended.

■ If text with a style sheet or sheets applied to it is pasted from another document using the Clipboard, drag-copied from another document, or retrieved from a library, the style sheet or sheets will be appended, with the above-mentioned name conflict being the only exception.

■ Style sheets can be appended from a document created in Microsoft Word 3.0 or later. The Microsoft Word filter must be in the QuarkXPress folder when the application is launched.

Append Style Sheets

Figure 13. *Click **Append** in the Style Sheets dialog box.*

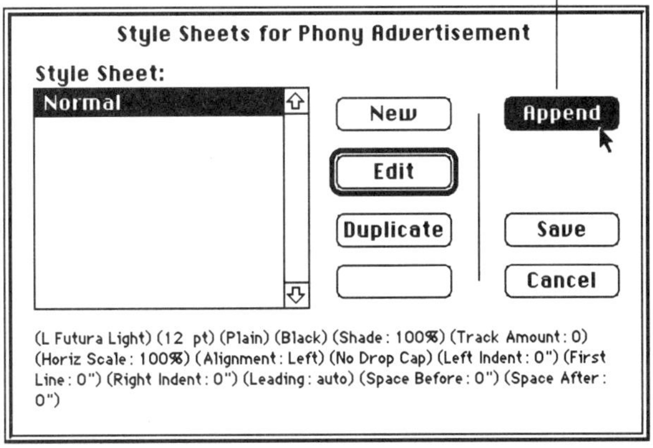

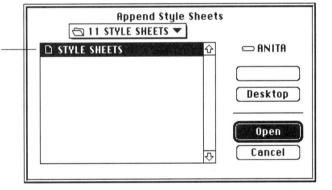

Figure 14. *Select the file to be appended from in the Append Style Sheets dialog box, then click **Open**.*

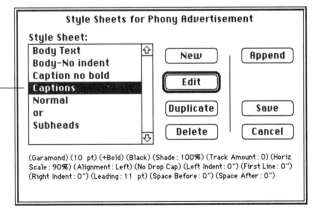

Figure 15. *The appended style sheets are now listed in the **Style Sheet** scroll list. Select and delete any style sheets you don't want to save, then click **Save**.*

About the Duplicate option:

The Duplicate command is used to create a copy of an existing style sheet. There is no linkage between a Duplicate style sheet and the original from which it is generated.

To duplicate a style sheet:

1. Select Style Sheets from the Edit menu **(Figure 16)**.

2. Select a style sheet name.

3. Click Duplicate **(Figure 17)**.

4. The Edit Style Sheet dialog box will automatically open, and the name of the style sheet will appear in the Name field, prefaced by "Copy of." Edit the name, if desired **(Figure 18)**.

5. Edit the new style sheet, if desired.

6. Click OK.

7. Click Save.

To delete a style sheet:

1. Select Style Sheets from the Edit menu.

2. Select a style sheet name.

3. Click Delete **(Figure 17)**.

4. When the prompt appears, click OK. Where the style sheet has been applied, it will be replaced with No Style.

5. Click Save.

✔ Tip

■ The Normal style sheet can be edited, but it cannot deleted.

Figure 16. *Select* **Style Sheets** *from the* **Edit** *menu.*

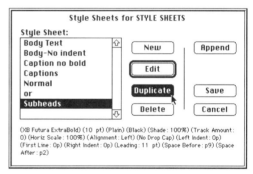

Figure 17. *Select a style sheet name, then click* **Duplicate**.

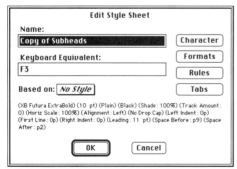

Figure 18. *The new style sheet name will be prefaced by "Copy of." A new name can be assigned.*

Duplicate or Delete a Style Sheet

Show Document Layout

The Document Layout palette is used throughout this chapter. Choose Show Document Layout from the View menu to display it **(Figure 1)**.

Figure 1. *Select* ***Show Document Layout*** *from the* ***View*** *menu.*

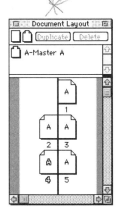

Figure 2. *The Document Layout palette of a* ***facing-page*** *document.*

Figure 3. *The Document Layout palette of a* ***single-sided*** *document.*

About master pages:

Items on a master page automatically appear on every document page to which the master is applied. You can use master pages to expedite the production of documents that contain repetitive elements — like headers, footers, page numbers, picture boxes, and lines. Items originating from a master page can be edited on individual document pages.

All new documents contain a Master A page. Up to 126 additional master pages can be created. Master pages are created, modified, and applied using the Document Layout palette.

(See also page 14)

Single-sided and facing-page documents:

If you check the Facing Pages box in the New dialog box, you can specify Inside and Outside margins. The first document page will be positioned by itself on the right side, and additional pages will be arranged in pairs along a central spine **(Figure 2)**. Facing master page and document page icons have turned-down corners. This format is used for book and magazine layouts.

If you uncheck the Facing Pages box in the New dialog box, you will create a single-sided document in which single pages are stacked vertically. Single-sided master page and document page icons have square corners **(Figure 3)**. To create a spread in a single-sided document, arrange document page icons side-by-side. *(See Figures 14a-b on page 56)*

To number pages automatically:

1. Double-click the Master A icon on the Document Layout palette **(Figure 4)**.

2. Select the Text Box tool. A

3. Press and drag to create a small text box for the page number.

4. Hold down Command (⌘) and press "3". You can type a prefix, such as "Page," before the page numbering command. Enter the command on both the left and right master pages for a facing-page document **(Figure 5)**.

5. Highlight the numbering command, then style it like a regular character — choose a font, point size, style, etc.

6. To display a document page, double-click its icon on the Document Layout palette.

✔ Tips

■ If you add or delete pages from the document, the page numbers will update automatically.

■ You can enter the Current Page Number command on a document page, but the page number will only appear on that page.

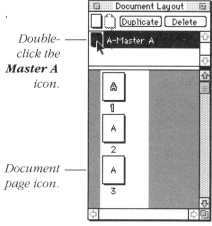

Double-click the Master A icon.

Document page icon.

Figure 4.

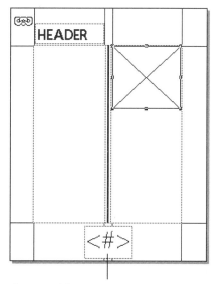

Figure 5. *The Current Page Number command displays as "<#>" on the master page. You can also place a header, picture box, vertical rule, or any other item on a master page.*

Automatic Page Numbering

Figure 6. *Double-click a master page icon.*

Blank page icon.

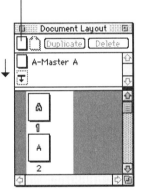

Figure 7a. *Press and drag a blank page icon into the master page area.*

Figure 7b. *Master Page B is renamed.*

To modify a master page:

1. Double-click a master page icon on the Document Layout palette **(Figure 6)**.

2. Add or modify any master item — header, footer, line, picture box, etc.

✔ Tips

■ Pages to which the master has already been applied will be modified. Previous master items that were locally modified in the document will not be affected by new modifications on the master page. *(See the second Tip on the next page)*

■ If Automatic Text Box was checked in the New dialog box when the document was created, an automatic text box will appear on the default Master A and on the document pages to which it is applied. Text cannot be entered in the automatic text box on a master page, but can be entered in any other text box.

■ In a facing-page document, every master page has a left and right page. Items placed on a the left master page will appear only on left (even-numbered) document pages, and vice versa.

To create a new master page:

Press and drag a blank single-sided or facing-page icon into the master page icon area on the Document Layout palette. The new master page will be labeled with the next letter of the alphabet **(Figures 7a-b)**.

To rename a master page:

1. Click on a master page name on the Document Layout palette.

2. Highlight and change the character preceding the hyphen and/or the characters following the hyphen **(Figure 7b)**.

Modify/Create/Rename a Master Page

To apply a master page to a document page:

1. Click on a document page icon on the Document Layout palette **(Figure 8a)**.

2. Hold down Option and click on a master page icon **(Figure 8b)**.

3. To display a document page, double-click its icon on the Document Layout palette.

✔ Tips

■ To apply a master page to multiple pages, click on the page icon of the first page in the series, hold down Shift and click on the last page icon in the series, then hold down Option and click on the master page icon. (To highlight non-consecutive page icons, hold down Command (⌘) instead of Shift.)

■ If Delete Changes is selected from the Master Page Items pop-up menu in the General Preferences dialog box, opened from the Edit menu, and a master page is applied or reapplied to a document page, locally modified and unmodified master items will be deleted from the document page. If Keep Changes is selected from the same pop-up menu, only unmodified master items will be deleted.

■ If you drag a page or pages from one file to another, any applied master pages will be appended.
(See the first Tip on page 58) (See the first Tip on page 58)

■ If an odd number of pages is added to or deleted from a facing-page document and document pages reshuffle, the corresponding left and right master pages will automatically be applied to the reshuffled pages.

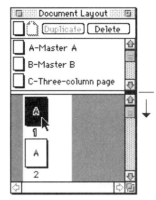

To enlarge the master page area, drag this little black bar downward.

Figure 8a. *To apply a master page, first click on a document page icon.*

Figure 8b. *Then hold down **Option** and click on a master page icon.*

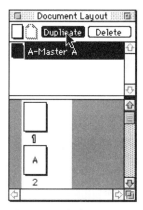

Figure 9. *Click on a master page icon, then click Duplicate (or Delete).*

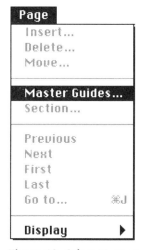

Figure 10. *Select Master Guides from the Page menu.*

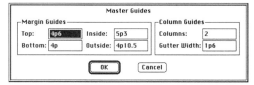

Figure 11. *Modify the non-printing Margin Guides and/or Column Guides in the Master Guides dialog box.*

To duplicate a master page:

1. Click a master page icon on the Document Layout palette **(Figure 9)**.

2. Click Duplicate.

To delete a master page:

1. Click a master page icon on the Document Layout palette **(Figure 9)**.

2. Click Delete.

To modify the non-printing margin and column guides:

1. Double-click a master page icon on the Document Layout Palette.

2. Select Master Guides from the Page menu **(Figure 10)**.

3. Modify the numbers in the Margin Guides fields **(Figure 11)**.
and/or
Modify the numbers in the Column Guides fields.

4. Click OK or press Return.

✔ Tips

■ If you modify a master page's guides, all pages to which that master page has been applied will display the new guides. Any automatic text box that fits exactly within the margin guides will resize to fit within the new margin guides, and will have the number of columns specified.

■ You can use the Display pop-up menu under the Page menu to display master pages and document pages. If you select Document when a master page is displayed, the last displayed document page will be displayed again.

About numbering sections:

Documents containing more than one section may require more than one page numbering format. For example, in this book, the lowercase Roman format is used for the Table of Contents and the numeric format is used for the pages that follow. A document that is divided into more than one file may also require special starting page numbers.

To number a section of a file:

1. To display the page where the new section is to begin, select Go to from the Page menu.

2. Enter the number of the page that is to begin the new section.

3. Click OK or press Return.

4. Select Section from the Page menu **(Figure 12)**.

5. Check the Section Start box **(Figure 13)**.

Steps 6-8 are optional.

6. Modify the default starting Number.

7. Enter a maximum of four characters in the Prefix field.

8. Select an alternate numbering Format.

9. Click OK or press Return.

✔ Tip

■ The number of the first page in a section will be marked with an asterisk in the current page number field and on the corresponding page icon in the Document Layout palette.
(See also the second Tip on page 32)

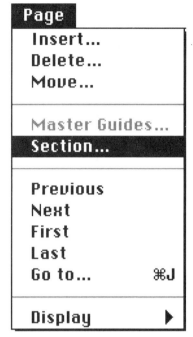

Figure 12. *Select **Section** from the **Page** menu.*

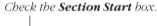
*Check the **Section Start** box.*

*Enter a **Prefix**.*

*Leave the default **Number** at 1 or enter a new number.*

*Select one of the five numbering **Formats**.*

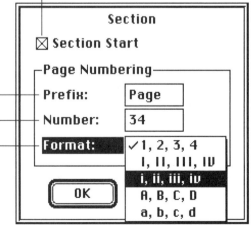

Figure 13. *The Section dialog box.*

Number Sections

COLOR 13

Edit

Can't Undo	⌘Z
Cut	⌘H
Copy	⌘C
Paste	⌘U
Clear	
Select All	⌘A
Subscribe To…	
Subscriber Options…	
Show Clipboard	
Find/Change	⌘F
Preferences	▶
Style Sheets…	
Colors…	
H&Js…	

Figure 1. *Select **Colors** from the **Edit** menu.*

About color:

Two basic methods are used for printing color: spot color and process color.

A separate plate is used to print each **spot color**. Spot color inks are mixed according to specifications defined in a color matching system, such as Pantone.

Four plates are used to print **process color**, one each for cyan (C), magenta (M), yellow (Y) and black (K). A layer of tiny colored dots is printed from each plate; the overlapping dots create an illusion of color.

Computer monitors display additive color by projecting light and printers produce subtractive color using ink. Because computer monitors do not accurately display ink equivalents, colors should be specified using formulas defined in process and spot color guides, and not mixed based on screen representations.

Spot and process colors can be combined in the same color palette in QuarkXPress. Up to 127 colors can be created per file.

To create a spot color:

1. Select Colors from the Edit menu **(Figure 1)**.

2. Click New **(Figure 2)**.

3. Select Pantone from the Model pop-up menu **(Figure 3)**.

4. Enter a number from a Pantone color guide in the Pantone No. field.
   or
   Select a color in the "swatch" window.

5. Make sure the Process Separation check box is **unchecked.**

6. Click OK or press Return.

7. Click Save **(Figure 4)**.

Create a Spot Color

(Continued on the following page)

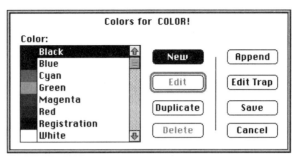

Figure 2. *Click* ***New*** *to create a new color.*

Figure 3. *Select* ***Pantone*** *from the* ***Model*** *pop-up menu in the Edit Color dialog box.*

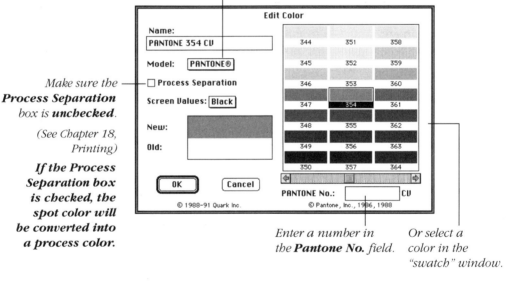

Make sure the ***Process Separation*** *box is* ***unchecked***.

(See Chapter 18, Printing)

If the Process Separation box is checked, the spot color will be converted into a process color.

Enter a number in the ***Pantone No.*** *field.*

Or select a color in the "swatch" window.

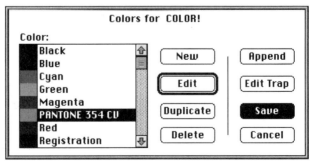

Figure 4. *The new Pantone color is now listed in the Colors dialog box, and is added to the Colors palette. Click* ***Save*** *to Exit.*

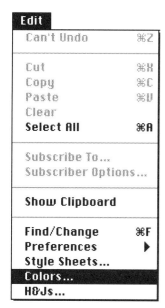

Figure 5. *Select **Colors** from the **Edit** menu.*

To create a process color:

1. Select Colors from the Edit menu **(Figure 5)**.

2. Click New **(Figure 2)**.

3. Select CMYK from the Model pop-up menu, enter percentages in the Cyan, Magenta, Yellow, and Black fields, then enter a name for the color in the Name field **(Figure 6)**.
   or
   Select Trumatch or Focoltone from the Model pop-up menu, then enter a number in the Trumatch No. or Focoltone No. field or click a color in the "swatch" window.

4. Make sure the Process Separation box is **checked**.

5. Click OK or press Return.

6. Click Save. The color will be added to the Colors palette.

✔ Tips

- If you create a color when no document is open, that color will appear on the Colors palette of subsequently created documents.

- Use the RGB Model if your document will be output on a film recorder or is solely for video monitor display.

*Enter a **Name** for a new **CMYK** color. A name will appear automatically for a Trumatch or Focoltone color.*

*Select **CMYK, Trumatch,** or **Focoltone** from the **Model** pop-up menu.*

*Make sure the **Process Separation** box is **checked**.*

*If the **Process Separation** box is unchecked, the process color will be converted into a spot color.*

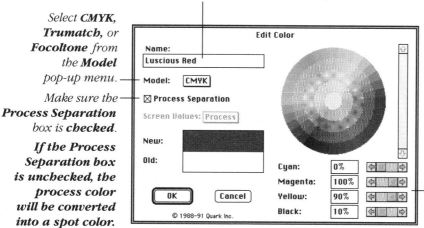

*For a **CMYK** color, enter **Cyan, Magenta, Yellow,** and **Black** percentages.*

Figure 6. *The **Edit Color** dialog box.*

To edit a process color:

1. Select Colors from the Edit menu.
or
Hold down Command (⌘) and click a color in the Colors palette.

2. Select a color in the Colors dialog box and click Edit **(Figure 7)**.
or
Double-click a color.

3. Modify any of the Cyan, Magenta, Yellow or Black percentages **(Figure 8)**.

4. Click OK.

5. Click Save.

*To append a color or colors from another QuarkXPress file, click **Append**. A color with the same name as a color in the active file will not be appended.*

Figure 7. *Select a color, then click **Edit**.*

*Click **Delete** to remove selected color from the color palette. Cyan, Magenta, Yellow, Black, White and Registration cannot be deleted.*

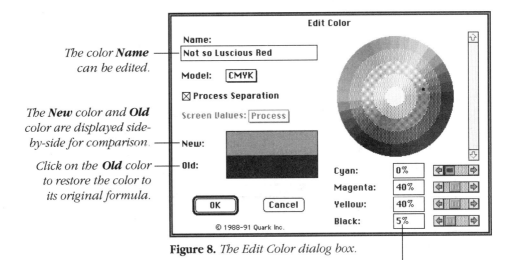

*The color **Name** can be edited.*

*The **New** color and **Old** color are displayed side-by-side for comparison.*

*Click on the **Old** color to restore the color to its original formula.*

Figure 8. *The Edit Color dialog box.*

*Modify any of the **Cyan, Magenta, Yellow,** or **Black** percentages.*

Edit a Color

*Select a **shade**. To apply a custom shade, select Other from the Shade pop-up menu under the Style menu.* ——

*Click the **text icon*** —— *to apply color to text.*

Click the —— ***frame icon*** *to apply color to a frame.*

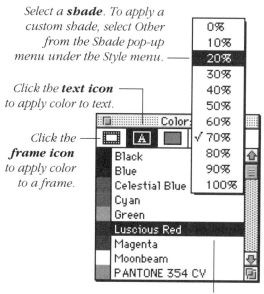

Figure 9. *The Colors palette when a **text box** is selected.*

*Select a **color**.*

To apply color to text:

1. Select Show Colors from the View menu to display the Colors palette **(Figure 15)**.

2. Select the Content tool.

3. Highlight the text to which color is to be applied.

4. Click the text icon in the Colors palette **(Figure 9)**.

5. Select a color.

6. Select a shade from the Shade pop-up menu **(Figures 10-11)**.

✔ Tip

■ A color or shade can also be applied to text using the Color or Shade pop-up menu under the Style menu, or using the Character dialog box, opened from the Style menu.

TWENTYPERCENT

THIRTYPERCENT

FORTY PERCENT

FIFTY PERCENT

SIXTY PERCENT

SEVENTYPERCENT

EIGHTYPERCENT

NINETYPERCENT

HUNDREDPERCENT

Figure 10. *A range of shades can be applied to type.*

CREATIVE MINDS
ALWAYS HAVE BEEN KNOWN TO SURVIVE ANY
KIND OF BAD TRAINING.
Anna Freud

Figure 11. *"Reversed" type.*

To apply color to a frame:

1. Select Show Colors from the View menu to display the Colors palette **(Figure 15)**.

2. Select the Item or Content tool.

3. Click on a text or picture box.

4. Click the frame icon in the Colors palette **(Figure 9)**.

5. Select a color.

6. Select a shade from the Shade pop-up menu.

✔ Tip

■ The frame width must be specified in the Frame dialog box, opened from the Item menu.

To apply color to a picture:

1. Select Show Colors from the View menu to display the Colors palette **(Figure 15)**.

2. Select the Content tool.

3. Click on a black-and-white bitmap, or TIFF or RIFF line art or grayscale picture.

4. Click the picture icon in the Colors palette **(Figure 12)**.

5. Select a color.

6. *Optional:* Select a shade percentage from the Shade pop-up menu for a black-and-white bitmap or TIFF or RIFF line art picture.

✔ Tips

■ A color can also be applied to a picture using the Color pop-up menu under the Style menu.

■ To color separate a TIFF picture from QuarkXPress, convert it to CMYK mode in another application before importing it.

Click the
picture icon.   *Select a* **shade**.

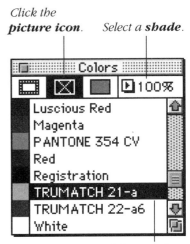

Select a **color**.

Figure 12. *The Colors palette when a* **picture box** *is selected.*

To apply color to a line:

1. Select Show Colors from the View menu to display the Colors palette **(Figure 15)**.

2. Select the Item or Content tool.

3. Select a line.

4. Click the line icon in the Colors palette **(Figure 13)**.

5. Select a color.

6. Select a shade percentage from the Shade pop-up menu.

✔ Tip

■ A color can also be applied to a line using the Color pop-up menu under the Style menu.

Click the
line icon.   *Select a* **shade**.

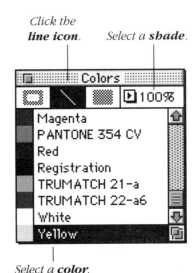

Select a **color**.

Figure 13. *The Colors palette when a* **line** *is selected.*

Apply Color

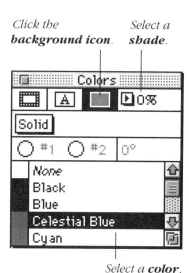

Click the **background icon.** *Select a* **shade.**

Select a **color.**

Figure 14. *The background icon is available on the Colors palette when a* **text box** *or* **picture box** *is selected.*

View

Fit in Window	⌘0
50%	
75%	
Actual Size	⌘1
200%	
Thumbnails	
Hide Guides	
Show Baseline Grid	
Snap to Guides	
Hide Rulers	⌘R
Show Invisibles	⌘I
Hide Tools	
Hide Measurements	
Show Document Layout	
Show Style Sheets	
Show Colors	
Show Trap Information	
Show Value Converter	
Windows	▶

Figure 15. *Select* **Show Colors** *from the* **View** *menu.*

To apply color to the background of a box:

1. Select Show Colors from the View menu to display the Colors palette **(Figure 15)**.

2. Select the Item or Content tool.

3. Click on a text or picture box.

4. Click the background icon in the Colors palette **(Figure 14)**.

5. Select a color.

6. Select a shade percentage from the Shade pop-up menu.

✔ Tip

■ When coloring type white, or returning "reversed type" to black-on-white, change the type color before changing the background color, so the text will be easy to highlight.

About linear blends:

Two-color linear blends can be created in QuarkXPress 3.1. A blend can be applied to the background of a text box or picture box, but not to text, lines or frames.

To create a linear blend:

1. Select the Item tool.

2. Click a text or picture box.

3. Select Show Colors from the View menu to open the Colors palette **(Figure 15)**.

(Continued on the following page)

Apply Color; Create a Linear Blend

4. Click the Background icon **(Figure 18)**.

5. Select Linear Blend from the Fill-type pop-up menu.

6. Click the button for the #1 color, select a color, and select a percentage from the Shade pop-up menu.

7. Click the button for the #2 color, select a color, and select a percentage from the Shade pop-up menu **(Figure 19)**.

8. *Optional:* Enter an angle between -360° and 360° in increments as small as .001° in the Angle field **(Figures 16-17)**.

✔ Tip

■ A linear blend will be displayed in a deselected box, or in a selected box when the Item tool is selected. A linear blend will not be displayed in a selected box if the Content tool is selected.

Figure 16. *A black & white linear blend at a 90° angle.*

Figure 17. *A black & white linear blend at a 125° angle.*

Figure 18. *Select* **Linear Blend** *from the Fill-type pop-up menu.*   *Click the* **background icon**.   *Select a* **shade**.   *The* **angle** *of the blend can be modified.*

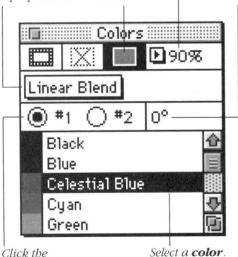

Click the **#1 color** *button.*   *Select a* **color**.

Figure 19. *Click the* **#2 color** *button, then select a* **color** *and* **shade**.

Figure 1. *Select **Library** from the **Utilities** menu.*

About libraries:

Libraries are special files that store items that can be drag-copied onto any Quark-XPress page. Each library is displayed as a floating palette and can contain up to 2,000 entries. An unlimited number of libraries can be created.

(If you are using QuarkXPress Version 3.2, see page 188)

To create a library:

1. Select Library from the Utilities menu **(Figure 1)**.

2. Click New **(Figure 2)**.

3. Enter a name for the library in the New Library field **(Figure 3)**.

4. Select a drive or folder in which to save the library.

5. Click Create. A new library palette will be displayed.

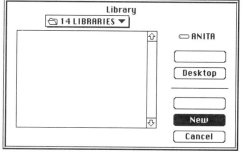

Figure 2. *Click **New** in the **Library** dialog box.*

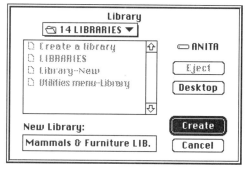

Figure 3. *Enter a name in the **New Library** field, then click **Create**.*

To open a library from within QuarkXPress:

1. Select Library from the Utilities menu **(Figure 4)**.

2. Select a library file.

3. Click Open **(Figure 5)**.

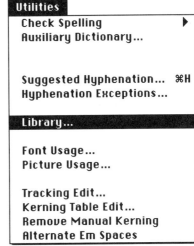

Figure 4. *Select **Library** from the **Utilities** menu.*

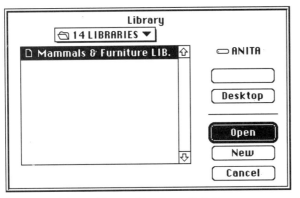

Figure 5. *Select a library file, then click **Open**.*

To open a library from the Desktop:

Double-click a library icon **(Figure 6)**.

Figure 6. *Double-click a library icon from the Finder desktop.*

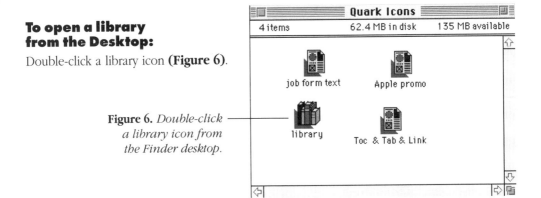

To add an entry to a library:

1. Open a library.
(Instructions on the previous page)

2. Select the Item tool.

3. Press and drag any item or group into the library **(Figures 7-9)**.

✔ Tip

■ A library is saved each time an entry is added to it if the Auto Library Save box is checked in the Application Preferences dialog box, opened from the Edit menu. Otherwise, a library is saved only when it is closed.

To delete an entry from a library:

1. Select the Item or Content tool.

2. Click on a library entry.

3. Select Clear from the Edit menu.
or
Press Delete.

Figure 7. *Press and drag an item into a library with the **Item** tool.*

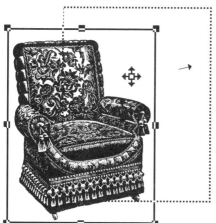

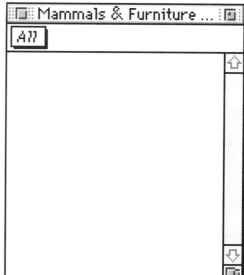

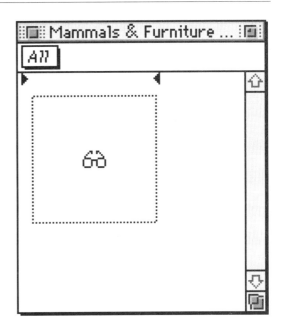

Figure 8. *The cursor turns into an eyeglasses icon as an entry is dragged into a library.*

Click the Close box to close a library palette.

Figure 9. *The entry is automatically duplicated, and the original is left intact. Entries can be rearranged within a library by pressing and dragging them.*

To retrieve an entry from a library:

1. Select the Item or Content tool.

2. Press and drag an item from a library onto a document page **(Figure 10)**.

✔ Tips

■ When an item with a color applied to it is retrieved from a library, the color is appended to the color palette of the active file.

■ When text with a style sheet applied to it is retrieved from a library, the style sheet is appended to the active file.

■ When a picture is added to a library, the path to the original picture file is stored with the library entry. When a picture is retrieved from a library, the picture's path is also stored with the document. The original picture file must be retained to print properly. *(See also Chapter 9, Import a Picture and Picture Usage)*

Click the Zoom box to display the library entries in horizontal rows.

Figure 10. *Press and drag an entry onto a document page.*

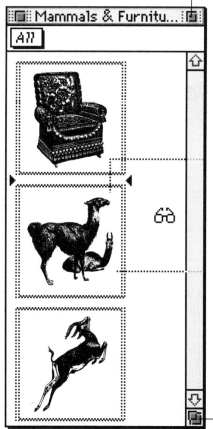

Press and drag the resize box to resize the palette.

About labeling library entries:

Labeling related library entries helps organize them. The same label can be applied to numerous entries so that when a label is selected from the Label pop-up menu, all entries with that label are displayed. The Label pop-up menu always displays "All" and "Unlabeled." When a new label is created, it is added to the Label pop-up menu.

To label a library entry:

1. Double-click a library entry.

2. Enter a name in the Label field **(Figure 11)**.

or

Select an existing label from the Label pop-up menu.

3. Click OK or press Return.

✔ Tip

■ The same label can be re-entered for different entries, but it is easier to select an existing label.

To display entries with the same label:

Select a label from the pop-up menu in the library palette. Any number of labels can be displayed at a time **(Figure 12)**.

Select All from the pop-up menu to display all the entries in a library.

To hide entries with the same label:

Re-select a selected label from the pop-up menu in the library palette. A selected label has a check mark next to it **(Figure 12)**.

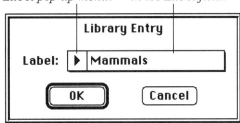

Figure 11. *Double-click a library entry and select an existing label from the* **Label** *pop-up menu.* *Or enter a new label in the* **Label** *field.*

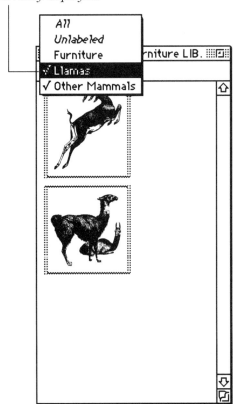

Figure 12. *A check mark indicates that entries with that label are currently displayed.*

Victorian decorative initial

Figure 1a. *Drag a marquee over multiple items with the Item tool.*

Victorian decorative initial

Figure 1b. *The handles indicate that both items are selected.*

Item	
Modify...	⌘M
Frame...	⌘B
Runaround...	⌘T
Duplicate	⌘D
Step and Repeat...	
Delete	⌘K
Group	**⌘G**
Ungroup	⌘U
Constrain	
Unlock	⌘L
Send to Back	
Bring to Front	
Space/Align...	
Picture Box Shape	▶
Reshape Polygon	

Figure 2. *Select **Group** from the **Item** menu.*

About the Group command:

Items that are grouped using the Group command remain associated as a unit until the Ungroup command is selected. For example, a picture and caption can be grouped so that they can be moved as a unit. Individual items within a group can be modified.

To group items:

1. Select the Item tool.

2. Hold down Shift and click once on each item to be included in the group. (To deselect an item from a multiple-selection and keep the remaining items selected, hold down Shift and click on the item.)

or

Position the cursor outside all the items to be included in the group, then press and drag a marquee around them. It is only necessary to drag over a portion of all the items **(Figures 1a and 1b)**.

3. Select Group from the Item menu **(Figures 2-3)**.

or

Hold down Command (⌘) and press "G".

Victorian decorative initial

Figure 3. *A dotted border surrounds a group that is selected with the Item tool.*

Group Items

To move an item within a group:

1. Select the Content tool.

2. Hold down Command (⌘), press on an item to be moved, pause briefly for the item to redraw, then drag the item **(Figure 4)**.

To delete an item from a group:

1. Select the Content tool.

2. Select an item to be deleted.

3. Select Delete from the Item menu.
or
Hold down Command (⌘) and press "K".

4. After the warning prompt appears, click OK or press Return **(Figure 5)**.

To ungroup items:

1. Select the Item tool.

2. Select a group.

3. Select Ungroup from the Item menu **(Figure 6)**.
or
Hold down Command (⌘) and press "U".

✔ Tips

■ Select the Content tool to modify the size or contents of an item in a group.

■ Groups can be multiple-selected and grouped into larger groups.

■ The background color and shade, angle of rotation, and position of a group can be modified by selecting the group with the Item tool, selecting Modify from the Item menu, and modifying any of the Group Specifications. Runaround options must be selected individually for each item in a group.

Figure 4. *Select the Content tool, hold down Command (⌘) and press and drag an item. Note the Item tool icon.*

Figure 5. *This prompt will appear if you attempt to delete an item from a group.*

This will delete an item from a group and cannot be undone. OK to continue? — OK / Cancel

Figure 6. *Select* **Ungroup** *from the* **Item** *menu.*

Item	
Modify...	⌘M
Frame...	⌘B
Runaround...	⌘T
Duplicate	⌘D
Step and Repeat...	
Delete	⌘K
Group	⌘G
Ungroup	⌘U
Constrain	
Lock	⌘L
Send to Back	
Bring to Front	
Space/Align...	
Picture Box Shape	▶
Reshape Polygon	

Figure 7. *Select **Lock** from the **Item** menu.*

Item	
Modify...	⌘M
Frame...	⌘B
Runaround...	⌘T
Duplicate	⌘D
Step and Repeat...	
Delete	⌘K
Group	⌘G
Ungroup	⌘U
Constrain	
Unlock	⌘L
Send to Back	
Bring to Front	
Space/Align...	
Picture Box Shape	▶
Reshape Polygon	

Figure 8. *Select **Unlock** from the **Item** menu.*

About Locking:

Locking is a safety command that can be applied to any item — header, vertical rule, page number, etc. A locked item can only be moved or resized using the Measurements palette or a dialog box.

To lock an item:

1. Select the Item or Content tool.
2. Select an item to be locked.
3. Select Lock from the Item menu **(Figure 7)**.

To unlock an item:

1. Select the Item or Content tool.
2. Select an item to be unlocked.
3. Select Unlock from the Item menu **(Figure 8)**.

✔ Tips

■ When a locked item is selected with the Item tool, the cursor turns into a Padlock icon **(Figure 9)**.

■ The contents of a locked text box or picture box and the attributes of a line, such as style and width, can be edited.

■ Beware: a locked item **can** be deleted.

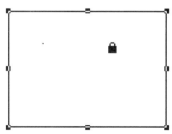

Figure 9. *The Padlock icon is displayed when a locked item is selected with the Item tool.*

To duplicate an item:

1. Select the Item tool.

2. Select a text box, picture box, group, or line to be duplicated **(Figure 10)**.

3. Select Duplicate from the Item menu **(Figures 11-12)**.

or

Hold down Command (⌘) and press "D".

✔ Tips

■ Duplicates are positioned according to the offsets last used in the Step and Repeat dialog box.

■ A linked text box cannot be duplicated.

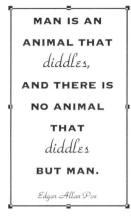

Figure 10. *Select an item to be duplicated.*

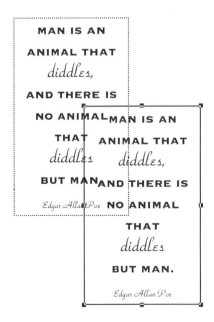

Figure 12. *A duplicate is made.*

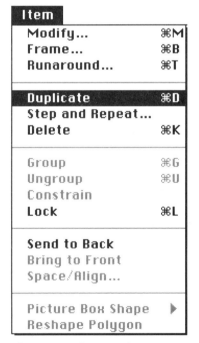

Figure 11. *Select **Duplicate** from the **Item** menu.*

Figure 13. *Select an item.*

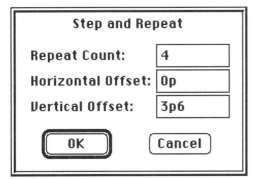

Figure 14. *The Step and Repeat dialog box.*

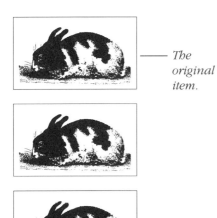

—— *The original item.*

About Step and Repeat:

With the Step and Repeat command, multiple duplicates can be made at one time and the duplicates can be placed at a specified distance from each other.

To Step and Repeat an item:

1. Select the Item or Content tool.
2. Select a text box, picture box, group or line **(Figure 13)**.
3. Select Step and Repeat from the Item menu **(Figure 11)**.
   or
   Hold down Command (⌘) and Option and press "D".
4. Enter a number between 1 and 99 in the Repeat Count field for the number of duplicates to be made **(Figure 14)**.
5. Enter a number in the Horizontal Offset field. Enter a minus sign before the number to step and repeat items to the left of the original.
6. Enter a number in the Vertical Offset field. Enter a minus sign before the number to step and repeat items above the original.
7. Click OK or press Return **(Figure 15)**.

✔ Tips

■ If an alert prompt appears, reduce the repeat count and/or offset numbers so the duplicated items will fit within the limits of the pasteboard.

■ A linked text box cannot be duplicated with the Step and Repeat command.

Figure 15. *A Repeat Count of 3, Horizontal Offset of 0, and Vertical Offset of 5p5 was used to Step and Repeat this picture box.*

Step and Repeat

To copy an item from one document to another:

1. Open two QuarkXPress files.

2. Resize both document windows so that they are side-by-side on the screen.

3. Select the Item tool.

4. Press and drag an item or group from one document window into the other. A duplicate is made automatically **(Figures 16-17)**.

✔ Tips

■ A linked text box cannot be duplicated with this method.

■ Items cannot be copied between documents in Thumbnails view.

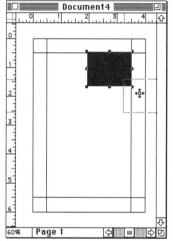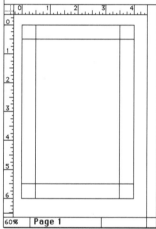

Figure 16. *Open two files, select the Item tool and press and drag an item from one file into the other.*

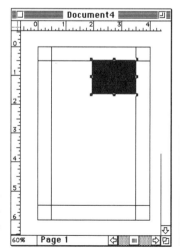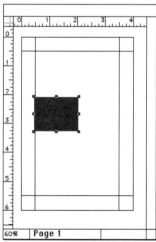

Figure 17. *A duplicate is made automatically as the item is dragged. The original item is unchanged.*

Copy an Item Between Documents

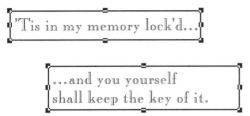

Figure 18. *Select two or more items.*

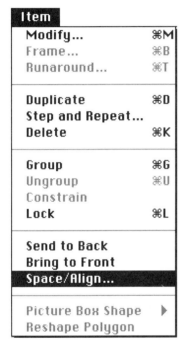

Figure 19. *Select **Space/Align** from the **Item** menu.*

To multiple-select items for aligning or distributing:

1. Select the Item tool.

2. Hold down Shift and click on each item to be multiple-selected.

or

Position the cursor outside the items to be multiple-selected, then press and drag a marquee around them.

To align items:

1. Multiple-select two or more items using the method outlined above **(Figure 18)**.

2. Select Space/Align from the Item menu **(Figure 19)**.

3. Check the Horizontal or Vertical box **(Figure 20)**.

4. Click the Space button.

5. Enter a positive or negative number between 0" and 10" in any measurement system in increments as small as 001. in the Space field to stair-step the items left or right if Horizontal is checked, up or down if Vertical is checked.

or

Enter 0 to align the items along their edges or centers.

6. Select an option from the Between pop-up menu.

7. Click Apply to preview.

8. Click OK or press Return **(Figure 21)**.

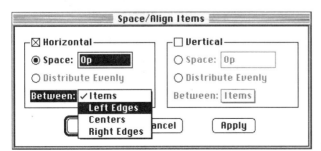

Figure 20. *The Space/Align Items dialog box.*

'Tis in my memory lock'd...

...and you yourself shall keep the key of it.

Figure 21. *Two text boxes are aligned along their left edges.*

Align Items

Distribute Items

To distribute items:

1. Multiple-select three or more items **(Figure 22)**.
   (See instructions on the previous page)

2. Select Space/Align from the Item menu **(Figure 19)**.

3. Check the Vertical or Horizontal box **(Figure 23)**.

4. Click Distribute Evenly.

5. Select an option from the Between pop-up menu.

6. Click Apply to preview.

7. Click OK or press Return **(Figure 24)**.

Figure 22. *Select three or more items.*

✔ Tip

■ The topmost and bottommost or leftmost and rightmost boxes remain stationary and the remaining items are distributed between them.

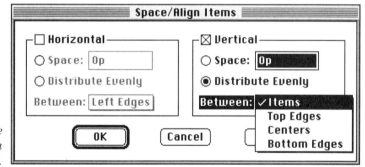

Figure 23. *The Space/Align Items dialog box.*

About multiple-selected items:

The position, number of columns, angle of rotation, background color, and other specifications can be modified for multiple-selected items. Modification options vary depending on whether the items are all text boxes, all picture boxes, all lines, or a combination thereof. Multiple-selected items can also be moved with the Item tool.

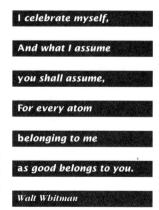

Figure 24. *These items are evenly distributed vertically.*

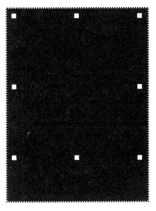

Figure 25. *A gray box in back of a black box is selected, as indicated by the eight handles.*

About Layering:

The most recently created item is automatically placed in front of all other items. The following commands can be used to change the stacking order.

To select an item that is behind another item:

1. Select the Item or Content tool.

2. Hold down Command (⌘), Option, Shift and click on an item. Each click will select the next item behind in succession **(Figure 25)**.

To send an item to the back or bring an item to the front:

1. Select the Item or Content tool.

2. Select an item.

3. Select Send to Back or Bring to Front from the Item menu **(Figures 26-27)**.

To send an item backward or bring an item forward:

1. Select the Item or Content tool.

2. Select an item.

3. Hold down Option and Select Send Backward or Bring Forward from the Item menu. This command will move an item backward or forward one layer at a time.

Item	
Modify...	⌘M
Frame...	⌘B
Runaround...	⌘T
Duplicate	⌘D
Step and Repeat...	
Delete	⌘K
Group	⌘G
Ungroup	⌘U
Constrain	
Lock	⌘L
Send to Back	
Bring to Front	
Space/Align...	
Picture Box Shape	▶
Reshape Polygon	

Figure 26. *Select **Bring to Front** from the **Item** menu.*

Figure 27. *The gray box is now in front of the black box.*

Anchor a Box

About anchored boxes:

A text or picture box can be pasted into a text box as an inline graphic. It thereafter functions like a character, and remains anchored to the text. The contents of an anchored box can be edited. Lines and groups cannot be anchored.

To anchor a box:

1. Select the Item tool.

2. Click on a text or picture box.

3. Select Copy or Cut from the Edit menu.

4. Select the Content tool.

5. Click in a text box to create an insertion point.

6. Select Paste from the Edit menu **(Figures 28-29)**.

✔ Tip

■ Don't anchor a box into an indented paragraph.

To align an anchored box:

1. Select the Item or Content tool.

2. Click on an anchored box.

3. Click the Ascent icon on the Measurements palette to align the top of the anchored box with the ascent of the character to its right **(Figure 30)**.
or
Click the Baseline icon to align the bottom of the anchored box with the baseline of the line of text in which it is anchored.

To delete an anchored box:

1. Select the Content tool.

2. Click just to the right of the anchored box. The blinking cursor will be the height of the anchored box.

3. Press Delete.

have mastery yet to chant the wonder at the wayside given to kings. Still by God's grace there surges within me singing magic grown to my life and power, how the wild bird portent hurled forth the Achaeans' twin-stemmed power single hearted, lords of the youth of Hellas, with spear and hand of strength to the land of Teucrus.

Aeschylus

Figure 28. *An anchored picture box,* **Ascent** *aligned.*

Figure 29. *An anchored picture box,* **Baseline** *aligned.*

The **Ascent** *icon on the Measurements palette.*

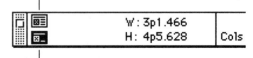

Figure 30. *The* **Baseline** *icon.*

SEARCH & REPLACE

Figure 1. *Select* **Word** *from the* **Check Spelling** *pop-up menu.*

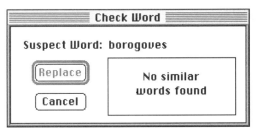

Figure 2. *Neither the word "borogoves" nor similar words have been found in the QuarkXPress dictionary.*

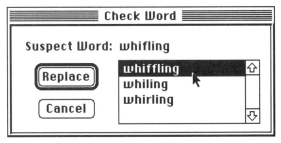

About Check Spelling:

A word, story or document can be checked for spelling accuracy. The QuarkXPress dictionary contains 120,000 words and cannot be edited. However, custom auxiliary dictionaries can be created to work in conjunction with the QuarkXPress dictionary.

To check the spelling of a word:

1. Select the Content tool.

2. Click or double-click a suspect word.

3. Select Word from the Check Spelling pop-up menu under the Utilities menu **(Figure 1)**.
or
Hold down Command (⌘) and press "W".

4. If the Suspect Word is not found in the QuarkXPress dictionary or any open auxiliary dictionary and no similar words are found, the Check Word dialog box will display "No similar words found." Click Cancel to exit the Check Word dialog box **(Figure 2)**.

If the Suspect Word and/or similar words are found in the QuarkXPress dictionary or any open auxiliary dictionary, they will be displayed. The Suspect Word, if found, will be highlighted. Double-click a replacement word; or highlight a word and click Replace; or click Cancel to leave the Suspect Word unchanged **(Figure 3)**.

Figure 3. *Double-click a replacement word.*

About the Auxiliary Dictionary feature:

Custom auxiliary dictionaries can be created to work in conjunction with the QuarkXPress dictionary. Only one auxiliary dictionary can be open at a time, but a document can be checked for spelling several times, each time with a different auxiliary dictionary open. Unlike the QuarkXPress dictionary, auxiliary dictionaries can be edited.

To create an auxiliary dictionary:

1. Select Auxiliary Dictionary from the Utilities menu **(Figure 4)**.

2. Click New **(Figure 5)**.

3. Enter a name in the New Auxiliary Dictionary field **(Figure 6)**.

4. Select a location in which to save the dictionary, then click Save.

✔ Tip

■ If an auxiliary dictionary is created when no document is open, it will be the default auxiliary dictionary for all subsequently created documents.

To open an existing auxiliary dictionary:

1. Select Auxiliary Dictionary from the Utilities menu **(Figure 4)**.

2. Select an auxiliary dictionary **(Figure 5)**.

3. Click Open.

✔ Tip

■ The last auxiliary dictionary that is open when a document is saved will remain open until another auxiliary dictionary is opened for that document.

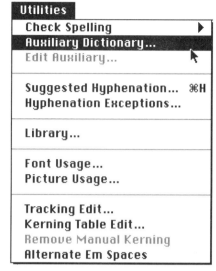

Figure 4. *Select **Auxiliary Dictionary** from the **Utilities** menu.*

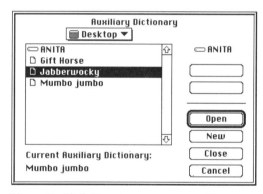

Figure 5. *Click **New** to create an auxiliary dictionary or select an existing auxiliary dictionary and click **Open**.*

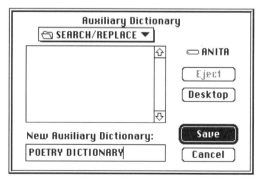

Figure 6. *Select a location in which to save the new auxiliary dictionary, then click **Save**.*

Check Spelling

Figure 7. *Select **Edit Auxiliary** from the **Utilities** menu.*

To edit an auxiliary dictionary:

1. Select Edit Auxiliary from the Utilities menu **(Figure 7)**.

2. Type a new word in the entry field and click Add. No spaces or punctuation are permitted, and all characters are saved in lowercase **(Figure 8)**.
   or
   Select a word and click Delete.

3. Click Save.

✔ Tips

- A Suspect Word can also be added to an open auxiliary dictionary by clicking Keep in the Check Story or Check Document dialog box.

- Words cannot actually be edited in the Edit Auxiliary Dictionary dialog box, they can only be deleted or added.

Figure 8. *This scroll list displays all the words in the Auxiliary Dictionary. To delete a word, select it and click **Delete**.*

*To add a new word, type a word in the entry field and click **Add**.*

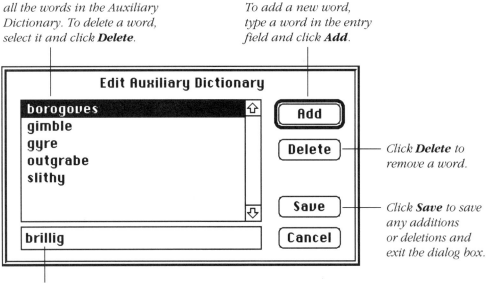

*Click **Delete** to remove a word.*

*Click **Save** to save any additions or deletions and exit the dialog box.*

Type a new word in the entry field.

To check the spelling of a story or document:

1. *Optional:* Open an auxiliary dictionary. *(See instructions on page 166)*

2. Select the Content tool.

3. To Check Spelling in a **story**, click in a story. Then select Story from the Check Spelling pop-up menu under the Utilities menu **(Figure 9)**.

or

To Check Spelling in a **document**, select Document from the Check Spelling pop-up menu under the Utilities menu. Spelling will automatically be checked from the beginning of the document.

4. When the Word Count box appears, click OK or press Return **(Figure 10)**.

5. Click Lookup to see a list of similar words. Double-click a similar word, or click a similar word and click Replace **(Figures 11-12)**.

or

Click Skip to skip over a word.

or

Click Keep to add the Suspect Word to the open auxiliary dictionary.

or

Click the Suspect Word, correct its spelling in the "Replace with" field, then click Replace.

✔ Tips

■ After the spelling of a word is checked once, all other instances of the word are treated in the same manner.

■ Text cannot be edited manually in the document while the Check Story or Check Document dialog box is open.

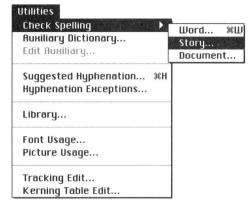

Figure 9. *Select* **Story** *or* **Document** *from the* **Check Spelling** *pop-up menu under the* **Utilities** *menu. (Check Spelling keyboard shortcuts for Version 3.2 are on page 187. Shortcuts for prior versions are on page 184)*

The **Total** number
of words in the story.

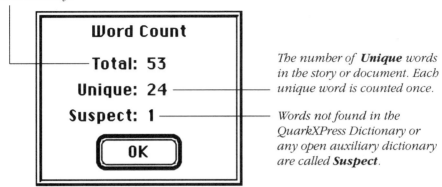

The number of **Unique** words
in the story or document. Each
unique word is counted once.

Words not found in the
QuarkXPress Dictionary or
any open auxiliary dictionary
are called **Suspect**.

Figure 10. *Click OK to proceed to the Check
Story or Check Document dialog box.*

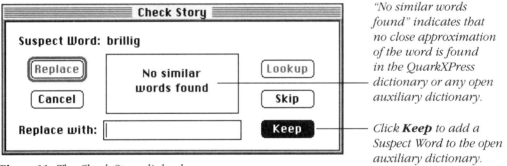

*"No similar words
found" indicates that
no close approximation
of the word is found
in the QuarkXPress
dictionary or any open
auxiliary dictionary.*

Click **Keep** to add a
Suspect Word to the open
auxiliary dictionary.

Figure 11. *The Check Story dialog box.*

Double-click a suggested
word to substitute it for a
Suspect Word.

Figure 12. *The Check Story dialog box.*

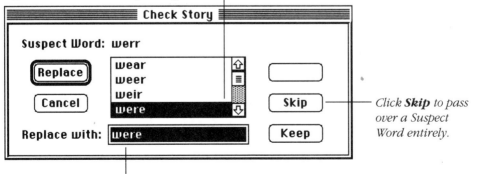

Click **Skip** to pass
over a Suspect
Word entirely.

Or type a word in the **Replace with** field and click **Replace**.

169

About Find/Change:

The Find/Change utility can be used to search for and replace text or attributes. The fields and check boxes on the left side of the Find/Change dialog box define the text or attributes to be searched for, and the fields and check boxes on the right side define what the text or attributes will be changed to.

To find and change spaces, characters, words, or attributes:

1. To search a story, select the Content tool and click in a story. To search a document, make sure no text boxes are selected.

2. Select Find/Change from the Edit menu **(Figure 13)**.
or
Hold down Command (⌘) and press "F".

3. Enter a maximum of 80 characters or spaces in the Find what field **(Figure 14)**.

4. Enter a maximum of 80 characters or spaces in the Change to field.
or
Leave the Change to field blank to delete the Find what text.

5. Check the Document box to search the whole document.

Steps 6 through 8 are optional.

6. Uncheck the Whole Word box to search for any instances of the Find what text that are embedded in a larger word.

7. Uncheck Ignore Case to search for only an exact match of the upper and lowercase configuration entered in the Find what field.

8. Uncheck the Ignore Attributes box to Find/Change attributes. Check the Font box or boxes to search for and/or

(Continued on the following page)

*Figure 13. Select **Find/Change** from the **Edit** menu.*

*Uncheck the **Ignore Attributes** box to expand the dialog box to Find/Change Font, Size, and Style attributes.*

Click the Zoom box to reduce the dialog box.

Figure 14.
The Find/Change dialog box.

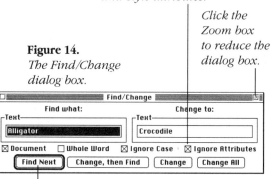

*Hold down Option to convert the **Find Next** button into the **Find First** button.*

Find/Change

Enter these keystrokes to Find/Change non-printing characters.

Character	Keystroke	Field will display
Tab	⌘ Tab	\t
New paragraph	⌘ Return	\p
New line	⌘ Shift-Return	\n
New column	⌘ Enter	\c
New box	⌘ Shift-Enter	\b
Current page #	⌘ 3	\3
Next box page #	⌘ 4	\4
Previous box page #	⌘ 2	\2
Wild card	⌘ ?	\?
Space	Space bar	

change a font, then select from the font pop-up menus **(Figure 15)**.
and/or
Check the Size box or boxes and enter a size or sizes.
and/or
In the Find what area, a checked Style will be found; an unchecked Style will not be found; a grayed style may or may not be found, but will not be changed.

In the Change to area, a checked Style will be applied to the text; an unchecked style will be removed from the text; a grayed style will not be changed.

9. Hold down Option and click Find First to find the first instance in the document of the Find what text.
or
Click Find Next to find the next instance of the Find what text from your current location in the document.

10. Click Change, Then Find to change an instance and find the next instance.
or
Click Change to change one instance.
or
Click Change All to change all instances at once. A prompt will appear indicating the number of instances found.

11. Click the close box to exit Find/Change.

Find what area.   *Change to area.*

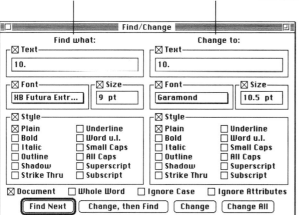

Figure 15. *Uncheck the **Ignore Attributes** box to include **Font, Size,** and **Style** attributes in a search.*

Find/Change (side tab)

✔ Tip

■ To display a list of fonts used in an active document, select Font Usage from the Utilities menu and press on the Font pop-up menu on the left side. This utility is useful for making a font list when sending a file to a service bureau **(Figures 16-17)**.

To use the Font Usage dialog box to search for and replace fonts, follow the instructions for Find/Change beginning on page 170.

Figure 16. *Select **Font Usage** from the **Utilities** menu.*

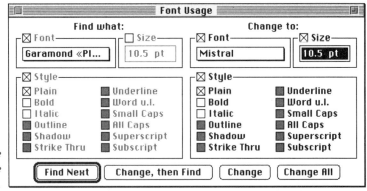

Figure 17. *The Font Usage dialog box.*

File

New...	⌘N
Open...	⌘O
Close	
Save	⌘S
Save as...	
Revert to Saved	
Get Text/Picture...	⌘E
Save Text...	
Save Page as EPS...	
Document Setup...	
Page Setup...	
Print...	⌘P
Quit	⌘Q

Figure 1.
*Select **Print**
from the
File menu.*

To print a document:

1. Select Print from the File menu **(Figure 1)** or hold down Command (⌘) and press "P".

2. Leave the default setting on All to print all the document pages.
   or
   Enter numbers in the From and To fields to print a range of pages **(Figure 2)**.

3. Click Print or press Return.

✔ Tip

■ If a missing pictures prompt appears, click List Pictures, click Update, locate the picture, then click Open.

(See also "To modify printer settings" on the following page)

Figure 2. *The Version 3.2 **Print** dialog box.*

*Click **Color/Grayscale** if your document contains grayscale or color elements.*

*Choose **Low Resolution Output** to print a document containing pictures more quickly. Choose **Rough** to suppress picture printout.*

*To print a separate sheet of film or paper for a color, choose **Separation On**. Then select from the **Plate** pop-up menu (on the right).*

*Enter the number of **Copies** to be printed. 1 is the default.*

*Leave the default setting on **All** or enter numbers in the **From** and **To** fields. You can type "End" in the To field.*

*Click **Print** or press Return when you are ready to print.*

LaserWriter "Pierre 2f"	7.1.1

[Print] **[Cancel]**

Copies: 1   Pages: ○ All ● From: 2 To: end

Cover Page: ● No ○ First Page ○ Last Page

Paper Source: ● Paper Cassette ○ Manual Feed

Print: ○ Black & White ● Color/Grayscale

Destination: ● Printer   ○ PostScript® File

Page Sequence: [All]   ☐ Collate   ☐ Back to Front

Output: [Normal]   ☐ Sprea | All Plates
Tiling: [Automatic]   Overlap: | Black
Separation: [On]   Plate: | Cyan
Registration: [Centered] OPI: | ✓Magenta
Options: ☐ Calibrated Output | Registration
          ☒ Include Blank Pages ☐ Print Colors as Grays | Yellow

*Choose **Centered Registration** to print crop marks and registration marks. Your page size should be smaller than the paper size.*

*Click **Print Colors as Grays** to print gray simulations of color.*

Printing

To print pages that are larger than the printer's paper size:

An oversized document can be printed in sections on more than one sheet of paper using Auto or Manual Tiling. To print an oversized document on one sheet of paper, reduce the printout size **(Figure 4)**.

To print using Auto Tiling:

1. Select the appropriate Orientation icon in the Page Setup dialog box, opened from the File menu **(Figure 4)**.

2. Select Print from the File menu.

3. Check the Auto Tiling box **(Figure 2)**.

4. Enter a number in the Auto, overlap field.

5. Click Print.

To modify printer settings:

1. Select Page Setup from the File menu.

2. Make any desired modifications **(Figure 4)**.

3. Click OK or press Return.

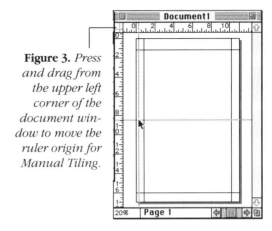

Figure 3. *Press and drag from the upper left corner of the document window to move the ruler origin for Manual Tiling.*

To print an 11" x 17" page on two sheets of paper.

Check the landscape Orientation icon in the Page Setup dialog box **(Figure 4)**. Print the page with the Tiling box unchecked. Then press and drag the ruler origin to 8.5" on the vertical ruler to move the position from which the document will begin printing **(Figure 3)**, and Print again with the Manual Tiling box checked **(Figure 2)**.

Figure 4. *The **Page Setup** dialog box.*

*Click one of the **Paper** size buttons.*

*Enter a number between 25% and 400% to **Reduce** or **Enlarge** the printout size.*

*Click an **Orientation** icon to print a document in portrait or landscape format.*

*Select a printer from the **Printer Type** pop-up menu.*

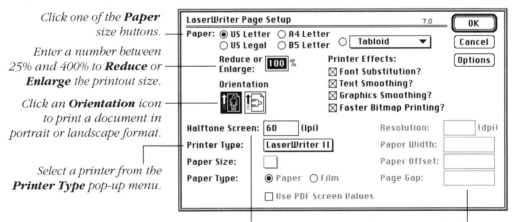

*Enter an lpi (lines per inch) setting between 15 and 400 in the **Halftone Screen** field. A setting between 65 and 85 is usually required by newspapers; a setting between 120 and 150 is used for magazines; books require higher settings. A setting of 60 is recommended for printing to a Laserwriter.*

These dimmed fields are available when an imagesetter is selected from the Printer Type pop-up menu.

Printing

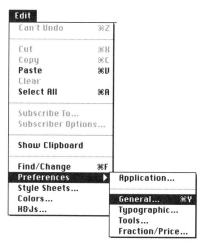

Figure 1. *Select **Application, General, Typographic, Tools,** or **Fraction/Price** (if available) from the **Preferences** pop-up menu under the **Edit** menu.*

About defaults:

Default settings are the values that automatically apply when a feature or tool is used. For example, when the Line tool is used, a line is automatically drawn in a particular width. That width is the default setting. Default settings can be customized.

Select Application from the Preferences pop-up menu under the Edit menu to set application-wide defaults. For example, the Page Grabber Hand is available in all documents when turned on in Application Preferences **(Figure 1)**.

Select General, Typographic, Tools, or Fraction/Price (with the FeaturesPlus XTension) without a document open to set application-wide defaults; select with a document open to set defaults for that document only.

Set defaults for Style Sheets, Colors, H&Js, and Auxiliary Dictionaries in their individual dialog boxes. For example, a style sheet created with no document open will appear on the Style Sheets palette of subsequently created documents.

Instructions for setting defaults are also set forth in other chapters.

(The EfiColor Preferences dialog box is discussed on page 217)

Set Defaults

Typographic Preferences for DEFAULT SETTINGS

Superscript	Subscript	Baseline Grid
Offset: 33%	Offset: 33%	Start: 3p
VScale: 100%	VScale: 100%	Increment: 12 pt
HScale: 100%	HScale: 100%	
		Auto Leading: 20%
Small Caps	Superior	Flex Space Width: 50%
VScale: 80%	VScale: 50%	☒ Auto Kern Above: 8 pt
HScale: 75%	HScale: 50%	☒ Maintain Leading

Ligatures: On   1
Hyphenation Method: Enhanced
Character Widths: Fractional   OK   Cancel
Leading Mode: Typesetting

Figure 2. *In the **Typographic Preferences** dialog box, you can set **Superscript, Subscript, Small Caps,** and **Superior** position and scaling values, turn **Ligatures** on or off, and, in the **Auto Kern Above** field, specify the point size above which character pairs kern automatically.*

"By the time she had caught the flamingo and brought it back, the fight was over..." *Lewis Carroll*

Figure 3. *The "fl" and "fi" ligatures. A ligature is a pair of characters kerned tightly so they join.*

Key to the General Preferences dialog box.

1-2 Choose default Horizontal and Vertical Measures separately. Select Inches, Inches Decimal, Picas, Points, Millimeters, Centimeters, or Ciceros. *(See page 16)*

3 With Auto Page Insertion, pages will be added at End of Story, End of Section, End of Document, or not at all (Off). *(See pages 51-53)*

4 Framing can be applied to the Inside or Outside edges of a box.

5 Set Ruler Guides to display In Front of or Behind page elements. *(See page 99)*

6 The Master Page Items options, Keep Changes and Delete Changes, affect whether modified items from the previously applied master page are kept or deleted when a new master page is applied to a document page. *(See page 138)*

7 Auto Picture Import options include Off, On, and On (verify). *(See page 119)*

8 With Greek Pictures checked, pictures are displayed only when selected. Otherwise, they display as solid gray boxes. Greeking speeds up screen redraw.

9 Greek Below indicates the point size below which text displays as solid gray bars.

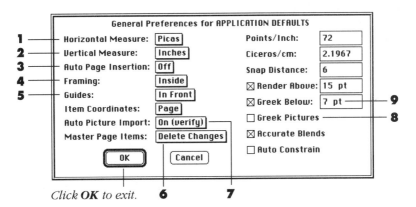

*Click **OK** to exit.*

Figure 4. *The **General Preferences** dialog box. Choose options on the left side from pop-up menus.*

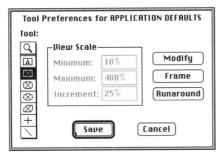

Figure 5. *To open the **Tool Preferences** dialog box, select **Tools** from the Preferences pop-up menu under the Edit menu or double-click the Zoom tool or any Item creation tool. Click **Modify, Frame,** or **Runaround** to modify default settings.*

Set Defaults

Glossary

Ascender	The part of a lowercase letter that extends above the x-height, as in the letters *b, d, f, h* and *l*.
Baseline	The invisible line on which most uppercase and lower-case letters sit.
Baseline Shift	Raise or lower one or more characters above or below the baseline.
Bleed	An item that extends beyond the edge of the page.
Condense Type	Make characters narrower than normal.
Descender	The part of a lowercase letter that extends below the baseline, as in the letters *p* and *j*.
Em Space	The width occupied by two zeros in a given font.
En Space	The width occupied by one zero in a given font.
EPS	Encapsulated Postscript, a picture file format.
Extend Type	Make characters wider than normal.
File	An electronic document. A QuarkXPress file can consist of one or more pages.
Folio	Page number.
Hanging Indent	A format in which the first line of a paragraph is aligned flush left and the remaining lines are indented.
Horizontal Scale	Character width.
Imagesetter	A high resolution printer.
Kern	Adjust the space between two characters.
Leading	The space measured from baseline to baseline between lines of type.
Line	A line of type, *or,* a line that is drawn with a Line tool.
Link	To connect text boxes into a chain so that text flows continuously from one box into another.
Orphan	The first line of a paragraph that falls at the bottom of a column.
Pica	A unit of measure used in graphic arts. Six picas equals 1 inch; 1 pica equals 12 points.

Glossary

Paragraph   Any number of characters followed by a Return.

Point   The unit used to measure type size, leading and rules. In the example "2p8," the numbers before the p indicate picas and the numbers after the "p" indicate points.

Polygon   A closed shape composed of three or more straight sides.

Resolution   The degree of sharpness of detail that a printer can achieve (dots per inch).

Rule   A line that is anchored to text using the Paragraph Rules feature.

Ruler Origin   The intersection of the horizontal and vertical rulers, usually positioned at the upper left corner of the page.

Sans Serif Font   A font with no finishing strokes projecting from the ends of its characters.

Serif Font   A font with short finishing strokes projecting from the ends of its characters.

Spread   Two or more pages displayed or printed side-by-side.

Story   Text that is contained in one box or a series of linked boxes. A document can contain more than one story.

TIFF   A picture file format used for saving scanned images (Tag Image File Format).

Track   Adjust the space to the right of one or more highlighted characters.

Typeface   A distinctive type design, such as Optima. The Optima typeface includes the Optima Regular, Optima Oblique, and Optima Bold fonts.

Widow   The last line of a paragraph that falls at the top of a column.

X-height   The height of the lowercase "x" in a particular font.

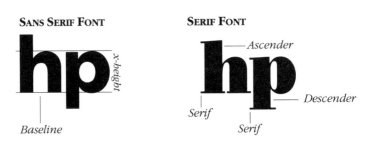

SANS SERIF FONT

SERIF FONT

x-height

Baseline

Ascender

Descender

Serif

Serif

Appendix B: **List of Keyboard Shortcuts by Chapter**

```
                    KEY
   🖱       Click
   🖱🖱      Double-click
   ┈┈🖱     Press and drag
```

Chapter 1: **The Basics**

Tool palette

Show Tools or select next tool	⌘ Tab
Show Tools or select previous tool	⌘ Shift Tab
Keep a tool selected	Option click on tool
Tool preferences...	🖱🖱 Item creation or Zoom tool
Move item with Item tool not selected	⌘ ┈┈🖱
About QuarkXPress (Help)	⌘ ? or ⌘ /

Measurements palette

Display Measurements palette/ highlight first field	⌘ Option M
Highlight field	🖱🖱
Highlight next field	Tab
Highlight previous field	Shift Tab
Cancel/Exit	⌘ Period
Apply/Exit	Enter or Return
Revert to original values	⌘ Z

Dialog boxes

OK (or heavy bordered button)	Return
Cancel	⌘ Period
Apply	⌘ A
Continuous Apply	⌘ Option A or Option 🖱 Apply
Yes	⌘ Y
No	⌘ N
Highlight field	🖱🖱
Highlight next field	Tab
Highlight previous field	Shift Tab
Revert to original values	⌘ Z

Rulers

Show/Hide Rulers	⌘ R

Chapter 3: **Create a Document**

New...	⌘ N
Open...	⌘ O
Save	⌘ S
Save As...	⌘ Option S

Quit	⌘ Q
Close all document windows	Option ↖ Close box

Chapter 4: **Getting Around**

Change view sizes

Fit in Window view	⌘ Zero
Page/spread and pasteboard	Option Fit in Window view
Actual Size view	⌘ 1
Enlarge view size	Control ↖ or Control ┈↖
Reduce view size	Control Option ↖

Move through a document

Go To...	⌘ J
Start of document	Control A or Home
End of document	Control D or End
Scroll up one screen	Control K or Page Up
Scroll down one screen	Control L or Page Down
Scroll to first page	Control Shift A or Shift Home
Scroll to last page	Control Shift D or Shift End
Scroll to previous page	Control Shift K or Shift Page Up
Scroll to next page	Control Shift L or Shift Page Down
Page Grabber Hand	Option ┈↖

Chapter 5: **Text Input**

Show/Hide Invisibles	⌘ I

Highlight Text

One word	↖↖
One line	↖↖↖
One paragraph	↖↖↖↖
Entire story (Select All)	↖↖↖↖↖ or ⌘ A

Move the cursor

(Hold down Shift to highlight while moving.)

Character-by-character	Left & Right Arrows
Line-by-line	Up & Down Arrows
Word-by-word	⌘ Left & Right Arrows
Paragraph-by-paragraph	⌘ Up & Down Arrows
Start of line	⌘ Option Left Arrow
End of line	⌘ Option Right Arrow
Start of story	⌘ Option Up Arrow
End of story	⌘ Option Down Arrow

The Clipboard

Cut	⌘ X
Copy	⌘ C
Paste	⌘ V

Text Boxes

Frame...	⌘ B
Modify... (Item Specifications)	⌘ M
Delete box	⌘ K

Chapter 6: **Text Flow**

Get text...	⌘ E
Current text box page number	⌘ 3
Previous text box page number	⌘ 2
Next text box page number	⌘ 4

Chapter 7: **Paragraph Formats**

Formats...	⌘ Shift F
Leading...	⌘ Shift E
Tabs...	⌘ Shift T
Rules...	⌘ Shift N
Increase leading 1 point	⌘ Shift "
Decrease leading 1 point	⌘ Shift :
Increase leading 1/10 point	⌘ Option Shift "
Decrease leading 1/10 point	⌘ Option Shift :
Indent Here character	⌘ \
Delete all tab stops	Option ⬆ tabs ruler
Right-Indent tab	Option Tab
Suggested Hyphenation	⌘ H

Chapter 8: **Typography**

Character...	⌘ Shift D
Display Measurements palette/ highlight Font field	⌘ Option Shift M
Increase Horizontal Scaling 5%	⌘]
Decrease Horizontal Scaling 5%	⌘ [
Baseline Shift up 1 point	⌘ Option Shift +
Baseline Shift down 1 point	⌘ Option Shift Hyphen

Resize text

Increase point size to preset sizes	⌘ Shift >
Decrease point size to preset sizes	⌘ Shift <
Increase point size by 1 point	⌘ Option Shift >
Decrease point size by 1 point	⌘ Option Shift <
Other size...	⌘ Shift \

Style text

Plain text	⌘ Shift P
Bold	⌘ Shift B
Italic	⌘ Shift I
Underline	⌘ Shift U
Word Underline	⌘ Shift W

Keyboard Shortcuts

Strike Thru	⌘ Shift /
Outline	⌘ Shift O
Shadow	⌘ Shift S
All Caps	⌘ Shift K
Small Caps	⌘ Shift H
Superscript	⌘ Shift +
Subscript	⌘ Shift Hyphen
Superior	⌘ Shift V

Horizontal alignment

Left alignment	⌘ Shift L
Right alignment	⌘ Shift R
Center alignment	⌘ Shift C
Justified alignment	⌘ Shift J

Tracking and kerning

Increase Kerning/Tracking 10 units	⌘ Shift }
Decrease Kerning/Tracking 10 units	⌘ Shift {
Increase Kerning/Tracking 1 unit	⌘ Option Shift }
Decrease Kerning/Tracking 1 unit	⌘ Option Shift {

Word space tracking

For use only with FeaturesPlus XTension.

Increase Word Space 10 units	⌘ Shift Control }
Decrease Word Space 10 units	⌘ Shift Control {
Increase Word Space 1 unit	⌘ Option Shift Control }
Decrease Word Space 1 unit	⌘ Option Shift Control {

Special characters

Insert one Zapf Dingbats character	⌘ Shift Z
Insert one Symbol character	⌘ Shift Q
New paragraph	Return
New line	Shift Return
Discretionary new line	⌘ Return
Discretionary hyphen	⌘ Hyphen
Nonbreaking standard hyphen	⌘ =
Nonbreaking standard space	⌘ Space bar
New column	Enter
New box	Shift Enter
Breaking en space	Option Space bar
Nonbreaking en space	⌘ Option Space bar
Breaking flex space	Option Shift Space bar
Nonbreaking flex space	⌘ Option Shift Space bar
Nonbreaking em dash	⌘ Option =
Breaking em dash	Option Shift Hyphen
Nonbreaking en dash	Option Hyphen

Chapter 9: **Pictures**

Import a picture

Get Picture...	⌘ E

In Get Picture dialog box:

Import picture at 72 dpi if Low Resolution Tiff is checked in Application Preferences dialog box	Shift Open
Import picture at 36 dpi if Low Resolution Tiff is unchecked in Application Preferences dialog box	Shift Open
TIFF line art to grayscale	Option Open
TIFF grayscale to line art	⌘ Open
TIFF color to grayscale	⌘ Open

Pictures and picture boxes

Center picture in box	⌘ Shift M
Frame...	⌘ B
Modify... (Item Specifications)	⌘ M
Delete box	⌘ K
Move picture in box 1 point	Arrow keys
Move picture in box 1/10 point	Option Arrow keys
Fit picture to box	⌘ Shift F
Fit picture to box (maintain aspect ratio)	⌘ Option Shift F
Enlarge picture in 5% increments	⌘ Option Shift >
Reduce picture in 5% increments	⌘ Option Shift <
Constrain box to square or circle	Shift ⋯↖
Resize box (maintain aspect ratio)	Option Shift ⋯↖
Scale picture and box	⌘ ⋯↖
Scale picture and box (maintain aspect ratio)	⌘ Option Shift ⋯↖

Style a picture

Other Contrast...	⌘ Shift C
Other Screen...	⌘ Shift S
Negative	⌘ Shift Hyphen
Normal contrast	⌘ Shift N
High contrast	⌘ Shift H
Posterized contrast	⌘ Shift P

Text wrap

Runaround...	⌘ T

Modify a polygon picture box or Runaround polygon

Create a handle	⌘ ↖ on line segment
Delete a handle	⌘ ↖ on handle
Constrain line or handle movement to 0°, 45°, 90°	Shift ⋯↖
Temporarily suspend text reflow	Space bar
Delete Runaround polygon	⌘ Shift ↖

Keyboard Shortcuts

Chapter 10: **Lines**

Increase width in preset range	⌘ Shift >
Decrease width in preset range	⌘ Shift <
Increase width by 1 point	⌘ Option Shift >
Decrease width by 1 point	⌘ Option Shift <
Other width	⌘ Shift \
Constrain resizing/rotating to 0°/45°/90°	Shift ````↖
Constrain to same angle	Option Shift ````↖

Chapter 11: **Style Sheets**

Style Sheets...	⌘ ↖ style sheet name in Style Sheets palette
Apply No Style, then style sheet	Option ↖ style sheet name in Style Sheets palette

Chapter 12: **Master Pages**

Automatic page numbering command	⌘ 3

Chapter 13: **Color**

Colors...	⌘ ↖ color in Colors palette

Chapter 15: **Multiple Items**

Group	⌘ G
Ungroup	⌘ U
Lock/Unlock	⌘ L
Duplicate	⌘ D
Step and Repeat...	⌘ Option D
Select through layers	⌘ Option Shift ↖
Bring Forward one level	Option Item menu
Send Backward one level	Option Item menu
Move item 1 point	Arrow keys
Move item ¹⁄₁₀ point	Option Arrow keys

Chapter 16: **Search & Replace**

Check Spelling: Word...	⌘ W
Check Spelling: Story...	⌘ Option W
Find/Change...	⌘ F
Change Find Next button to Find First	Option (in Find/Change dialog box)

Chapter 17: **Printing**

Page Setup...	⌘ Option P
Print...	⌘ P
Print Status	Shift Print

Chapter 18: **Default Settings**

General Preferences...	⌘ Y
Typographic Preferences...	⌘ Option Y

Appendix C: **QuarkXPress 3.2**

The new Box Skew feature was used to produce this cube.

QUARK**XP**RESS **3.2** includes many welcome additions and improvements. There are new design tools: you can flip text or a picture, scale text vertically, skew text, and resize text by resizing its box.

Other additions save steps. You can use the Drag and Drop feature to move text without using the Clipboard. And there are over 35 new keyboard shortcuts that open and close palettes, open dialog boxes, highlight the View Percent field, close windows, scale text in 1% increments, etc.

There are also new (and long-awaited) typesetting features: Smart Quotes, which makes curly quotes appear automatically when the quote key is pressed, and Forced Justify alignment, which justifies every line in a paragraph, including the last line.

The Collect for Output command places the current QuarkXPress file and associated picture files in a folder. It also creates a Report file containing information about the document, such as the fonts used.

Among the many other new features are Next Style, for chaining style sheets, Stack Documents and Tile Documents for arranging document windows, a Line width pop-up menu on the Measurements palette, a PhotoCD Import XTension, backup features — Auto Save and Auto Backup — and the EfiColor XTension, an important breakthrough in color management. Finally, Version 3.2 is noticeably faster than Version 3.1 — in itself a time-saver.

Note: The Document Layout palette was revamped and is covered on pages 14, 33, 55-58, and 135-139. All the other new features are covered in this appendix, which overrides relevant portions of the main text.

'THREE QUARKS FOR MUSTER MARK!'

James Joyce, *Finnegans Wake*

KEYBOARD SHORTCUTS

F KEYS*

F1	Undo
F2	Cut
F3	Copy
F4	Paste
F5	Bring to Front
Option F5	Bring Forward
Shift F5	Send to Back
Option Shift F5	Send Backward
F6	Lock/Unlock (no longer ⌘ L)
F7	Show/Hide Guides
Shift F7	Snap to Guides
Option F7	Show/Hide Baseline Grid
F8	Show/Hide Tool palette
Shift F8	Select Item tool/Content tool
Option F8	Select next tool
Option Shift F8	Select previous tool
F9	Show/Hide Measurements palette
Shift F9	Highlight font field
Option F9	Select next font
Option Shift F9	Select previous font
F10	Show/Hide Document Layout palette
F11	Show/Hide Style Sheets palette
Shift F11	Style Sheets dialog box
Option Shift F11	H&Js dialog box
F12	Show/Hide Colors palette
Shift F12	Colors dialog box
Option F12	Trapping Information palette
Option Shift F12	Trapping Preferences dialog box
F13	Font Usage dialog box (open/close)
Option F13	Picture Usage dialog box

*If you choose an F key as a Keyboard Equivalent for a
style sheet, it will override the default F key command.*

KEYBOARD SHORTCUTS

RESIZE TEXT AND BOX
⌘	Drag handle
⌘ Option Shift	Drag handle (maintain text scaling and aspect ratio of box)

VIEW PERCENT FIELD
Control V	Highlight View Percent field

DOCUMENT WINDOWS
⌘ W	Close active document
⌘ Option W	Close all documents
Shift	Press on document title bar to choose Windows options

CHECK SPELLING
⌘ L	Check Word
⌘ Option L	Check Story
⌘ Option Shift L	Check Document

FORCED JUSTIFY
⌘ Option Shift J	Forced Justify alignment

HORIZONTAL/VERTICAL SCALE
⌘ [	Decrease scale 5%
⌘]	Increase scale 5%
⌘ Option [	Decrease scale 1%
⌘ Option]	Increase scale 1%

FIND/CHANGE
\.	Search for flex space

DIALOG BOXES
⌘ Option N	New Library
⌘ Option E	Save Text
⌘ Option Shift S	Save Page as EPS
⌘ Option Shift P	Document Setup
⌘ Option Shift Y	Application Preferences
⌘ Option H	H&Js
⌘ ,	Space/Align Items

Multiplication and division

To multiply numbers in a field, enter *, then the multiplier.

To divide numbers in a field, enter /, then the divider **(Figure 1)**.

The Width will be divided by 2 when Return is pressed.

| X: 1.542" | W: 1.75"/2 | ⊿ 0° |
| Y: 1.486" | H: 0.569" | Cols: 1 |

Figure 1.

Chapter 3

Convert a file to Version 3.2

1. Launch QuarkXPress 3.2.

2. Choose Open from the File menu.

3. Highlight the file.

4. Click Open.

5. Select Save from the File menu.

New file/new library

The New dialog box and Library dialog box now open from a pop-up menu under the File menu.

To create a new document, select Document from the New pop-up menu under the File menu **(Figure 2)**.
or
Hold down Command (⌘) and press "N".

To create a new library, select Library from the same pop-up menu.
or
Hold down Command (⌘) and Option and press "N."

✔ Tip

■ To open a library, use the Open dialog box, opened from the File menu. If you highlight a library name in the Open dialog box, a library icon and the word "Library" will appear in the lower left corner.

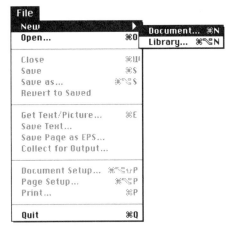

Figure 2. *From the **New** pop-up menu under the **File** menu, select **Document** to create a new file or **Library** to create a new library.*

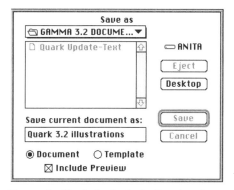

Figure 3. *Check the* **Include Preview** *box in the* **Save As** *dialog box when you first save a document.*

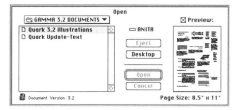

Figure 4. *If the* **Preview** *box is checked, you'll see a thumbnail of the first page of the document in the* **Open** *dialog box.*

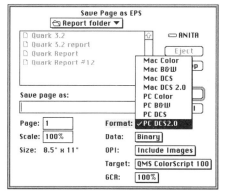

Figure 5. *In the* **Save Page as EPS** *dialog box, you can choose from several file* **Formats***.*

Document preview

Check the Include Preview box in the Save As dialog box when you first save a document **(Figure 3)**.

If you subsequently open the document using the Open dialog box and the Preview box is checked, you'll see a thumbnail of the first page of the document **(Figure 4)**

Save page as EPS options

The Save Page as EPS dialog box converts QuarkXPress pages into picture files *(See pages 112-113)*. Several new Macintosh and PC file formats are available under the Format pop-up menu **(Figure 5)**.

To color separate a page before printing, you can save it in either of two DCS (Desktop Color Separation) file formats: DCS 1.0, which consists of five files (cyan, magenta, yellow, black, and a PICT preview), or the new DCS 2.0, which consists of separations combined in one file, and can include spot color plates.

✓ Tips

■ Ask your service provider which file format to select for your target output device.

■ Binary Data files print more quickly than ASCII files, and are smaller in file size. Choose ASCII only in circumstances where Binary files cannot be used.

(See also "Save Page as EPS" on page 217)

Replace fonts

If you open a document that uses fonts not installed or not currently available in your system, a prompt will appear.

1. Click **List Fonts** to see a list of missing fonts **(Figure 6)**.

2. To replace a font, click on a Missing Font **(Figure 7)**.

3. Click Replace.

4. Select a font from the Replacement Font pop-up menu **(Figure 8)**.

5. Click OK.

6. Repeat steps 2-5 for each missing font you wish to replace.

7. Click OK or press Return.

✓ Tips

■ If you click **Continue**, the missing fonts will display in Chicago. If you subsequently open the document on a system in which a missing font is available (or you open the font suitcase using Suitcase or another font utility), the font will display properly.

■ If you change your mind after replacing a font, click on the replacement font, then click Reset.

■ An asterisk in the Replacement Font column indicates that font has not been replaced.

Figure 6. *The missing fonts prompt. Click **List Fonts** to substitute fonts. Click **Continue** to display missing fonts in Chicago.*

Figure 7. *In the **Missing Fonts** dialog box, click a font name, then click **Replace**.*

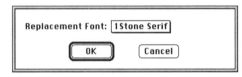

Figure 8. *Choose from the **Replacement Font** pop-up menu.*

Network support of templates

Network users can open the same template file, and it may be opened an unlimited number of times.

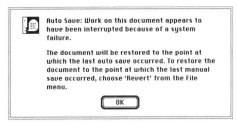

Figure 9. *The Auto Save prompt.*

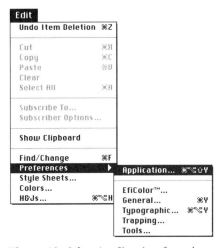

Figure 10. *Select Application from the Preferences pop-up menu under the Edit menu.*

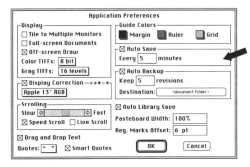

Figure 11. *Turn Auto Save on or off in the Application Preferences dialog box. Enter a frequency for Auto Save in the Every __ minutes field.*

Auto save

It is always a good idea to save your document frequently as you work, in case a system or power failure occurs. With the new Auto Save option enabled, modifications are saved in a temporary file every five minutes, or at another interval you specify. If a system or power failure occurs while you are modifying a document and you restart, then reopen the document, a prompt will appear **(Figure 9)**. Click OK. The last Auto saved version will open. To restore the last manually saved version, choose Revert to Saved from the File menu.

Note: Application Preferences settings apply to all documents.

1. Select Application from the Preferences pop-up menu under the Edit menu **(Figure 10)**.

2. Check the Auto Save box **(Figure 11)**.

3. *Optional:* Modify the number in the "Every __ minutes" field.

4. Click OK or press Return.

✔ Tips

■ To overwrite the permanent file, use the Save command, as usual. Select Revert to Saved to restore the last manually saved version.

■ There may be a short interruption while Auto Save occurs.

Auto Save

Auto backup

Unlike Auto Save, which saves only modifications made to a document in a temporary file, Auto Backup creates a backup version of the entire document when you execute the Save command. Progressively higher numbers are appended to the backup names.

You can specify how many backup versions will be created before the oldest backup version is deleted. Backup versions are placed in the current document folder, unless you specify a different destination.

Note: Application Preferences settings apply to all documents.

1. Select Application from the Preferences pop-up menu under the Edit menu **(Figure 10)**.

2. Check the Auto Backup box **(Figure 12)**.

3. Enter a number between 1 and 100 in the "Keep __ revisions" field.

Optional: To select a different Destination, follow steps 4-6.

4. Click the destination name.

5. Locate and open an existing folder **(Figure 13)**.
or
Click New Folder, enter a name, then click Create **(Figure 14)**.

6. Click Select.

7. Click OK or press Return.

✔ Tip

■ To reset the Destination as the current document folder, click the Destination name in Application Preferences, then click Use Document Folder.

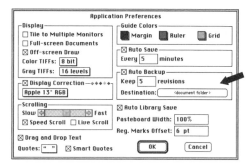

Figure 12. *In the **Application Preferences** dialog box, check the **Auto Backup** box, specify the number of backups in the **Keep __ revisions** field, and choose a **Destination**.*

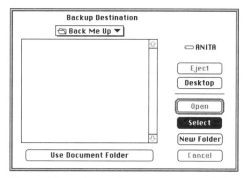

Figure 13. *In the **Backup Destination** dialog box, choose an existing folder for the backups, create a **New Folder**, or click **Use Document Folder**, then click **Select**.*

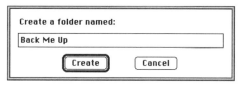

Figure 14. *Enter a name for the folder, then click **Create**.*

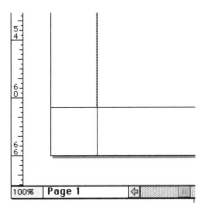

Figure 15. *Hold down **Control** and press "V" to highlight the **View Percent** field.*

Chapter 4

View percent field shortcut

To quickly change the display size of your document, use a keystroke to highlight the View Percent field, then enter a percentage.

1. Hold down Control and press "V" **(Figure 15)**.

2. Enter a number between 10 and 400. You do not need to enter the percent symbol.
or
Enter "T" for Thumbnails view.

3. Press Return.

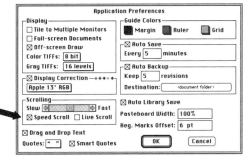

Figure 16. *Check the **Speed Scroll** box in the **Application Preferences** dialog box.*

Speed scroll

For faster scrolling, turn on Speed Scroll. Pictures and blends will be greeked (displayed as solid gray) while you scroll, then redrawn when you stop scrolling.

1. Select Application from the Preferences pop-up menu under the Edit menu **(Figure 10)**.

2. Check the Speed Scroll box **(Figure 16)**.

3. Click OK.

✓ Tip

■ Check the Live Scroll box to have the screen redraw as you drag a scroll box. Check the Off-screen Draw box to have the screen redraw all at once, instead of in sections.

Windows pop-up menu

You can Stack, Tile, or activate open document windows or dialog boxes via the new Windows pop-up menu. Access it from the View menu **(Figure 17)**, or by holding down Shift and pressing on a document name in its title bar **(Figure 18)**.

Select Stack Documents to stack document windows at full size in front of one another **(Figure 19)**.
or
Select Tile Documents to arrange document windows next to each other **(Figure 20)**. Choose this option before drag-copying items or pages between documents *(see page 160 and the first tip on page 58)*.
or
Select an open document or dialog box to activate it. For example, select Find/Change from the Windows pop-up menu to activate the Find/Change dialog box if it is already open.

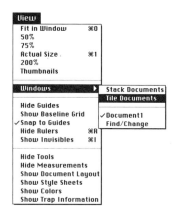

Figure 17. *From the* **Windows** *pop-up menu under the* **View** *menu, select* **Stack Documents** *or* **Tile Documents,** *or activate an open document or dialog box.*

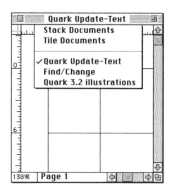

Figure 18. *Hold down* **Shift** *and press on a document title bar to access Windows commands.*

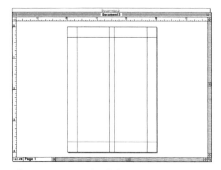

Figure 19. *Stacked documents.*

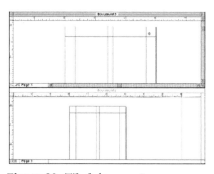

Figure 20. *Tiled documents.*

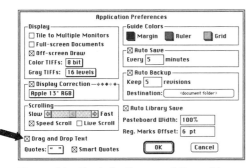

Figure 21. *Check the* **Drag and Drop Text** *box in the* **Application Preferences** *dialog box.*

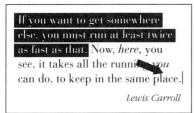

Now, *here*, you see, it takes all the runni...you can do, to keep in the same place.|

Lewis Carroll

Figure 22a. *To move (Drag and Drop) text, highlight it and release the mouse. Then press on the highlighted text and drag the blinking cursor to a new position.*

"Now, *here*, you see, it takes all the running *you* can do, to keep in the same place. If you want to get somewhere else, you must run at least twice as fast as that..."

Lewis Carroll

Figure 22b. *The sentences in reverse order.*

Chapter 5

Drag and drop text

Use the new Drag and Drop Text feature to move or copy text quickly without using the Clipboard commands. You can Drag and Drop text within a box or within a chain of linked boxes.

To turn the Drag and Drop Text feature on, select Application from the Preferences pop-up menu under the Edit menu **(Figure 10)**, check the Drag and Drop Text box **(Figure 21)**, then click OK.

To Drag and Drop text:

1. Select the Content tool.

2. Highlight the text you wish to move or copy *(see page 39)* **(Figure 22a)**.

3. Release the mouse.

4. To move the text, press on the highlighted text, drag the blinking cursor to a new location, then release the mouse **(Figures 22a-b)**.
or
To move a copy of the text, press on the highlighted text, hold down Shift and drag the blinking cursor to a new location.

✔ Tips

■ To move text when the Drag and Drop Text box is unchecked, hold down Command (⌘) and Control, highlight and drag the text. To copy text when the Drag and Drop Text box is unchecked, hold down Command (⌘), Control, and Shift, highlight and drag the copy.

■ Text that is moved or copied using the Drag and Drop feature is automatically placed on the Clipboard.

■ Double-click, then drag to the right to highlight multiple words. Triple-click, then drag downward to highlight multiple lines.

Drag and Drop Text

Skew a text box or picture box

1. Select the Item or Content tool.

2. Click on a text box or picture box.

3. Select Modify from the Item menu.
or
Hold down Command (⌘) and press "M."

4. Enter a number between -75 and 75 in the Box Skew field **(Figure 23)**. Enter a positive number to skew to the right. Enter a negative number to skew to the left.

5. Click OK or press Return **(Figures 24-25b)**.

✔ Tips

■ To skew a picture without skewing its box, select the Content tool, then enter a number between -75 and 75 in the Skew field on the Measurements palette (lower right corner).

■ Skewed text and pictures are editable.

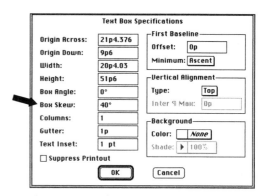

Figure 23. *To skew a text box or picture box, select **Modify** from the **Item** menu, then enter a number in the **Box Skew** field.*

Figure 24. *A text box skewed 40%.*

Figure 25a. *A picture box.*

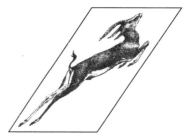

Figure 25b. *The same box skewed 35%.*

Chapter 7

Larger automatic drop caps

An automatic drop cap can be up to 16 lines high; 8 is the maximum Line Count in prior versions.

"Oh, I'm not particular as to size," Alice hastily replied; "only one doesn't like changing so often, you know."

Figure 26a. *The original text.*

"Oh, I'm not particular as to size," Alice hastily replied; "only one doesn't like changing so often, you know."

Figure 26b. *To resize text while preserving its scale and the proportions of its box, hold down* **Command** *(⌘),* **Option, Shift** *and drag a handle.*

"Oh, I'm not particular as to size," Alice hastily replied; "only one doesn't like changing so often, you know."

Lewis Carroll

Figure 26c. *To resize text while changing its scale and the proportions of its box, hold down* **Command** *(⌘) and drag a handle. The text will condense or expand to fit the box.*

Chapter 8

Interactive text resizing

1. Select the Item or Content tool.

2. To resize text while preserving its horizontal/vertical scale and the proportions of its box, hold down Command (⌘), Option, Shift and drag a handle **(Figures 26a-b)**.

or

To resize text while changing its scale and the proportions of its box, hold down Command (⌘) and drag a handle **(Figure 26c)**.

✔ Tips

■ Text in a linked box cannot be resized using this technique.

■ To restore normal scaling to the text, highlight it, select Horizontal/Vertical Scale from the Style menu, then enter 100 in the Scale field.

Forced justify

To justify all the lines in a paragraph — including the last line — select the new Forced alignment option **(Figures 29a-b)**. Make sure the paragraph has a Return character (¶) at the end.

1. Select the Content tool.

2. Highlight one or more paragraphs.

3. Click the Forced Justify icon on the Measurements palette **(Figure 27)**.
or
Hold down Command (⌘), Option, Shift and press "J".
or
Select Forced from the Alignment pop-up menu under the Style menu **(Figure 28)**.

✔ Tip

■ Justified text looks better with hyphenation on *(see page 83)*.

Figure 27. *Click the **Forced Justify** alignment icon on the **Measurements** palette.*

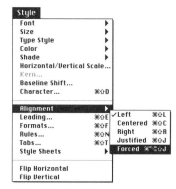

Figure 28. *Select **Forced** from the **Alignment** pop-up menu under the **Style** menu.*

Benedict	And, I pray thee now, tell me, for which of my bad parts didst thou first fall in love with me?
Beatrice	For them all together; which maintained so politic a state of evil that they will not admit any good part to intermingle with them. But for which of my good parts did you first suffer love for me?
Benedict	*Suffer love;* a good epithet! I do suffer love, indeed, for I love thee against my will.

Figure 29a. *Justify alignment.*

Benedict	And, I pray thee now, tell me, for which of my bad parts didst thou first fall in love with me?
Beatrice	For them all together; which maintained so politic a state of evil that they will not admit any good part to intermingle with them. But for which of my good parts did you first suffer love for me?
Benedict	*Suffer love;* a good epithet! I do suffer love, indeed, for I love thee against my will.
	Shakespeare

Figure 29b. *Forced Justify alignment.*

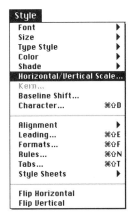

Figure 30. *Select Horizontal/Vertical Scale from the Style menu.*

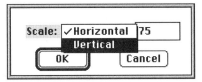

Figure 31. *Select Horizontal or Vertical from the Scale pop-up menu, then enter a number.*

Horizontal/vertical scale

What was formerly the Horizontal Scale dialog box is now the Horizontal/Vertical Scale dialog box. You cannot modify the horizontal and vertical scale of the same characters. You can, of course, change their point size.

1. Select the Content tool.

2. Highlight one or more characters *(see page 39)*.

3. Select Horizontal/Vertical Scale from the Style menu.

4. Select Horizontal or Vertical from the Scale pop-up menu **(Figure 30)**.

5. Enter a number between 25 and 400 **(Figure 31)**.

6. Click OK or press Return **(Figure 32a-d)**.

✓ Tip

■ To condense text in 5% increments using the keyboard, hold down Command (⌘) and press "[". To extend text, hold down Command (⌘) and press "]". Add the Option key to scale in 1% increments. The scaling will be horizontal or vertical depending on which option is currently selected in the Horizontal/Vertical Scale dialog box.

"It was much pleasanter at home," thought poor Alice, "when one wasn't always growing larger and smaller, and being ordered about by mice and rabbits."

Figure 32a. *100% horizontal and vertical scale.*

"It was much pleasanter at home," thought poor Alice, "when one wasn't always growing larger and smaller, and being ordered about by mice and rabbits."
  Lewis Carroll

Figure 32b. *80% horizontal scale.*

"It was much pleasanter at home," thought poor Alice, "when one wasn't always growing larger and smaller, and being ordered about by mice and rabbits."

Figure 32c. *75% vertical scale.*

"It was much pleasanter at home," thought poor Alice, "when one wasn't always growing larger and smaller, and being ordered about by mice and rabbits."

Figure 32d. *110% horizontal scale.*

Smart quotes

Now it is easy to input the curly, "smart" quotes that professional typesetters use **(Figure 35)** and foreign language quotes, like guillemets (« »). If you press ' or " with the Smart Quotes option on, quotes appear in the style specified in the Application Preferences dialog box.

As in prior versions of QuarkXPress, if you import text with the Convert Quotes box checked in the Get Text dialog box, smart quotes are substituted for straight quotes. In version 3.2 you can also specify the quotes style.

Follow the instructions below to turn on Smart Quotes or to choose a different Quotes style.

1. Select Application from the Preferences pop-up menu under the Edit menu.

2. Check the Smart Quotes box to produce quotes in the style chosen from the Quotes pop-up menu.

3. Select a style from the Quotes pop-up menu **(Figure 33)**.

4. Click OK or press Return.

✔ Tips

■ To produce an inch mark when the Smart Quotes option is enabled, hold down Control and press ' **(Figures 34a-b)**. To produce a foot mark, hold down Control and Shift and press ".

■ Uncheck the Smart Quotes box to produce inch and foot marks when you press ' and ". To produce smart quotes when the Smart Quotes box is unchecked, hold down Control and press ' or ".

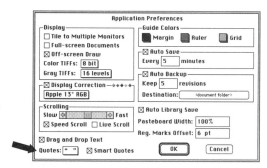

Figure 33. *In the **Application Preferences** dialog box, choose a style from the **Quotes** pop-up menu and check the **Smart Quotes** box.*

The woman is 5'6" tall.

Figure 34a. *Use straight quotes only for foot and inch marks.*

The woman is 5′6″ tall.

Figure 34b. *Or, better yet, use oblique foot and inch marks, called prime marks. To produce a foot mark, choose the Symbol font, then hold down Option and press 4. To produce an inch mark, hold down Option and press ,.*

"HATE THE SIN AND LOVE THE SINNER"

Mohandas Gandhi

Figure 35. *Use Smart Quotes for quotations (and apostrophe marks).*

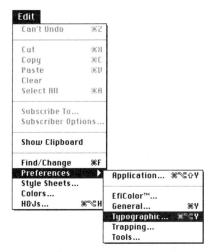

Figure 36. *Select* **Typographic** *from the* **Preferences** *pop-up menu under the* **Edit** *menu.*

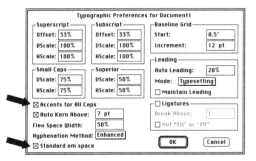

Figure 37. *The* **Accents for All Caps** *box and* **Standard em space** *box in the* **Typographic Preferences** *dialog box.*

Accent *n.:* a mark (as **É, À, Õ, Ü**) used in writing or printing to indicate a specific sound value, stress, or pitch.

Figure 38. *With* **Accents for All Caps** *on, accents can be inserted above uppercase characters in the All Caps style.*

Accents for all caps

You can produce accent marks on characters to which the All Caps style has been applied.

1. Select Typographic from the Preferences pop-up menu under the Edit menu **(Figure 36)**.

2. Check the Accents for All Caps box **(Figure 37)**.

3. Click OK **(Figure 38)**.

✔ Tip

◼ Hold down Option as you open a document created without the Accents for All Caps option to prevent the text from reflowing.

ALL CAPS WITH ACCENT MARKS

Ä	Option - u, *then* A
À	Option - `, *then* A
Ã	Option - n, *then* A
É	Option - e, *then* E
Ñ	Option - n, *then* N
Ö	Option - u, *then* O
Õ	Option - n, *then* O
Ü	Option - u, *then* U

Standard em space

An em space as defined by QuarkXPress is equal to the width of two zeros in a particular font. With the "Standard em space" option on, an em space is equal to the point size you are using. An en space is half the width of an em space.

1. Select Typographic from the Preferences pop-up menu under the Edit menu **(Figure 36)**.

2. Check the "Standard em space" box **(Figure 37)**.

3. Click OK.

(Special character and space keystrokes are on page 182)

Accents for All Caps; Em Space

Chapter 9

Flip a picture or text

The flip commands flip the entire contents of a box. Flipped text and pictures can be modified.

1. Select the Content tool.

2. Click on a picture box or text box.

3. Select Flip Horizontal or Flip Vertical from the Style menu **(Figure 39)**.
or
Click the Flip Horizontal icon or Flip Vertical icon on the Measurements palette **(Figures 40-41c)**.

Figure 39. *Select **Flip Horizontal** or **Flip Vertical** from the **Style** menu.*

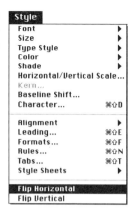

Flip Horizontal icon.

Flip Vertical icon.

Figure 40.

Figure 41a. *The text box containing the gray "Narcissus" was flipped vertically.*

It's a poor sort of memory that only works sqɹɐʍʞɔɐq

Lewis Carroll

Figure 41b. *"Backwards" was typed in a separate text box, then flipped horizontally.*

Figure 41c. *The picture in the bottom box was flipped vertically and lightened using the Other Contrast dialog box (Style menu).*

Flip a Picture or Text

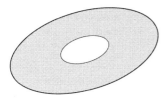

PhotoCD filter

If the PhotoCD Import XTension is in the QuarkXPress folder, you can import Kodak PhotoCD pictures from a PhotoCD disk using the Get Picture dialog box.

Windows file formats

Windows Metafile (.WMF) and Bitmap (.BMP) picture files can be imported.

Update multiple pictures

Figure 42. *Click OK to update other missing pictures in the same folder.*

If you update a picture using the Picture Usage dialog box or by responding to an Auto Picture Import prompt and other missing pictures are located in the same folder, a prompt will appear **(Figure 42)**. If you click OK, all missing pictures in that folder will be updated.

(See pages 119-120)

Chapter 10

Line width pop-up menu

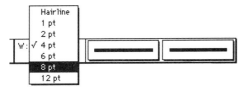

Figure 43. *The new **line width** pop-up menu on the Measurements palette.*

You can choose a line width from a new pop-up menu on the Measurements palette **(Figures 43-44)**.

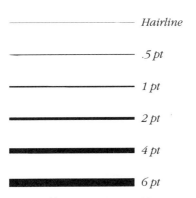

Hairline

.5 pt

1 pt

2 pt

4 pt

6 pt

Figure 44. *Sample line widths.*

File Formats; Update Multiple Pictures

Chapter 11

Next style

You can chain one style sheet to another style sheet using the Next Style option. When you press Return, the Next Style sheet is applied automatically to the next paragraph you type **(Figure 45)**.

To assign a Next Style to an existing style sheet:

1. Select Style Sheets from the Edit menu.

2. Click a style sheet name.

3. Click Edit.

4. Select from the Next Style pop-up menu **(Figure 46)**.

5. Click OK.

6. Click Save.

Figure 45. *Use the Next Style feature to apply successive style sheets automatically as you input text.*

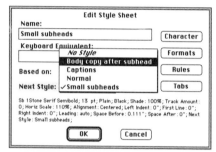

Figure 46. *Select from the **Next Style** pop-up menu in the **Edit Style Sheet** dialog box.*

Local changes

As before, you can make local changes (manually style or format text) in a paragraph to which a style sheet has been applied. In Version 3.2, if you insert the cursor in or highlight locally styled text, a plus sign will appear on the Style Sheets palette next to the name of the style sheet applied to that paragraph **(Figure 47)**.

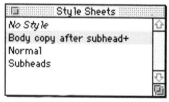

Figure 47. *A plus sign next to a style sheet name indicates the currently highlighted characters are locally formatted.*

Figure 48. *Click* **Rename New Style** *to append a style sheet with the same name as a style sheet in the current document.*

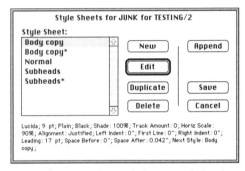

Figure 49. *Asterisks mark the appended style sheets.*

Figure 50. *If this prompt appears, select a replacement style sheet from the* **Replace with** *pop-up menu, or select* **No Style**.

Rename an appended style sheet

In QuarkXPress 3.2, you can append a style sheet with the same name as a style sheet in the current document. *(Instructions for appending style sheets are on pages 132-133)*

If you attempt to append a style sheet with a duplicate name, a warning prompt will appear **(Figure 48)**. Click **Rename New Style** to append the style sheet. An asterisk will appear after its name in the Style Sheets dialog box **(Figure 49)**.

If you click **Use Existing Style**, the style sheet will not be appended.

✔ Tip

■ To rename a style sheet, highlight it in the Style Sheets dialog box, click Edit, then type in the Name field.

Replace a deleted style sheet

If you delete a style sheet that has been applied to one or more paragraphs in your document, a prompt will appear. Select a replacement style sheet from the "Replace with" pop-up menu to apply to that text, or select No Style (your only choice in prior versions), then click OK **(Figure 50)**. *(See page 134)*

✔ Tip

■ If you delete an H&J, a similar prompt will appear.

Chapter 13

Pantone color sets

You can choose from three new Pantone color models in the Edit Color dialog box: Pantone Process (four-color process colors), Pantone ProSim (four-color process colors that simulate spot colors for coated stock), and Pantone Uncoated (spot colors for uncoated stock) **(Figure 51)**.

Note: To access the new Pantone color sets, the Pantone Colors file must be in the QuarkXPress folder when the program is launched.

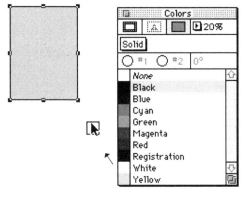

Figure 51. *Choose **Pantone Process, Pantone ProSim,** or **Pantone Uncoated** from the **Model** pop-up menu in the **Edit Color** dialog box.*

Drag color

Use the Drag Color feature to preview and apply color.

1. Select **any** item in your document.

2. Drag a swatch from the Colors palette over a text box, picture box, frame, or line **(Figure 52a-b)**.

3. Release the mouse over the item to apply the color.
or
Keep the mouse button down and move the cursor away from the item to leave its color unchanged.

✔ Tips

■ A color will be applied in the default shade percentage of an item if you have not changed its color or in the shade of the color last applied to the item. If that shade is 0%, it will remain so. To apply a new shade, click the corresponding icon on the Colors palette, then select a percentage from the Shade pop-up menu.

■ Hold down Option while dragging a swatch to apply a 100% shade of a color.

■ When applying a color to a frame or line, release the mouse when the tip of the arrow is directly over it.

Figure 52a. *Drag a swatch from the Colors palette over an item. (The Drag Color feature applies color to the background of a picture box or text box, not to a picture or text.)*

Figure 52b. *The box background turns White.*

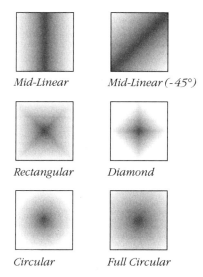

Mid-Linear *Mid-Linear (-45°)*

Rectangular *Diamond*

Circular *Full Circular*

Figure 53. ***Cool Blends***. *White is the #1 color; 70% gray is the #2 color.*

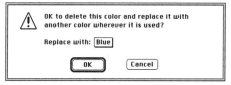

Figure 54. *Select a replacement color from the* ***Replace with*** *pop-up menu.*

Cool Blends

Cool Blends is a free XTension included with QuarkXPress 3.2. Using it, you can create Mid-Linear, Rectangular, Diamond, Circular, and Full Circular blends in picture boxes and text boxes via the Colors palette **(Figure 53)**. To use the Cool Blends XTension, it must be in the QuarkXPress folder when the program is launched.

To create a cool blend, follow the instructions on pages 147-148. For step 5, choose a cool blend option from the pop-up menu on the Colors palette.

✔ Tip

■ To render blends on screen without banding, check the Accurate Blends box in the General Preferences dialog box, opened from the Edit menu. The screen redraw speed is slower when this option is checked.

Replace a deleted color

If you delete a color via the Colors dialog box that has been applied to any element in the active document, a prompt will appear. Select a replacement color from the "Replace with" pop-up menu **(Figure 54)**.

Chapter 15

Copy, paste, duplicate linked boxes

In Version 3.2, you can copy, paste, or duplicate a linked text box. You can also drag-copy a linked box between documents or into a library. Text preceding the box in the chain will not be copied, but overflow text will.

Linked boxes in a group or multiple selection can be copied using any method described in the previous paragraph, as long as *all* the boxes in the chain are in the group or multiple selection.

Chapter 19

Collect for output

If you send a document to a service provider, you must also send the picture files used in the document. You also need to supply information about the document, such as its name, date, dimensions, and fonts used. The Collect for Output command gathers all these elements together automatically.

1. With a document active, select Collect for Output from the File menu **(Figure 55)**. If any picture files are missing, a prompt will appear. Click List Files to update them *(see page 120)*.

(see page 120)

If you modified the document after saving it, a prompt will appear. Click Save or Don't Save **(Figure 56)**.

2. Click Desktop or choose another location for the folder.

3. Click New Folder **(Figure 57)**.

4. *Optional:* Modify the folder name **(Figure 58)**.

5. Click Create.

6. *Optional:* Modify the Report Name.

7. Click Collect.

8. A folder containing the current document, associated picture files, and a detailed report file will appear in the location you chose.

✔ Tip

■ If you make a PostScript file of your document, your service provider will not need your original picture files. First prepare your document as per your service provider's instructions. Click PostScript® File in the Print dialog box, choose a location for the file, enter a name, then click Save.

You should also send along the "live" (non-PostScript) file, just in case, and send the report file generated by the Collect for Output command so your service provider will know which fonts you used.

Figure 55. *Choose* **Collect for Output** *from the* **File** *menu.*

Figure 56. *If you modified the document after saving it, this prompt will appear. Click* **Save** *or* **Don't Save**.

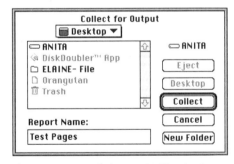

Figure 57. *First click* **New Folder** *in the* **Collect for Output** *dialog box, then later click* **Collect**.

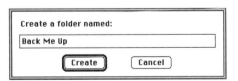

Figure 58. *Rename the folder, if desired, then click* **Create**.

Collect for Output

Output request template

After using the Collect for Output command, you can flow the report file into the Output Request template.

1. Open the Output Request template located in the QuarkXPress folder.

2. Select Save As from the File menu, rename the file, then click Save.

3. Fill out the top portion of the Electronic Output Request **(Figure 59)**.

4. Select the Content tool.

5. Click on the text box on the bottom of page 1.

6. Select Get Text from the File menu.

7. Locate and select the report file.

8. Click Open. New pages will be added automatically to accommodate the text.

9. Print the document and give it to your service provider, along with your computer file.

Fill out the top portion of page 1.

ELECTRONIC OUTPUT REQUEST

CLIENT INFORMATION
Contact Person: _____
Company: _____
Address: _____
City, ST, Zip: _____
Office Phone: _____
Home Phone: _____

DELIVERY INFORMATION
__ Deliver   __ Hold For Pickup   __ Call When Complete
Delivery Address: _____
City, ST, Zip: _____

TURNAROUND INFORMATION
__ Normal   __ Rush   __ Emergency

FONT INFORMATION
__ Adobe/Linotype   __ Font Company   __ Agfa Compugraphic
__ Bitstream   __ Monotype

COPYRIGHT INFORMATION
All that appears on the enclosed medium (including, but not limited to, floppy disk, modem transmission, removable media) is unencumbered by copyrights. We, the customer, have full rights to reproduce the supplied content.
Signature: _____
Date: _____

OUTPUT MEDIA (CHECK ALL THAT APPLY)
__ Film   __ RC Paper   __ Color Proof
__ Laser Print   __ Color Slides
__ Negative   -or-   __ Positive
__ Emulsion Down -or-   __ Emulsion Up

OUTPUT SPECIFICATION
__ Output All Pages
__ Output The Following Specified Pages.
From: _____ To: _____

CROP MARKS
__ Yes   __ No

RESOLUTION/DPI
__ 1200/1270   __ 2400/2540   __ 3000+

SCREEN RULING/LPI
__ 65   __ 85   __ 120
__ 133   __ 150

COLOR SEPARATION PLATES
__ Cyan   __ Magenta   __ Yellow   __ Black

COLOR PROOF SPECIFICATION
__ Proof All Pages
__ Proof The Following Specified Pages.
From: _____ To: _____

LASER PROOF PROVIDED WITH JOB?
__ Yes   __ No

OTHER INFORMATION
Type information about the job here.

QUARK REPORT
@doc info: Source Pathname: ANITA: QUARK 3.2 UPGRADE:GAMMA 3.2 DOCUMENTS:Quark 3.2
Destination Pathname: ANITA:Desktop Folder:Report folder:
Last modified: 12:23 PM; 7/7/93
Document Size: 116K
Most recently saved version: 3.20G2
Document has been saved by the following versions of QuarkXPress:
     3.20G1
     3.20G2
Total Pages: 2
Page Width: 51p
Page Height: 66p

REQUIRED XTENSIONS:
Cool Blends

ELECTRONIC OUTPUT REQUEST FOR: YOUR COMPANY NAME HERE   PAGE 2

ACTIVE XTENSIONS:
Kern/Track Editor;   Cool Blends 1.23;   Multiple Master Utilities (3.2);   Xstyle™ 1.5

DOCUMENT FONTS
EXTERNAL NAME	INTERNAL NAME	PS FILENAME
I Garamond LightItalic	Garamond-LightItalic	GaramLigIta
Garamond	Garamond-Light	GaramLig
Kuenstler Script Black	KuenstlerScript-Black	KuensScrBla
Helvetica	Helvetica	Helve
Lucida	Lucida	Lucid
BauerBodoni	BauerBodoni-Roman	BauerBodRom
Blk ITCKabel Book	ItcKabel-Book	ItcKabBoo
Futura Book	Futura-Book	FuturBoo

PICTURE FONTS
PICTURE	EXTERNAL NAME
Blends EPS	No fonts used.

GRAPHICS
(EDGE VALUES MEASURED FROM TOP-LEFT OF PAGE.) PATHNAME

TYPE	PAGE	SIZE	BOX ANGLE	PIC ANGLE	SKEW	XSCALE	YSCALE	TOP EDGE	LEFT EDGE	DPI	TYPE
ANITA: QUARK 3.2 UPGRADE:Appendix C 3.2:Blends EPS											
EPSF	2	42K	0°	0°	0°	100%	100%	21p9	25p9.723		
ANITA: QUARK 3.2 UPGRADE:Appendix C 3.2:Flip Horizontal											
PICT	2	38K	0°	0°	0°	100%	100%	20p3	24p3.723		
ANITA: QUARK 3.2 UPGRADE:Appendix C 3.2:Colors palette-blends											
PICT	2	24K	0°	0°	0°	100%	100%	7p5.49	26p6.962		

STYLE SHEETS
Normal
Subheads
Body Text
Captions
Chapter #s

H AND J'S
Standard

COLORS
     Black
     Blue
     Cyan
     Registration
     White
     Yellow

TRAPPING (UNLESS NOTED, COLORS ARE TRAPPED AUTOMATICALLY)
     Trapping Preferences Information:
     Auto Method: Absolute
     Auto Amount: 0.144 pt
     Indeterminate: 0.144 pt
     Overprint Limit: 95%
     Ignore White: On
     Process Trap: On

COLOR PLATES
Black

Figure 59. *Import the **report file** into the bottom box.*

Output Request Template

Suppress printing

You can suppress printing of any picture using the Picture Usage dialog box.

1. Select Picture Usage from the Utilities menu.

2. Click a check mark in the Print column to suppress printing of that picture **(Figure 60)**. (Click again to turn printing back on.)

3. Click the Close box in the upper left corner when you are finished.

Figure 60. *Click a check mark in the **Print** column to suppress printing of that picture.*

Low-resolution printing

A document containing a large, high-resolution picture may take a long time to print. To speed printing, select Low Resolution from the Output pop-up menu in the Print dialog box **(Figure 61)**. The low-resolution version of the picture that is part of the QuarkXPress file will print instead of the original picture file.

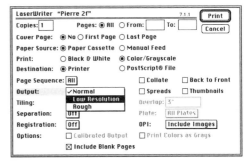

Figure 61. *Select **Low Resolution** from the **Output** pop-up menu in the **Print** dialog box. (Several radio buttons have been replaced with pop-up menus in this dialog box.)*

Print status

In Version 3.2, a Print Status box will appear automatically while your document is printing **(Figure 62)**. To disable Print Status, hold down Shift as you click the Print button. (In Version 3.1, a Print Status box will appear if you hold down Shift and click Print.)

✔ Tip

■ If the number of fonts used in your document exceeds printer memory (an error message will appear when you try to print), select Page Setup from the File menu, check the Options box, then check the "Unlimited Downloadable Fonts in a Document" box. Printing much slower with this option on. A better solution is to buy more RAM for your printer.

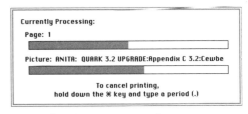

Figure 62. *The **Print Status** box opens automatically while a document is printing.*

The EfiColor XTension

This is a brief introduction to the EfiColor XTension. For more information, consult your QuarkXPress documentation.

What is the EfiColor XTension?

The EfiColor XTension is a color management system created by EFI (Electronics for Imaging, Inc.). It makes color rendering more consistent from device to device — monitor to **digital color printer*** to **imagesetter**. The EfiColor XTension will make the screen display of a picture and a digital color proof of the same picture look more like the final print. (Perfect color matching is impossible, however, due to inherent limitations of each hardware device.)

How does the EfiColor XTension work?

The rendering of **color objects** in a QuarkXPress document is *device dependent,* because every hardware device — scanner, monitor, and printer — interprets and renders color differently, depending on manufacturer specifications.

The EfiColor XTension uses precise color definitions developed by the Commission Internationale de l'Eclairage (CIE) to standardize color rendering and output from different hardware devices. The EfiColor XTension relates all devices to the CIE standard to make color rendering *device independent.*

The EfiColor XTension uses **device profiles** for various scanner, monitor, and printer models that contain information about how each device defines color and what colors it can read, display, or print. By assigning each color object a device profile and a **rendering style**, the EfiColor XTension can perform a **color transformation** that takes into account the differences between devices. A profile and rendering style can be assigned to a picture in another application or in QuarkXPress.

**Boldface words are defined in the glossary (left).*

EFICOLOR GLOSSARY

COLOR OBJECT
A color picture or an item (text box, picture box, frame, or line) to which color has been applied.

COLOR TRANSFORMATION
The translation of colors from the color space of one device to the color space of another device.

DIGITAL COLOR PRINTER
A device that produces composite color "proofs" from computer files. Thermal wax, color laser, inkjet, and dye sublimation are types of digital color printers. The IRIS SmartJet, Fiery/Canon CLC 500, and QMS ColorScript are digital color printers.

DEVICE PROFILE
The color information for a particular output device.

GAMUT
The range of colors a device is capable of rendering or printing.

IMAGESETTER
A high-resolution device that produces paper or film output. The Linotronic and Scitex/Dolev are imagesetters.

RENDERING STYLE
The method for translating colors from one gamut to another. Photographic rendering preserves the relative range of colors. Solid Color renders a color exactly if it falls within the gamut of the target output device and substitutes the closest match if it is "out-of-gamut."

Each device has a different **gamut**. The EfiColor XTension automaticaly transforms colors in an object if they fall outside the gamut of a target output device. The EfiColor XTension performs color transformations for RGB TIFF, CMYK TIFF, and PICT picture files.

If you create a color in QuarkXPress that is "out of gamut" for your target output device, the EfiColor XTension will display a Gamut Alarm. You can substitute a printable color.

To use the EfiColor XTension, it must be in the QuarkXPress folder when the application is launched. A core group of color profiles for monitors, scanners and printers is included with the EfiColor XTension. You can obtain other profiles from EFI or an EFI reseller.

Note: Pictures may take longer to import and print when the EfiColor XTension is on.

The first step in color management is to select your monitor profile so color rendering on your screen will more closely match output color. The EfiColor XTension will not calibrate your monitor. For the best results, calibrate your monitor using an external calibration device and maintain consistent lighting conditions.

To choose a monitor profile:

1. Select Application from the Preferences pop-up menu under the Edit menu **(Figure 63)**.

2. Check the Display Correction box **(Figure 64)**.

3. Select the EfiColor monitor profile for your monitor. Ask EFI which profile to use if your monitor model is not listed.

4. Click OK or press Return. This setting only affects screen color. It does not affect print output.

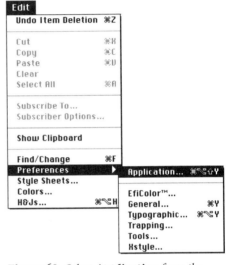

Figure 63. *Select **Application** from the **Preferences** pop-up menu under the **Edit** menu.*

Figure 64. *In the **Application Preferences** dialog box, check the **Display Correction** box and choose a **monitor profile** from the pop-up menu.*

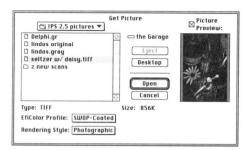

Figure 65. *In the **Get Picture** dialog box, select an **EfiColor Profile** and **Rendering Style**.*

If a picture was not "tagged" with an EfiColor profile in another application, you can assign a profile to it as you import it. The EfiColor XTension can convert a CMYK TIFF, RGB TIFF, or PICT file. EPS, OPI, and DCS picture files are not convertible.

To assign a profile/rendering style when importing a picture:

1. Select the Content tool.

2. Click on a picture box.

3. Select Get Picture from the File menu.

4. Select a color picture **(Figure 65)**.

5. Select your final output device from the EfiColor Profile pop-up menu.

If the profile name is underlined, the picture is already tagged and the EfiColor XTension has chosen the correct profile.

If the profile name is gray, the profile assigned to the picture is not available in your system.

6. Select Photographic from the Rendering Style pop-up menu for a continuous tone photograph to preserve its relative color range.
or
Select Solid Color for more exact color matching — if the picture contains matching system colors (Trumatch, Pantone, etc.), for example, or is a CMYK TIFF.

7. Click Open.

✔ Tip

■ If you don't know which EfiColor Profile to choose, leave the default selection as is.

EfiColor XTension

You can assign a profile to a TIFF or PICT that is already in QuarkXPress.

To assign a profile/rendering style to a picture in Quark:

1. Select the Content tool.

2. Click on a color picture.

3. Select Profile from the Style menu **(Figure 66)**.

4. Select an EfiColor Profile.

5. Select a Rendering Style **(Figure 67)**.

6. Click OK or press Return.

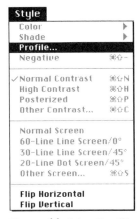

Figure 66. *Select* **Profile** *from the* **Style** *menu.*

When you mix a color, you can use the Gamut Alarm to determine if it is within the gamut for your target output device.

To use the Gamut Alarm:

1. Create a new color or open the Edit Color dialog box for an existing color. *(See pages 143-144)*

2. In the Edit Color dialog box, check the Gamut Alarm box **(Figure 68)**.

3. Choose your target output device from the Target pop-up menu.

4. If the color is out-of-gamut, an exclamation point will appear next to it. A slash mark through a Pantone, Focoltone, or Trumatch swatch indicates that color is out-of-gamut. You can change the CMYK percentages or choose a different color.

5. For a process color (Process Separation on), select a Rendering Style. Select Solid Color to exactly match an in-gamut color. Photographic may produce better results for an out-of-gamut color.

6. Click OK.

7. Click Save.

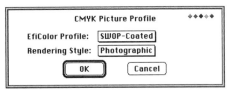

Figure 67. *Select an* **EfiColor Profile** *and/or* **Rendering Style** *in the* **Picture Profile** *dialog box. (If you select an RGB picture, this box will be labeled "RGB Picture Profile.")*

This line bounds the gamut of printable color for the currently selected color Model. Few RGB colors are printable.

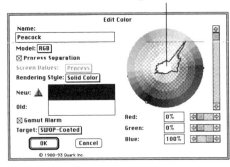

Figure 68. *In the* **Edit Color** *dialog box, check the* **Gamut Alarm** *box, and choose your target output device from the* **Target** *pop-up menu.*

Figure 69. *In the **Page Setup** dialog box, select a **Printer Type** and **EfiColor Profile**.*

GCR

GCR (short for Gray Component Replacement) is the replacement of a percentage of Cyan, Magenta, and Yellow inks with black ink. GCR lowers printing costs and produces richer blacks.

If the EfiColor Profile you chose involves color separations, select a Gray Component Replacement percentage from the GCR pop-up menu. Ask your print shop which setting to use. GCR only affects RGB pictures the EfiColor XTension converts to CMYK. Imported CMYK pictures are not affected by this setting.

The EfiColor XTension improves image-setter and digital color printer output. Make sure you select the appropriate Printer Type and EfiColor Profile in the Page Setup dialog box. Make sure you also select the correct printer in the Chooser (opened from the Apple menu) if you are printing in-house.

To prepare a document for a PostScript printer:

1. Select Page Setup from the File menu.

2. Select your target output device from the Printer Type pop-up menu **(Figure 69)**.

3. Select the profile for that output device from the EfiColor Profile pop-up menu. If you select None, the EfiColor XTension will not transform colors for this printout.

4. If you selected a color printer from the Printer Type pop-up menu, the box in the lower right corner of the dialog box will be labeled Use EfiColor Screen Values. Check this box to use EfiColor XTension screen angles. Uncheck this box to use default QuarkXPress screen angles.

If you selected a black-and-white printer or imagesetter from the Printer Type pop-up menu, the same box will be labeled Use PDF Screen Values. Check this box to use printer-defined screen angles. Uncheck to use default QuarkXPress screen angles.

Consult with your service provider regarding screen angle settings.

5. Click OK or press Return. Your document is ready for printing.

EfiColor XTension

If you try to print a document that uses an assigned profile that is not available in your system, a prompt will appear. You can assign a different profile using the Missing Profiles dialog box.

To replace profiles for printing:

1. Select Print from the File menu.

2. Click Print. If there is a missing profile in your system, a prompt will appear. Click List Profiles.

3. In the Missing Profiles dialog box, click "Pictures" in the Objects column.

4. To replace all occurrences of the missing profile, click Replace All.
or
To replace profiles one picture at a time, click Show First, then click Replace.

5. Select an EfiColor Profile (**Figure 70**).

6. Select a Rendering Style, if necessary.

7. Click OK or press Return.

8. If you are replacing profiles one picture at a time, click Show Next and repeat steps 5-7 until you have replaced all the profiles.

9. Click OK.

✔ Tips

■ If you open a document with missing profiles, a prompt will appear. If you click OK, the Profile Usage dialog box will open (**Figure 71**). You can also open the Profile Usage dialog box directly from the Utilities menu.

■ If you click Replace All, then select the Photographic Rendering Style, that style will be used for any object with the same EfiColor Profile.

■ If you click OK (instead of List Profiles) when the prompt appears, the default profiles selected in the EfiColor Preferences dialog box will be used.

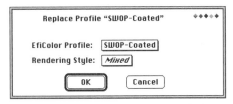

Figure 70. *In the **Replace Profile** dialog box, select an **EfiColor Profile** and/or **Rendering Style**.*

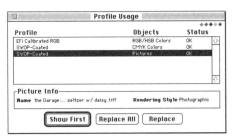

Figure 71. *Click **Pictures** in the **Profile Usage** dialog box.*

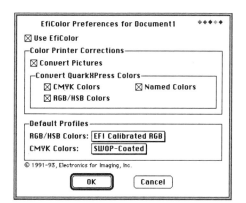

Figure 72. *In the **EfiColor Preferences** dialog box, check the **Use EfiColor** box to turn on the EfiColor XTension, then choose **Color Printer Correction** and **Default Profile** options.*

Save Page as EPS

If you open the Save Page as EPS dialog box when the EfiColor XTension is enabled, you can choose an output device from the Target pop-up menu. Once you click Save, the Target of the EPS file cannot be changed. To assign a different Target, create a new EPS file from the original Quark-XPress document.
(See pages 112 and 189)

Follow these instructions to turn on the EfiColor XTension or to change default settings. The default settings you select will be used for a picture only if it does not have an assigned profile. You can assign a non-default profile to an individual picture or color *(see page 214)*.

To set EfiColor preferences:

1. Select EfiColor from the Preferences pop-up menu under the Edit menu.

2. Check the Use EfiColor box to turn on the EfiColor XTension **(Figure 72)**.

3. Check the Convert Pictures box to have the EfiColor XTension transform TIFF and PICT pictures.

4. Check the QuarkXPress color models you wish to have transformed — colors created in QuarkXPress. TRUMATCH and FOCOLTONE colors are CMYK colors. PANTONE spot colors are Named Colors.

5. Select the Default RGB/HSB Profile that corresponds to your monitor.

6. Select the Default CMYK Profile that corresponds to your target output device.

7. Click OK or press Return.

✓ Tip

■ EfiColor Preferences selected with no document open will be the default settings for subsequently created documents. Settings chosen with a document open will apply to that document only.

EfiColor XTension

For information about **Quark XTensions**, call **XChange 800-788-7557**. Outside the U.S. 303-229-0656.

Appendix D: **QuarkXPress 3.3**

> 'After that I suppose we shall have pretty nearly finished rubbing off each other's angles,' he reflected; but the worst of it was that May's pressure was already bearing on the very angles whose sharpness he most wanted to keep.
>
> *Edith Wharton*

Figure 1. *Click on a text box.*

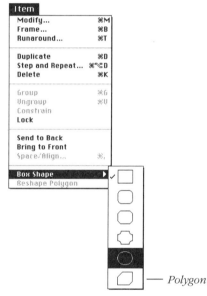

Figure 2. *Choose any shape from the **Box Shape** pop-up menu under the **Item** menu.*

QUARK**XP**RESS **3.3** incorporates a few new features and a few improvements to existing features. For example, you can now create non-rectangular text shapes, you can use a shortcut to deselect multiple items, and you can choose from two new spot color models — Toyo and DIC. The Document Layout palette has also been slightly altered from Version 3.2.

There are several improvements in picture handling. If you import an EPS picture with spot colors, those colors are automatically appended to the Colors palette in the QuarkXPress document. You can apply a Shade percentage to a grayscale TIFF. And you can import a picture in the JPEG or PCX file format if the corresponding filter is installed.

Chapter 5

To create a non-rectangular text shape:

1. Select the Item or Content tool.

2. Click on a text box **(Figure 1)**.

3. Choose any shape from the Box Shape pop-up menu under the Item menu **(Figures 2-3)**.

(Instructions for reshaping a polygonal text shape are on the following page)

> 'After that I suppose we shall have pretty nearly finished rubbing off each other's angles,' he reflected; but the worst of it was that May's pressure was already bearing on the very angles whose sharpness he most wanted to keep.
>
> *Wharton*

Figure 3. *An oval text box with a 5 pt. Text Inset.*

Text Shapes

To reshape a polygonal text shape:

1. Select the Item or Content tool.

2. Click on a polygonal text shape.

3. Choose Reshape Polygon from the Item menu **(Figure 4)**.

4. Press and drag a handle or line segment **(Figure 5)**.

or

Hold down Command (⌘) and click on a handle to delete it.

or

Hold down Command (⌘) and click on a line segment to add a handle.

(Figures 6-7)

✔ Tips

■ For the most uniform text fill, justify the text and choose a small point size relative to the box.

■ If the Vertical Alignment of a rectangular text box is Centered, Bottom, or Justified and you then convert it to a non-rectangular shape other than a polygon, the Vertical Alignment will revert to Top. You cannot change the Vertical Alignment of a non-rectangular text box. If you reshape a polygonal text box, its Vertical Alignment reverts to Top.

Figure 4. *Choose **Reshape Polygon** from the **Item** menu.*

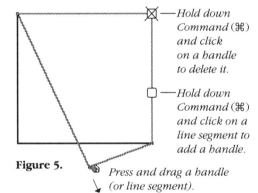

Hold down Command (⌘) and click on a handle to delete it.

Hold down Command (⌘) and click on a line segment to add a handle.

Figure 5. *Press and drag a handle (or line segment).*

'After that I suppose we shall have pretty nearly finished rubbing off each other's angles,' he reflected; but the worst of it was that May's pressure was already bearing on the very angles whose sharpness he most wanted to keep.

Figure 6. *A reshaped polygonal text box with a frame.*

'After that I suppose we shall have pretty nearly finished rubbing off each other's angles,' he reflected; but the worst of it was that May's pressure was already bearing on the very angles whose sharpness he most wanted to keep.

Figure 7. *A reshaped polygonal text box with no frame.*

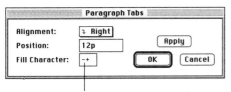

Figure 8. *You can enter one or two characters in the **Fill Character** field in the **Tabs** dialog box.*

Steamed vegetable dumplings 3.50	
Shrimp rolls 4.00	
Steamed vegetable dumplings - - - - - - - 3.50	
Shrimp rolls - - - - - - - - - - - - - - - 4.00	

Figure 9. *To create a dot leader with extra space between the dots, enter a period and a space in the **Fill Character** field. To create a dashed line with extra space between the dashes, enter a hyphen and a space.*

Chapter 7

Two-character tab leader

You can enter any two characters in the Fill Character field in the Paragraph Tabs dialog box **(Figures 8-9)**. (In previous versions, only one character could be entered.)

Chapter 9

EPS spot colors

When you import an EPS picture into a QuarkXPress 3.3 document, spot colors from the picture are automatically appended to the document's Colors palette. (In previous versions, if you imported an EPS picture containing a spot color, to color separate the picture, you had to create a spot color with the same name in the QuarkXPress document.)

✔ Tip

■ Hold down Command (⌘) as you click Open in the Get Picture dialog box to *prevent* colors from being imported with an EPS picture.

Tab Leaders; EPS Spot Colors

To apply a shade to a grayscale TIFF:

1. Select the Content tool.

2. Click on a grayscale picture **(Figure 10)**.

3. If the Colors palette is not already open, choose Show Colors from the View menu.

4. Click the picture icon on the Colors palette **(Figure 11)**.

5. Click a color name.

6. Choose a shade percentage **(Figure 12)**.

✓ Tip

■ You can also choose a percentage from the Shade pop-up menu under the Style menu.

Figure 10. *The original picture.*

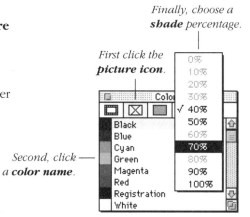

First click the **picture icon**.

Second, click a **color name**.

Finally, choose a **shade** *percentage.*

Figure 11. *The* **Colors** *palette.*

XTension folder

In QuarkXPress 3.3, filters and XTensions can be installed in the QuarkXPress folder on the same level as the application, or in a folder labeled "XTension," which will be created automatically when you install version 3.3 (do not rename this folder).

Import JPEG or PCX picture

You can import a picture in the JPEG (Joint Photographic Experts Group) or PCX (from the PC platform) file format if the corresponding filter is installed in the QuarkXPress folder or the new XTension folder.

Figure 12. *The same picture in a lighter shade.*

Shade a Grayscale TIFF

*To duplicate a master page, click the master page icon, then click the **duplicate** icon.*

*To delete a document or master page, click its icon, then click the **delete** icon.*

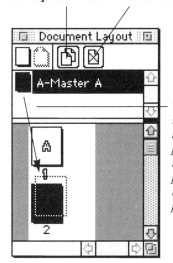

*To **apply** a master page to a document page, drag the master page icon over the document page icon.*

Figure 13. *The **Document Layout** palette.*

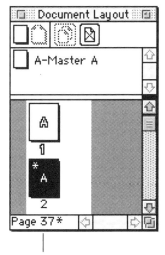

Figure 14. *The applied **section number** of the highlighted document page icon. Click this number to open the **Section** dialog box.*

Chapter 12

Document Layout palette

The Document Layout palette is changed again! *(The QuarkXPress version 3.2 equivalents for these functions are discussed on pages 138-140)*

- As in QuarkXPress versions prior to 3.2, you can apply a master page to a document page by dragging the master page icon over the document page icon **(Figure 13)**.

- To duplicate a master page, click on the icon of the master page you wish to duplicate, then click on the duplicate icon **(Figure 13)**.

- To delete a document or master page, click on its icon, then click on the delete icon **(Figure 13)**.

- If you click on a document page icon that has an applied section page number, that number will appear in the lower left corner of the Document Layout palette. To open the Section dialog box, click on the section number **(Figure 14)**.

Document Layout Palette

Chapter 13
Toyo and DIC spot colors

You can choose from two new spot color matching system models: Toyo and DIC **(Figure 15)**. Toyo and DIC inks are used in Japan.

An asterisk next to a Toyo or DIC color number indicates that the appearance of the color on screen differs from the same color when it is printed. Two asterisks indicate an even greater discrepancy.
(Instructions for creating a spot color are on pages 141-142)

✓ Tip
■ Ask your print shop if they can mix Toyo or DIC inks before choosing from either color model.

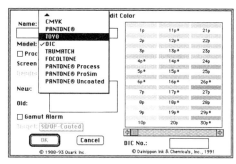

Figure 15. *In the **Edit Color** dialog box, you can choose from two Japanese matching system models: **Toyo** and **DIC**.*

Chapter 15
Undo multiple-item deletion

If you delete a group or choose Delete when more than one item is selected, you can choose the Undo command from the Edit menu.

✓ Tips
■ If you delete multiple text boxes that are linked to other text boxes that you don't delete, a prompt will warn you that the links to and from the deleted boxes cannot be reestablished using the Undo command **(Figure 16)**. If you delete *all* the text boxes in a linked chain and then choose the Undo command, the entire chain will be restored.

■ The layering position of the deleted items may be different when they reappear.

Deselect multiple items

To quickly deselect all currently selected items, select the Item tool, then press Tab.

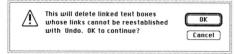

Figure 16. *This prompt will appear if you delete multiple linked text boxes but don't delete all the boxes in the chain.*

Zapf Dingbats font

Key	Zapf	Shift	Option	Option Shift	Key	Zapf	Shift	Option	Option Shift
A	❁	✡	{	)	Y	❘	✳	⑨	▶
B	❂	⊹	❺	➪	Z	❙	✴	❽	➾
C	✳	⊹	}	(	1	☞	✂	②	➚
D	❄	✜	❶	➬	2	☛	✠	♥	➙
E	❅	✛	♠		3	✓	✄	❣	➝
F	❆	◆	⑤	➩	4	✔	✁	❢	→
G	✳	✧	◆	➦	5	✗	☎	⑤	➛
H	✣	★	➡	➮	6	✘	✿	♥	➟
I	✤	☆	✒		7	✗	©	☙	➠
J	✼	✪	⑦	➱	8	✘	☜	❀	❡
K	❊	✩	➤		9	✚	✈	❻	➡
L	●	✫	③	➫	0	✎	✉	❼	➢
M	○	✬	⑩	➥	`	✿	✾	❀	
N	■	✭	✤		-	✍	✿	❼	❽
O	❑	✮	⑩	④	=	†	☞	②	⑥
P	❐	✯	❹	❸	[	✳	‘	⑨	⑩
Q	❒	✽	❻	❺	]	✳	"	→	→
R	❏	✺	♣	➤	\	✳	’	⑧	⑨
S	▲	✲	❧	➪	;	✛	✚	⑩	➲
T	▼	✴			'	♻	✂	❾	③
U	◆	✳	①		,	✌	✣	⑦	➾
V	❖	✦	④	↕	.	✏	✞	⑧	➶
W	❥	✱	❷	➢	/	✐	✟	↔	①
X	❘	✳	⑥	⇒	Space bar			❶	❶

Special characters

¡	Option **1**	©	Option **g**	Σ	Option **w**
/	Option Shift **1**	"	Option Shift **g**	„	Option Shift **w**
™	Option **2**	·	Option **h**	≈	Option **x**
¤	Option Shift **2**	Ó	Option Shift **h**	˛	Option Shift **x**
£	Option **3**	î	Option **i**, *then* **i** (a,e,o,u)	¥	Option **y**
‹	Option Shift **3**	^	Option Shift **i**	Á	Option Shift **y**
¢	Option **4**	Δ	Option **j**	Ω	Option **z**
›	Option Shift **4**	Ô	Option Shift **j**	¸	Option Shift **z**
∞	Option **5**	°	Option **k**	à	Option `, *then* **a** (e,i,o,u)
fi	Option Shift **5**		Option Shift **k**	`	Option Shift `
§	Option **6**	¬	Option **l**	–	Option -
fl	Option Shift **6**	Ò	Option Shift **l**	—	Option Shift -
¶	Option **7**	µ	Option **m**	≠	Option =
‡	Option Shift **7**	Â	Option Shift **m**	±	Option Shift =
•	Option **8**	ñ	Option **n**, *then* **n** (or a, o)	"	Option [
°	Option Shift **8**	~	Option Shift **n**	"	Option Shift [
ª	Option **9**	ø	Option **o**	'	Option]
·	Option Shift **9**	Ø	Option Shift **o**	'	Option Shift]
º	Option **0**	π	Option **p**	«	Option \
‚	Option Shift **0**	∏	Option Shift **p**	»	Option Shift \
å	Option **a**	œ	Option **q**	…	Option ;
Å	Option Shift **a**	Œ	Option Shift **q**	Ú	Option Shift ;
∫	Option **b**	®	Option **r**	æ	Option '
ı	Option Shift **b**	‰	Option Shift **r**	Æ	Option Shift '
ç	Option **c**	ß	Option **s**	≤	Option ,
Ç	Option Shift **c**	Í	Option Shift **s**	¯	Option Shift ,
∂	Option **d**	†	Option **t**	≥	Option .
Î	Option Shift **d**	ˇ	Option Shift **t**	˘	Option Shift .
é	Option **e**, *then* **e** (a,i,o,u)	ü	Option **u**, *then* **u** (a,e,i,o)	÷	Option /
´	Option Shift **e**	¨	Option Shift **u**	¿	Option Shift /
ƒ	Option **f**	√	Option **v**		
Ï	Option Shift **f**	◊	Option Shift **v**		

Index

Index

*Do you have any
comments, compliments,
or corrections that
you'd like to share
with the author?*

Elaine Weinmann
*c/o Peachpit Press
2414 Sixth Street
Berkeley, CA 94710*

More from Peachpit Press

Beyond the Mac is not a typewriter

Robin Williams

Think of this as the typography equivalent of Strunk and White's The Elements of Style. Expanding upon the content of its phenomenally popular predecessor The Mac is not a typewriter, this little book not only defines the principles governing type but explains the logic behind them, to help you see and understand what looks best and why. Armed with this knowledge, and putting into practice the secrets best-selling author Robin Williams reveals for making type readable and artistic, you can then go on to create beautiful, sophisticated, professional-looking pages on your computer. *$16.95 (224 pages)*

Elements of Web Design

Darcy DiNucci, Maria Giudice, and Lynne Stiles

This book introduces graphic designers to the opportunities and pitfalls of Web design. *Elements of Web Design* includes chapters on every step of assembling pages — from practical issues, such as pulling together a team with the appropriate skills and creating contracts to reflect the ever-changing nature of Web pages, to the technical and design issues involved in creating HTML, graphics, and interactivity. *$39.95 (208 pages)*

Home Sweet Home Page

Robin Williams and Dave Mark

Best-selling authors Robin Williams and Dave Mark have teamed up to bring you this family-and-friends approach to creating personal Web sites and using them as a collaborative, interactive, and inexpensive means to stay in touch. WIth a clear, non-technical approach and extensive illustrations, this books offers design examples and ideas you can use to create professional-looking Web pages with personal flair. *$14.95 (184 pages)*

The Illustrator 6 Wow! Book

Sharon Steuer

This new edition of the best-selling Illustrator Wow! Book includes eye-catching and time-saving techniques and tips for beginning through advanced users of Adobe Illustrator. The works of over 70 of the country's best Illustrator artists are included. The content throughout is updated to cover the latest features and techniques in Illustrator 6, which include: new import capabilities, such as direct import of TIFF, Photoshop, and EPS files; new production features, including the ability to interpret any PostScript file and built-in color separation; improved integration with Photoshop and other Adobe products; and new tools, filters, and palettes. The book is now accompanied by a CD-ROM packed with demo versions of Illustrator 6, Photoshop 3, all major plug-in filters, Illustrator tutorials, and many more specially-created goodies collected or created by the author. *$39.95 224 pages (w/ CD-ROM)*

The Macintosh Bible, 6th Edition

Edited by Jeremy Judson

This classic reference book is now completely updated. *The Macintosh Bible, 6th Edition* is crammed with tips, tricks, and shortcuts that will help you to get the most out of your Mac. Written by 12 of the top writers in computer journalism, The Macintosh Bible tackles every subject area with a clear vision of what Macintosh users need to know in an engaging, no-nonsense style. Use it to find the right Mac, printer, monitor, and hard disk. Discover when and how to upgrade your system, how to protect your data, and what to do when disaster strikes. Get the latest on fonts, word processing, spreadsheets, graphics, desktop publishing, data bases, communications, utilities, multimedia, games, and more—and benefit from hundreds of practical tips. *$29.95 (1,009 pages)*

The Painter 4 Wow! Book

Cher Threinen-Pendarvis

This full-color volume uses hundreds of stunning, original illustrations depicting Painter 4's full range of styles and effects. Step-by-step descriptions clearly explain how each piece was created. Users of all levels will find these techniques easy to integrate in their own work. The dual-platform CD includes custom brushes and textures, stock photos, video clips, filters, and demo software. *$44.95 (264 pages)*

Photoshop 4 for Macintosh: Visual QuickStart Guide

Elaine Weinmann and Peter Lourekas

Completely revised for Photoshop 4, this indispensible guide is ideal for Mac users who want to get started in Adobe Photoshop without having to wade through long-winded explanations. *Photoshop 4 for Macintosh* uses illustrated, step-by-step examples to cover Photoshop fundamentals, including how to use masks, filters, colors, and more. *$19.95 (326 pages)*

The QuarkXPress Book, 4th Edition (Mac Edition)

David Blatner and Eric Taub

This is the highest rated, most comprehensive, and best-selling QuarkXPress book ever published. Now totally updated to cover the newest version, this book is made for easy access, including a handy tear-out keystroke shortcut card. You'll find valuable information on XTensions, EfiColor, AppleEvent scripting and more. Winner of the 1991 Benjamin Franklin Award (computer book category). *$29.95 (784 pages)*

QuarkXPress Tips & Tricks, 2nd Edition

David Blatner, Phil Gaskill, and Eric Taub

The smartest, most useful shortcuts from *The QuarkXPress Book*—plus many more—are packed into this book. You'll find answers to common questions as well as insights on techniques that will show you how to become a QuarkXPress power user. Includes a CD-ROM with useful XTensions and demos. *$34.95 (448 pages, w/CD-ROM)*

Real World Photoshop 4

David Blatner and Bruce Fraser

Here's the only book that explicitly covers the production issues Photoshop users face daily. Using simple language, it details the essential concepts and techniques for producing great-looking images quickly and efficiently. Fully updated to cover every new feature of Photoshop 4, including Actions and Adjustments layers. *$39.95 (672 pages)*

Real World Scanning and Halftones

David Blatner and Steve Roth

Master the digital halftone process—from scanning images, to tweaking them on your computer, to imagesetting them. Learn about optical character recognition, gamma control, sharpening, PostScript halftones, Photo CD, and image-manipulating applications like Photoshop and PhotoStyler. *$24.95 (296 pages)*

Start with a Scan

Janet Ashford and John Odam

Start with a Scan shows designers and illustrators how to transform raw scanned images into high-quality finished illustrations. Using gorgeous, full-color illustrations, this book will give you step-by-step instructions on how to take a scan of almost anything and turn it into beautiful art, using programs like Photoshop, FreeHand, and Illustrator. *$34.95 (144 pages)*

Web Graphics, Tools, and Techniques

Peter Kentie

This richly illustrated book is an indispensable resource for Web site creators who need to master a variety of authoring and graphics tools. It covers basic web concepts in addition to the specifics of formatting graphics, text, and tables with HTML. Next, it moves deeper into graphics techniques and tools, explaining the use of Photoshop, Painter, Poser, KPT Welder, GIF Construction Set, and Director. Also covers tables, clickable maps, 3-D images, and user interaction. *$39.95 (320 pages)*

Order Form

USA **800-283-9444** • **510-548-4393** • FAX **510-548-5991**
CANADA **800-387-8028** • **416-447-1779** • FAX **800-456-0536** OR **416-443-0948**
WEB **http://www.peachpit.com**

Qty	Title	Price	Total
	SUBTOTAL		
	ADD APPLICABLE SALES TAX*		
	SHIPPING		
	TOTAL		

Shipping is by UPS ground: $4 for first item, $1 each add'l.

*We are required to pay sales tax in all states with the exceptions of AK, DE, MT, NH, and OR.
Please include appropriate sales tax if you live in any state not mentioned above.

Customer Information

NAME

COMPANY

STREET ADDRESS

CITY   STATE   ZIP

PHONE ( )   FAX ( )
[REQUIRED FOR CREDIT CARD ORDERS]

Payment Method

❏ CHECK ENCLOSED   ❏ VISA   ❏ MASTERCARD   ❏ AMEX

CREDIT CARD #   EXP. DATE

COMPANY PURCHASE ORDER #

Tell Us What You Think

PLEASE TELL US WHAT YOU THOUGHT OF THIS BOOK: TITLE:_____

WHAT OTHER BOOKS WOULD YOU LIKE US TO PUBLISH?

Kudos for *QuarkXPress: Visual QuickStart Guide*

"The terse, 1-2-3 instructions are to-the-point. No foot-dragging here."

Computer Book Review

"The text is direct and concise, and the book is organized as a reference volume so readers can go straight to the task at hand."

Art & Design News

"...shows rather than tells how to use the page layout software. Text supports the illustrations and moves the reader from one illustration to the next. The book is well-designed, with thumb tabs at the outer edges listing chapter heads and subheads."

Communications Manager

"This comprehensive 'how-to' on QuarkXPress serves as a great learning tool to this popular, but somewhat difficult, program. Since QuarkXPress is becoming the program of choice for many DTP users, this handy guide should prove to be an essential guide for Macintosh artists."

Carl Calvert
MacArtist

"This book's method of teaching you is so simple, it eliminates the fear factor.... I especially enjoyed the look of the *Visual Quickstart Guide QuarkXPress 3.1* because of the variety of the visual examples.... For the beginning Quark user, I recommend buying this book. It will ease you into Quark, giving you the basics you need to function in the program."

Kathleen Blavatt
Macintouch